Routledge
Taylor & Francis Group

U0722221

语言权力分析：实践指南

著 （英）汤姆·巴特利特
（Tom Bartlett）

译 秦川

重庆大学出版社

版贸核渝字（2022）第 174 号

图书在版编目（CIP）数据

语言权力分析：实践指南／（英）汤姆·巴特利特
（Tom Bartlett）著；秦川译. — 重庆：重庆
大学出版社，2024.5
书名原文：Analysing Power in Language—A
Practical Guide
ISBN 978-7-5689-3847-1

Ⅰ. ①语… Ⅱ. ①汤… ②秦… Ⅲ. ①功能（语言学）—
研究 Ⅳ. ①H0

中国国家版本馆 CIP 数据核字（2023）第 059538 号

语言权力分析：实践指南
YUYAN QUANLI FENXI：SHIJIAN ZHINAN
（英）汤姆·巴特利特（Tom Bartlett） 著
秦川 译

责任编辑：杨 琪 版式设计：宏 霖
责任校对：关德强 责任印制：赵 晟
＊
重庆大学出版社出版发行
出版人：陈晓阳
社址：重庆市沙坪坝区大学城西路 21 号
邮编：401331
电话：（023）88617190 88617185（中小学）
传真：（023）88617186 88617166
网址：http：//www. cqup. com. cn
邮箱：fxk@ cqup. com. cn（营销中心）
全国新华书店经销
重庆天旭印务有限责任公司印刷
＊
开本：720mm×1020mm 1/16 印张：16.75 字数：260 千
2024 年 5 月第 1 版 2024 年 5 月第 1 次印刷
ISBN 978-7-5689-3847-1 定价：68.00 元

致　谢

　　小马丁·路德·金(Martin Luther King Jr.)的《我有一个梦想》(*I Have a Dream*)演讲为版权材料,其重印已取得小马丁·路德·金遗产继承人的协商许可,由"作者之家"(Writers House)作为版权所有人代理人转交相关材料纽约州纽约市ⓒ 1963 小马丁·路德·金.ⓒ 1991 科丽塔·斯科特·金的版权。

　　塞巴斯蒂安·科勋爵向国际奥委会发表的讲话已通过与英国奥林匹克委员会和塞巴斯蒂安·科勋爵的协商取得重印许可。

　　《卡迪夫大学校规》及院长欢迎辞的摘录均为卡迪夫大学版权所有,并经卡迪夫大学和英语、传播与哲学学院院长许可转载。

　　所有其他语篇和摘录均来自作者自有数据或公共信息。

　　非常感谢我曾经的学生米莉·戴维斯和艾比·琼斯,他们让我了解到了查夫和塞巴斯蒂安·科勋爵的语篇。

　　最后,特别致谢圭亚那北鲁普努尼大草原的各个社区,尤其是亨利叔叔、沃尔特、尼古拉斯、戈登和莎拉(均为本书中化名)。

转录规则

W：现在［X 在说什么	重叠的言语
Eu：　　　［你必须	
＝	言词间听不见停顿
（xxx）	发音不清（大约每个音节一个 x）
（这里的短缺）	最佳猜测
（？如何）	不确定的猜测
［……］	省略数据
（（挂图纸的噪声））	转录者的评论
Eu：这是我们不理解的。	动作与一段言语同时出现
＜＜纸张的沙沙声＞＞	
far	远超预期的重音
……/（p）	讲话中的短暂停顿（大约 2 秒）
（11s）	言语中时长如数所示的停顿
↑	高于预期的音高
↓	低于预期的音高
瓦妮莎	声音比正常情况大
°这里,留下这个°	比正常情况小声
°°无论哪种方式°°	比正常情况下小声得多
＜这就是为什么此项行动＞	比正常情况下快
＞当前的解决方案＜	比正常慢
lo：gging	元音延长
＊你好＊	笑着说

关于语篇体式的注释

本书中的一些语篇是按原样呈现的,没有被划分为小句或其他单元。因此,当提到这些语篇的特定部分时,我将提及其"行号"。

然而,在必要或有用的地方,我会将语篇分为小句。这意味着主句、小句和限定投射小句都将独立成行,并分别编号。因此,在提到这些语篇的特定部分时,我将提及它们的"小句编号"。

当从语篇中选取个别小句来说明语法点时,我会将其和其他示例一起按顺序编号,但马丁·路德·金的语篇为例外,以避免重复分析几段语篇时每次都以不同的方式对语篇进行编号造成混淆的情况。

目 录

第1章 语篇作为话语分析的门户

1.1 引言

无论表现为纸面上的弯曲线条还是空气中传递的声波,语言都是可以打动我们的。这个道理,体现在葡萄牙作家何塞·萨拉马戈的小说《失明》中的一段话中。这段话是这样说的:

> 医生的妻子性格坚毅无匹,然而她却因为一个人称代词、一个副词、一个动词或是一个形容词这些个语法范畴而流下了眼泪……

语法居然能产生如此神奇的作用,这一观点可能会让一些人感到惊讶,但其实这个观点由来已久。从历史上看,英语中"glamour(魅力)"一词最初是"grammar(语法)"一词的变体,现在则用以表示风度和形体之美所产生的迷人魔力。时代和品位可能会改变,但本书的一个目标是让读者相信语法仍然具有神奇的魅力!

语言除了可以用来施展情感咒语,还可以用来实现更具体的目标,比如牧师或政府官员可以用语言宣布一对男女结为夫妻,法官也可以用语言宣布判处一名囚犯十年苦役。令人落泪或是判人入狱的力量是强大的,但我们能说,在这两种情况下,这种力量是源于所用的词句本身吗? 如果这些话从别人口中说出来,也会产生同样的效果吗? 或者如果听众或说话的场合发生了改变呢?

哲学家约翰·L.奥斯汀(J. L. Austin)(1962年)将"我宣布你们结为夫妻"之类的话语称为**行事性话语**(*performatives*),因为说出这些话语的言说行为本身就完成了其词句所描述的社会行为——当然,必须要满足特定的条件。奥斯汀将这些条件称为**合适性条件**(*felicity conditions*),以区别于**真值条件**(*truth conditions*),因为后者所判断的是一段话语是否可以被认为在事实上是**正确的**(*correct*)。奥斯汀认为也许我们可以判断诸如"法国国王是个秃子"这类的话语是否是真切的事实(尽管哲学家发现这个问题的棘手程度超乎想象!),但是判断"我宣布你们结为夫妻"这句话的真假却是没有意义的。不过,讨论使这句话能够执行说话人宣称正在执行的行为的必要条件,却是有意义的。就上述例子而言,说话人必须拥有经官方批准的可以批准他人婚姻行为的(宗教的或世俗的)权力,而且这对夫妇必须都想要并且有资格(同彼此)结婚。承诺则更为复杂:在没有附加任何条件的情况下,说"我承诺做这件事"算不算承诺? 如果说话人悄悄在背后交叉手指(以求神祇原谅自己撒谎)呢? 如果他们的处境让他们无法履行承诺呢? 如果受话人不想让行动付诸实施呢? 还有确切的措辞问题——如果他们只是说"我会那样做"呢? 这也算是承诺吗? 在这一点上,孩子们似乎和父母遵守着不同的规则。

再来谈谈语言的情感力量。每个人听到萨拉马戈笔下医生的妻子听到的话都会同样被感动吗? 首先,他们必须说同一种语言(虽然话语的声音通常就足以引起情绪),就像杰米·李·柯蒂斯在《一条叫旺达的鱼》(*A Fish Called Wanda*)中深情款款地回应约翰·克莱斯所说的俄语那样。这似乎有点显而易见,所以不妨再考虑一下语言风格是否恰当的问题,比如口语和官方语言在赢得听众喜爱这个方面会有不同的效果。哪一种风格更有效取决于多种因素,其中最重要的是受众的特征。我在这里提出的观点是,任何语言的使用行为都具有行事性(Baumann and Briggs,1990),行事的效果不仅取决于所使用的语言本身,还取决于与所使用的语言相联系的一系列社会和文化因素。换言之,与其说力量存在于语言之中,不如说力量是借由语言来实现的。这意味着如果要讨论语言的强大效力，或是讨论所行之事以及行事是否成功（有力）这些问题，我们需要研究的对象远不止语言本身。然而，作为语言学家，我们的出发点是所使用的语言，因此我在本书中将阐述各种分析和描述语言的方法，以引出更宏观的问题，即影响语言效果的社会和文化因素。那个可以打动医生妻子的副词到底是怎么回事？为什么一个人称代词会产生这样的效果？最合理的解释是，这些言词本身并不会产生太大的效果，巨大的效果来源于言词在特定语境中织缀在一起的方式。当词汇（口语或书面语）以有意义的方式交织在一起时，我们称之为**语篇**（*text*）——它与"**纺织**（*textile*）"一词有着相同的词根，来自拉丁语中一个意为"编织"的词。词汇从它们的上下文和包含它们的句式中获得意义，并且它们所积累的意义与说话人的关系和这种意义与受话人的关系有所不同。但我们无法仅从语篇本身判断人们会如何接受它，正如我们无法判断"我宣布你们结为夫妻"这句话是否是具有法律约束力的话语一样，我们需要更多地了解话语产生时的各种条件。反之，如果我们不理解所用的词汇，包括其含义、历史和彼此的关系，我们也无法对语境进行探讨。语言和语境相结合，便是所谓的**话语**（*discourse*）①，而对情境中的语言使用进行研究称为**话语分析**（*discourse analysis*）。语篇是口头或书面语言的记录，所以从语言学家的角度来看，语篇是进入话语分析的门户。

从上文中可以看出，笔者给出了一些答案，也提出了许多问题，这种讨论模式将贯穿本书其余部分。然而，本书的副标题既然是"实践指南"，只提出问题而不给出解答的建议或者提示思路，似乎是名不副实的；因此，在接下来的几章中，我将详述一些相当具体的方法，以方便读者对语篇本身进行详细分析，并且为话语分析打下基础。本书核心的描述性方法是一种被称为系统功能语言学（Systemic Functional Lingustics，简称 SFL）的语法理论。原因有几个，其中最重

---

① 这个词偏巧有很多相关的用法。在本书中，"话语"指的是"语境化的语言使用"。有关语篇和话语之间差异的讨论，请参见 Widdowson 2004。

要的是,系统功能语言学已经发展成为一种"**适用**(*appliable*)**语言学**"。你很可能需要在拼写检查器中添加"appliable"一词,否则当你不注意的时候,你的电脑会将其改为"applicable"。这是因为"适用语言学"一词是由系统功能语言学的创始人韩礼德(Michael Halliday)创造的,其目的是区分可适用于各种场合的一般性语言学描述理论,即适用语言理论,和应用于或适合于某些特定情况的语言学描述方法。换言之,系统功能语言学的明确宗旨就是将语言描述为一个产生社会意义的系统和一个社会符号学系统,因此基于系统功能语言学的语言或语篇描述可以让我们对语篇进行话语分析。因此,从本书的角度来看,虽然笔者要阐述的只是一种特定的话语分析方法,但读者从中获得的描述性技能可以应用于各种话语分析中,即使每种方法都有其各自的目标和宗旨。对于本书在接下来的几章中将详细讨论的语篇,笔者将不时提供自己完成的、超越语篇本身的实地调查分析,并试图解答这些调查所引出的更为宏观的问题;但有时候,笔者只能提出通过对语篇的详细分析所揭示出来的问题,而读者应本着探究的目的,对这些问题加以解决,才能理解作为话语记录的语篇。

1.2　语法、语篇、语境和话语

在本章的第一段,我言辞凿凿地谈论着语言作为"纸面上的弯曲线条"或"空气中传递的声波"的神奇特性,似乎概括了语言的全部。然而,虽然声音和图形是语言最显著的物理特征,但其功能是为语言更为抽象的属性提供平台。本文所引用萨拉马戈的那句话提到了下一个层面,即这些线条和声波所代表的"语法范畴"。我想补充一点:这里的"语法范畴"是指语法和词汇在这一层面上的共同作用,即所谓**词汇语法**(*lexicogrammar*)(本书附录词汇表中列出了正文中的斜体字)。用专业术语来说,我们可以说声音或图形信号**实现**(*realise*)了词汇语法范畴。但是,萨拉马戈肯定所言有误:让医生的妻子流泪(也许在教室里除外)的不是这些语法范畴,而是它们在口头或书面上所表达的意义,即**语义**

(*semantics*)。这让我们深入到另一个抽象层次,即词汇语法范畴在话语中串联在一起时所产生的意义。用专业术语来说,词汇语法实现了话语的语义。而且,哪怕冒着让你涕泗滂沱的风险,我还得说语言还有另一个抽象层次,即话语的语义如何协同作用以实现**语境**(*contexts*)(或与语境互相作用,如何看这个问题取决于你的视角)。

在上文中,我谈到了语篇(孤立的一段语言)与话语(语篇在社会语境中的产生和接纳)之间的重要区别。我还说过,本书的目标是让你能够进行详细的语篇分析,但这些分析应被视作话语分析的基础,是需要解答的问题,而不是答案本身。因此,本书的重点是词汇语法和语义之间的界面、词汇和语法如何创造**话语**(*utterances*)的意义和语义,以及语境之间的界面和语篇意义如何对社会意义作出贡献,但除此之外,还提出了语篇分析为何可以作为话语分析(对特定情境中动态的语篇的分析)的基础。用费尔克劳夫(Fairclough)(2001)的术语来讲,这意味着对语篇[作为语境中的**话语**(*utterances*)]的意义的解释,从对语篇语言的客观描述,转向解释语篇可能产生的原因及其可能产生的影响。这代表着对语言使用从客观描述到主观描述的转变,因为解读和解释是个人的产物,可能会引起激烈的争议。然而,如果我们能够将这些解释建立在对语言的客观描述的基础上,那么我们就有了更坚实的基础来构建我们的讨论。这意味着我们需要这样一种描述单词和句子(即词汇和语法)的方法,这种方法一方面是客观的,另一方面又提供了一个平台来构建我们的解读和解释。

1.3　语法的不同视角

一般来说,有三种主要的语法理念。① 首先是"传统的"或规定性语法理

---

① 韩礼德(2002:384—417)将研究语法的这门学科称为"语法学"。语法和语法学之间的关系正如语言和语言学之间的关系。

念,你可能在学校里学到过,这也是许多自助书籍所秉持的、代表一种教人"正确说话"的"良好语法"的观点。在这种理念下,人们被告知永远不要拆分不定式,一定不要把介词放在句末。然而,这些规则是基于别人希望我们说话的方式,而不是我们在现实生活中实际的说话方式。以他人认可的方式说话是一个重要的考虑因素,因为这会影响我们所说的话是否会被认为是正确的。的确,在话语分析中,了解被分析的话语是否是"标准英语"很有用处。但在这种情况下,我们需要探讨所使用的是何种语言,并且思考一下"为什么"——仅仅说某种语言"是错的"是不够的。

与之相对,描述性语法的理念则侧重于描述人们实际所说的语言背后的规则。因此,在这种理念看来,例1到例3是"合乎语法的",而例4则不合语法,因为(据笔者浅见)任何人的语法都不会产生这个句子:

1. I ain't got no money.
2. Me and her went down the shops.
3. See the footie last night?
4. Mat cat sat the the on.

在描述语法内,又有形式语法和功能语法两种理念的区别。形式语法的关注焦点并不是各种句子的意义,而是决定句子形式是否正确的(潜意识)规则。因此,从形式的角度来看,例4的形式不正确,因为英语的规则是,限定词"the"只能出现在名词[如"cat"或"mat"]前,或是形容词修饰的名词短语之前[如"the ugly cat"]。相比之下,例2的形式是正确的,因为如果毗连另一个主语的话,宾格的"me"也可以充当句子的主语(人们就是这么用的),尽管从规定性语法的角度来看,这会被认为是"糟糕的语法"。

尽管互有差异,但形式语法的理念和规定语法的理念不约而同地将语法视为一套构造形式正确的句子的规则,二者只是在判断正确句式的标准上有所不同。形式语法的理念止步于词汇语法,即名词、形容词和动词可以如何串在一起。单词和句子是语言的具体要素。与此相反,我们在本书中采用的视角是功能法,①将语法视为一种**意义潜势**(*meaning potential*)(Halliday 1978:39),是一组以不同方式表达自己的选项,这些选项随着我们人类进化而发展出来,以满足我们不断扩大的交际需求。以这种观点来看,语言是一种社会行为,是语境的创造,而更具体的语义、词汇语法和音韵/字形层面是为这一基本功能服务的。从这个角度来看,当我们把句子组合在一起时,我们可以"选择"②谈论特定的动物,例如猫(如果这符合我们的交流目的);如果我们这样做了,那么我们就有了更多的选择,比如,我们是否想把它描述为"丑陋的",或者我们想如何把它突出描述为"那只丑陋的猫""我的丑陋的猫"或"这丑陋的猫"。我们所做的选择将决定这个句子的形式。因此,形式语法只考虑语序的各种可能性,而我们将采用的功能语法则强调了词汇的功能,既包括"the""that"和"my"(指示哪只猫)三词在功能上的相似性,又包括它们之间的意义区别。从功能角度来看,不后接名词的独立"the"的可能性并不存在,因为使用"the"这一种功能选择,我们只有在已经做出谈论某物某事的选择之后才会面临。因此,虽然功能性方法仍然关注形式正确的句子,但它超越了形式语法,提供了与所做选择的交流功能相关的语篇描述,允许我们将所做的选择与可用但未被采用的选项进行对比。如果我们想把语篇描述作为话语分析项下所做的解读和解释的基础,那么上述这些都是非常重要的优势,笔者希望随着本书内容的展开,读者能逐渐清楚地感受到这些优势。

1.4　意义潜势的三个方面

　　系统功能语言学语言观的另一个重要特征(这一特征也影响了本书的结构

---

① 　语法有各种各样的功能方法,其中许多可以用于话语分析。我在这里使用的是韩礼德的方法,但这并不意味着其他方法不能用来解答我们将对语篇提出的相同问题。

② 　这并不一定表示有意识地选择。

布局)在于其认为语言中有三种不同类型的意义,这一特征既适用于话语的语义,也适用于词汇语法范畴的"意义"。在讨论语境时,它也有重要的影响。虽然这是一个复杂的概念,但可以通过以下示例简单地加以说明:

5. The cat sat on the mat.
6. Did the cat sit on the mat?
7. The mat was sat on by the cat.

正如你所看到的,这三个例子都指的是现实世界中的同一个活动,因此它们体现相同的**经验**(*experiential*)意义。这可以总结为"cat"是一个动作者(一个动作的行为者);"sit"是行为;"on the mat"告诉我们在哪里(称为位置情况)。整个小句的这种经验意义(语义)是通过词汇语法的特定方面来体现的:通过各个单词的意义;通过语序;通过介词"on"与**名词词组**(*nominal group*)"the mat"的组合来表示位置;在例7中,通过介词by告诉我们动作者是谁或什么。

然而,虽然例6的经验意义与例5相同,但例6是一个问题而不是一个陈述,其标志是将"did"放在"cat"之前。这表明,我们是在提问而不是告知,这是**人际**(*interpersonal*)意义的一个方面。所以,我们就有了通过词汇语法的特定特征来体现的第二种意义。

在例7中,有着与例5相同的经验意义(二者虽有所差异,但可暂且忽略)和人际意义,但我们将"the mat"放在了句首。[①] 通过观察一个孤立的句子很难看出这样做的目的,因为这类变形通常取决于周围的句子,即**上下文**(*cotext*):

8. The dog sat on the table but the cat sat on the mat.
9. My mum was very proud of her new floor coverings until the mat was sat on by the cat. [②]

---

① 这让我想起了一个很老的笑话:猫爪末端有尖爪,句子末端有停顿。(猫爪 paws 与停顿 pause 同音,尖爪 claws 与句子 clause 同音——译者注)

② 这个例子暗示了(我之前忽视的)经验意义上的差异,与例5和例6不同,它表明垫子在某种程度上受到了影响。

我们可以看到,在例 9 中,将"the mat"放在小句的开头,令其与"floor coverings"这个范畴联系起来,因此我们将这种变化称为**语篇**(*textual*)意义。其中,语篇这一连贯单位的语义由词汇语法的特征(在本例中是词序)体现的。

因此,我们可以说,这些小句体现了三种类型的意义,即经验意义、人际意义和语篇意义,而每种意义都有其特别的词汇语法领域。韩礼德(参见 Halliday and Matthiessen 2004:29-31)将这些意义领域称为**元功能**(*metafunctions*)。元语言是关于语言的语言(例如,名词、动词和小句等),因此元功能是功能的功能,它捕捉到这样一个观点,即虽然词汇语法和语义的不同元素都有各自的特定功能,但它们可以被归为三大类:经验意义、人际意义和语篇意义。

从小句进入关于语篇和语境的讨论中,这三种元功能之间的区别具有重要的影响,因为一般来说,语篇中的经验意义用于描绘话语**语场**(*field*)(正在做什么或谈论什么);人际意义体现了话语的**语旨**(*tenor*)(说话人之间的关系或他们对主题的态度);而语篇意义共同建立了话语**语式**(*mode*)(我们处理的语篇类型)。稍后,我们将依次研究每个元功能,描述词汇语法如何体现不同类型的意义,这些意义如何**构建**(*construe*)语境的不同方面,以及这样做的社会意义。

在继续讨论之前,我想提醒大家一点:虽然元功能或多或少是相互独立的,因为一个元功能项下的选择在理论上不受另一个元功能项下的选择的约束,但这并不意味着它们在话语中不会独立地起作用。正如我们将看到的,恰恰相反,这三种意义的结合才界定了语境创造这种社会活动。

所以,讲了这么多理论,让我们看一些语篇,并提出一些问题!

练习 1.1

请通读语篇 1.1,并用自己的话粗略地对篇章中的语言进行描述。本书的一个主要目的就是向读者介绍专业术语,以便更明确地指称读者可能已经对不同语篇特征所产生的想法,并为读者提供整合这些想法的系统方法,但目前你可以用自己的话来表达自己与众不同的想法!

在小组或课堂上讨论完自己的想法后,请回答后面更为具体的问题:

语篇1.1

1　The most pressing question we now face, we might well say,

2　is who and where we are as a society.

3　Bonds have been broken,

4　trust abused and lost.

5　Whether it's an urban rioter mindlessly burning down a small shop that serves his community

6　or a speculator turning his back on the question of who bears the ultimate cost for his

7　acquisitive adventures in the virtual reality of today's financial world,

8　the picture is of atoms spinning apart in the dark.

问题①

(1) What do you think of the style of the extract in general?

(2) Do you think the extract comes from a text that was (i) written to be read privately; (ii) spontaneous spoken speech; or (iii) written to be read aloud? What is the basis of your judgement?

(3) Would you say the text presents a positive, negative of neutral picture of society? Again, what is the basis of your judgement?

(4) Who do you think might be the author of the text and what do you think their goal is?

　　好,下面请看看该语篇是如何继续展开的(参见 228 页),然后讨论问题(5)至(16):

(5) Were you surprised by the speaker and the occasion? How does this knowledge fit in with your earlier ideas?

(6) What is the background to this text?

(7) What position does the speaker adopt with respect to:

---

① 　相关分析涉及英语原文相关特征,这些特征在中文译文中会被隐去或转换而无法保留,因此译者保留这些问题的英文原文以便读者进行相关分析。本书中类似情况不再一一说明。——译者注

（ⅰ）the background as subject matter?

（ⅱ）his listeners?

（8）Why do you think that the speaker refers to both rioters and bankers in the text?

（9）What effect do the speaker's clothing, the procession and the setting have on the text?

（10）How does the speaker's *status* affect the text?

（11）What role is the speaker taking on as part of his status?

（12）Is this a role that has always been seen as appropriate to someone of the speaker's status?

（13）What audience（s） is the speaker addressing?

（14）Will his various audiences respond to his words and his status in the same way?

（15）Through this text, do you think the speaker has a single goal or several?

（16）How does the speaker achieve an idea of continuity or *cohesion* across the two parts of the text?

对于这样的问题,没有硬性的答案,但由于本章的目的是向读者介绍话语分析中的一些核心主题和概念,笔者将提供一些可能的答案,供读者参考,详见附录。在以后的练习中,当需要读者进行语言学分析时,笔者都会在书后提供参考答案,但相关讨论将留予读者自行进行。

1.5　关键概念 1

如上所述,上述练习的目的不是对语篇进行任何明确的分析,而是引出一些有趣的问题,并在本书的其余部分予以讨论,同时介绍一些核心概念。术语表中给出了其中许多术语的简要定义,但在继续讨论之前,有必要在此对它们进行稍详细的介绍。

语篇（*text*）指的是一段连贯的语言,无论最初是书面语言还是口头语言。可以在不参考语篇外信息的情况下,纯粹根据所用词语的含义及其出现的结构和模式来分析语篇。单词和句子结构合称为**词汇语法**（*lexicogrammar*）。我们可以使用"语篇模式"一词来指代语篇中比小句大的各部分之间的关系。

上下文(*cotext*)指我们所讨论的特定单词或语段周围的语篇部分、可能会影响这些单词或语段的含义或解释。例如,本节选的第二部分提供的上下文改变了我们对第一部分的理解。

语境(*context*)指的是如何结合经验意义、人际意义和语篇意义来定义情景。这个概念难以一言说清,将在全文逐渐展开讨论。区分语境、上下文和环境(见下文)很重要,不同的作者使用这些术语的方式也有所不同。许多作者或多或少地使用语境来指我们称之为环境的东西,还有些作者将语境用作上下文的同义词。

在本书中,**环境**(*environment*)指的是任何与语篇有关系的非语篇背景。这是一个非常宽泛且往往较模糊的范畴,可以涵盖一系列特征,从"贴近"语篇的特征(例如围绕大主教布道的盛大仪式和说话人的身份)到不那么直接的特征,例如语篇的社会背景和英国教会在社会生活中不断变化的角色。第一个练习的目的之一是展示环境特征对于更为全面地解读语篇这种社会行为的重要性。本书其余章节的主要目标是提供一种系统的方式来探讨语篇、语境和环境之间的关系。

正如我们所看到的,**意义**(*meaning*)也是一个含义广泛而难以三言两语说清楚的概念。在某种程度上,我们可以讨论我们在词典中找到的单词的意义,我们也可以讨论特定语法结构的意义(比如"狗咬邮递员"和"邮递员咬狗"之间的区别,不过后者稍微麻烦一些),我们可以把这些称为基于语篇的意义,因为它们(通常)可以在孤立的语篇中读取出来。然而,我们也可以从目的或效果的角度来讨论语篇整体或部分的意义。这需要一些语篇外的信息,本书中把此类意义称为社会意义。意义难以捉摸的特点可以通过"meaning(意思、意义)"一词在下列短语中的不同意思来说明:"这个词是什么意思?""他的言语对我意义重大。""他意欲何为?"当然,这三个意思是联系在一起的。(这就是为什么英语中会使用同一个词!)本书的目的之一就是研究这些相互联系。

在所有这些观点的背后是语篇和**话语**（*discourse*）之间的区别，这也是本章的重点。语篇指的是产生的词语组合，因此两个人在不同的场合可以产生相同的语篇，一个语篇可以脱离其语境，而话语指的是语篇情景化的产生过程，即语篇在特定语境中、在特定场合下的使用。因此，话语与语篇不同，不能重复。Widdowson（2004：1-16）对语篇和话语之间的差异进行了翔实的讨论，而Blommaert①（2005：3）也给话语提出了颇有教益的定义，现引述如下：

> 话语……包括与语言使用相关的社会、文化和历史模式及发展相关的所有形式的有意义的符号性人类活动。

符号（*semiotic*）活动是指使用符号来表达意义的各种方式，但在本书中，我们将只讨论语言符号的使用。有许多关于**多模态**（*multimodal*）意义的好书，它们研究了图像和声音如何与语篇结合，但这些讨论超出了本书的范围，不过本书提出的许多观点在多模态分析中很有用。尤其需要指出，*Kress* 和 *Van Leeuwen*（2001）所提出的一个多模态分析的描述性框架所采用的一般范畴与我们稍后用于语篇分析的范畴相同。

总而言之，本书的目的是为读者介绍相关技巧，使读者能够完整地对语篇进行详尽分析，让读者明白这种分析的局限性，提出将语篇分析转化为话语分析的方法。在下一节中，笔者将介绍一个启发式模型，用于分析作为话语的语篇。"启发式"一词意味着，该模型并非旨在精准地反映现实，而是提供一个便捷但粗疏的工具，用以揭示语篇与社会之间的关系，使我们不得不对这些关系进行思考。因此，笔者认为将要阐述的方法既非详尽无遗，也非从语篇转向话语的唯一途径。这个模型的全部或部分将贯穿本书，并且笔者也将探讨如何采用这个模型来更充分地考察语言的不同特征。读者在阅读本书时，尤其是探讨练习中的问题时，也应将此模型牢记于心。

---

① 本书的确备受推崇，但不要被它的名字所欺骗，这本书内容相当复杂，绝不是书名中所说的"导论"。

1.6 定位

回顾语篇 1.1,我们可以说,大主教在他布道的过程中采取了一个或多个**定位**(*position*),在他发言时的英国时局**故事情节**(*storyline*)背景下,该定位的确是合理的。布道一经播出,他的定位就成了这个不断演进的故事情节的一部分。行为(在我们的案例中是话语行为)、定位和故事情节之间的这种三向关系是社会心理学中定位理论一脉(Harré and van Langenhove 1999)的基础。这种三向关系如图 1.1 所示。

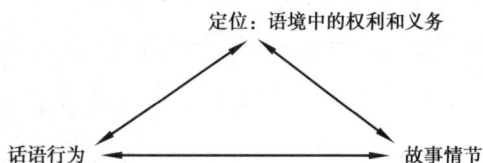

定位:语境中的权利和义务

话语行为 ⟷ 故事情节

图 1.1   定位三角,改编自 Harré and van Langenhove(1999)

然而,如果我们想研究采取话语定位怎样才能有效或有力,那么这个模型就存在一个问题,因为该模型似乎允许说话人在面对不断演变的故事情节时,可以自由地采取对他们最有利的立场。作为话语实践的模型,定位三角存在三个隐性的假设。第一个假设是,说话人有权采取他们所采取的定位,或者在受众眼中说话人被视为有此权利。显然,因为说话人的身份,语篇 1.1 中采取的立场是有效的;如果说话人是我或者理查德·道金斯,就不会产生相同的效果。借用布迪厄(Bourdieu 1977)的经济学比喻,我们可以将说话人的地位称作其**文化资本**(*cultural capital*),并且可以认为在正确的语境中,文化资本赋予了说话人的话语一种超越其内容本身价值的**符号资本**(*symbolic capital*)。第二个假设是,说话人可以掌控在当前语境中采取所欲定位所需的正确语言类型[称为**语码**(*code*)]。这就是为什么我在点一品脱啤酒和讲课时会说不同的话。第三个假设是,同一个话语行为在任何受众面前(或者继续使用布迪厄的经济术语来讲,在任何市场上)都具有相同的价值。正如对大主教讲道的分析所表明的那样,不同的听众可能以不同的方式对他的言语进行了解读。总之,我们可以说,虽然说话人的定位不能自动转化为权力,即完成事情的能力,但它可能永远是不同说话人的潜在属性;只有说话人在特定市场中拥有相应的文化资本,并且对相应的语码拥有相应的能力,才能在实践中实现权力(即采取有效定位),而这些约束条件未见于最初的定位三角中。因此,我们可以将包含文化资本、语码和市场三要素的第二个三角置于原始定位三角之上,以定位大卫之星为这些约束条件建立模型(见图 1.2;另见 Bartlet 2008, 2009, 2012a)。

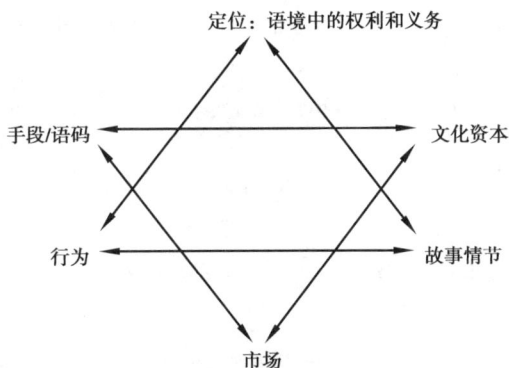

图 1.2　定位大卫之星

虽然一般来讲,文化资本、市场和语码这些变量可以说对不同说话人的定位施加了限制,但从另一个角度来看,也可以认为它们为说话人提供了机会(但并非没有限制)。例如,如果笔者想在派对上获得更高的声望,可以把话题切换成自己了解的话题;或者,如果一位政客想表现出自己很接地气,那么如果他拥有足够的底气,则可以将自己的语言风格改为当地方言。

正如我前文所说,定位大卫之星是一种启发式模型,是一种就语言作为话语的**约束性和允动性**(*constraints and affordances*)进行思考的方式。因此,整本书中都会适时运用它,但不会每做一点分析都用到模型的每个特征,有时候稍微聚焦一些会更好。在本介绍性章节的最后,让我们看看另一个语篇,并讨论它所展示的语篇特征,并适时使用定位大卫之星作为提示。

练习 1. 2

语篇 1. 2 是温斯顿·丘吉尔最著名的战时演讲之一的结语(*On the Beaches*)。尽可能多地阅读相关背景,以深入了解这篇演讲的内容、演讲者丘吉尔以及演讲的时期。然后,讨论后面的问题。

语篇 1. 2

1   Turning once again, and this time more generally, to the question of invasion, I would

2   observe that there has never been a period in all these long centuries of which we

3   boast when an absolute guarantee against invasion, still less against serious raids, could

4   have been given to our people. In the days of Napoleon, of which I was speaking

5   just now, the same wind which would have carried his transports across the Channel

6   might have driven away the blockading fleet. There was always the chance, and it is

7   that chance which has excited and befooled the imaginations of many Continental

8   tyrants. Many are the tales that are told. We are assured that novel methods will be

9   adopted, and when we see the originality of malice, the ingenuity of aggression,

10 which our enemy displays, we may certainly prepare ourselves for every kind of

11 novel stratagem and every kind of brutal and treacherous maneuvre. I think that no

12 idea is so outlandish that it should not be considered and viewed with a searching, but

13 at the same time, I hope, with a steady eye. We must never forget the solid assurances

14　of sea power and those which belong to air power if it can be locally exercised.

15　　　I have, myself, full confidence that if all do their duty, if nothing is neglected, and if

16　the best arrangements are made, as they are being made, we shall prove ourselves once

17　more able to defend our island home, to ride out the storm of war, and to outlive the

18　menace of tyranny, if necessary for years, if necessary alone. At any rate, that is what we

19　are going to try to do. That is the resolve of His Majesty's Government—every man of

20　them. That is the will of Parliament and the nation. The British Empire and the French

21　Republic, linked together in their cause and in their need, will defend to the death their

22　native soil, aiding each other like good comrades to the utmost of their strength.

23　　　Even though large tracts of Europe and many old and famous States have fallen

24　or may fall into the grip of the Gestapo and all the odious apparatus of Nazi rule, we

25　shall not flag or fail. We shall go on to the end. We shall fight in France, we shall

26　fight on the seas and oceans, we shall fight with growing confidence and growing

27　strength in the air, we shall defend our island, whatever the cost may be. We shall

28　fight on the beaches, we shall fight on the landing grounds, we shall fight in the

29　fields and in the streets, we shall fight in the hills; we shall never surrender, and if,

30　which I do not for a moment believe, this island or a large part of it were subjugated

31　and starving, then our Empire beyond the seas, armed and guarded by the British

32　Fleet, would carry on the struggle, until, in God's good time, the New World, with all its power and might, steps forth to the rescue and the liberation of the old.

问题

(1) What is the topic of the text? Is there one main topic? If there is more than one topic, is one topic more prominent than others, and how are the other topics related and how are they introduced in a coherent fashion?

(2) Would you describe the text as neutral or emotive? On what evidence? What different types of emotion are invoked? Do they relate to different subtopics and/or appeal to different groups of people?

(3) Who does Churchill refer to when he says "we" (or "us", or "our" or "ours")? Is this always the same group of people? Does it always include his audience? Is it always clear exactly who is being referred to? What is the effect of referring to a group of people as "we"? Who is in opposition to this "we" at each point? And what groups are referred to as "they" (or "them" or "their" or "theirs")?

(4) When does Churchill refers to himself (as "I" or "me" or "my" or "mine") rather than "we"? Is this done at strategic points? What is the effect?

(5) How strongly does Churchill make his various statements? Does he make use of *hedges* to downplay some of his comments and intensifiers to strengthen others?

(6) Churchill uses several different timeframes in this extract. How are these connected (logically and linguistically) and what is the effect of this?

(7) How would you describe the type of language Churchill uses in terms of formality?

(8) In what way is this text a *performance*?

(9) How important is Churchill's *status* as Prime Minister at the time in producing this performance? How would you describe the *position* or *stance* that Churchill takes in this text? Would such a position be open to other speakers? Would the effect of these words have been the same from different performers?

(10) How important is the political climate in which the speech was made in *legitimating* Churchill's position? Does it rely for its effect on the audience sharing certain views and opinions? What are these?

(11) It is said that just after he finished this speech, Churchill muttered to a colleague, "And we'll fight them with the butt ends of broken beer bottles because that's bloody well all we've got!" What do these words tell us about the speech

as a performance and Churchill as a performer?

(12) What would it mean to say this speech was *effective* or *powerful*? How would it be possible to measure this success? Are there other ways available to us today for judging the effect of this speech that were not available at the time?

(13) Could Churchill have made an entirely different type of speech at this point? What sort of speech?

(14) Do you think the status and roles of the Prime Minister today are the same as in Churchill's day? Would the Prime Minister, or leader in your country, today make such a speech "in the same way"?

(15) Is there anything else of interest in the speech (in this extract or elsewhere) that you would like to comment on or ask questions about?

　　这里有很多问题,我希望这些问题能引发很多讨论,并衍生出很多新问题！对于每一个问题,都可以写一篇完整的文章,来聚焦于丘吉尔修辞的一个特定方面。这种方法有时被称为"**摘选樱桃**(*cherry picking*)"(樱桃果小,且果农择熟而摘,其他不如意的则置之不理,所以这种说法很像中文中的"断章取义""挑三拣四""以偏概全"——译者注),因为有人说,不同政治信仰的话语分析人士可以在语篇中挑选出他们想在其中看到的东西,以支持他们自己先入为主的议程——Widdowson(2004)称之为他们的**先入篇见**(*pretext*)。虽然这种情况几乎是不可避免的,但本书就是旨在提供一种手段,以分析言语的各个方面、探讨这些方面如何共同作用而形成语篇,以及它们如何在更广泛的语境中组织成话语。如此一来,这种方法可以被称为一种**中观分析**(*mesoanalysis*),介于一些理论语言学研究的**微观分析**(*microanalysis*)和基于社会学方法的**宏观分析**(*macroanalysis*)二者之间。在这一章末,请允许我再举个文学的例子。博尔赫斯有一篇名为《关于科学的精确性》的短篇小说,主人公沉迷于绘制世界地图,他的地图越来越详细,越来越精准,终于成了一个全尺寸的世界复制品,每一处褶皱,每一条轮廓,一山一川都被复制得十分精确,甚至令人无法区分实物和复制品。这张地图很完美却毫无用处,因为地图不是世界本身,而是在特定尺度

上、出于特定目的对相关特征进行抽象表示的舆图。同样，语言学的描述也是对实时语言的抽象表示，旨在捕捉特定尺度上的某些特征。我们可以根据自己的目的选择尺度。如果我们过于拘泥于语篇的细节特征，就会忽视它们作为社会行为的要旨；但是，如果我们只聚焦于语篇的社会行为属性，而不考虑语篇是如何组合起来的，那么我认为我们就忽略了语篇之所以为语篇、之所以为语言的关键。不管对那些想要突出重点的人，还是对那些想要扩大关注点的人，希望这里介绍的中观描述层面能够成为他们研究的起点。

第 2 章　语场耕耘

2.1　引言

在本章和下一章中,我们将探讨说话人如何**构建话语语场**(*construe a field of discourse*)。话语语场是指讨论的话题或至少部分借助语言进行的任何活动,如预订假期或打桥牌;构建话语语场是指我们所做的语言选择如何共同作用——从而将一系列人、物、事融合成一个连贯且可识别的整体——的方式。"构建"这一概念在话语分析中非常重要,它暗示着在表述或表现同一事件时会存在个体差异,但并不暗示事件的任何特定版本比任何其他版本更接近真相,也不暗示任何说话人故意费心去歪曲主题或阻碍活动。在活动方面,不同的参与者可能对给定情境下的预期有不同的理解,因此一方可能试图将该活动构建为商务会议,另一方可能试图将其构建为社交活动。同样,当两个人重构过去的事件时,他们可能会产生非常不同的画面,因为每个人记忆中特别突出的人物和活动都是不同的。他们很可能会围绕这些不同的人物和活动来赋予各自的构建过程以结构,以致产生非常不同但同样真实的版本。同样,当讨论抽象主题时,不同的说话人会围绕不同的方面进行构建,但每个人都会觉得自己构建的画面是准确的。因此,构建比**表征**(*representation*)的内涵更丰富,因为表征意味着捕捉一个预先存在的现实,而构建这一概念则意味着这个现实是在话语行为本身的过程中被重新创造的,每个说话人根据当时的交际需要和目的,赋予事件的不同方面以"相关性"（Hasan，2009：177）。这些目的不一定都是自觉的或是有策略性的，但无论怎样，它们都让我们可以瞥见不同的社会行为者如何将自己和他人定位为特定场合中的行为者、信息提供者或受众，抑或既是行为者又是告知者，下文将对此进行介绍。

对话语语场的分析将分为两章。在本章中，我们将研究说话人建立和推进话语语场的总体方式，而在第 3 章中，我们将更具体地研究说话人如何构建不同参与者在所表征或开展的活动中的参与情况。这需要比较深入地介绍英语的及物性系统。

本章的内容分为两部分。在第 2.1 节中，我们将更详细地讨论一个观点，即话语语场可以指讨论的主题，可以指进行的活动，或兼而有之。另外，我们还将探讨**直接语境**（*immediate context*）和**移位语境**（*displaced context*）之间的差异以及这些语境在多大程度上为语言所定义。

在第 2.2 节中，我们将重温一个比喻，即将语篇比作缕缕丝线编织而成的整块整块的布料。我们将研究那些用以赋予"布料"整体性的语言手段，以及那些构造独特"花样"的语言手段。

在每一节中，笔者都会对一些示例进行分析，并就如何基于此类分析来讨论作为话语的语篇给出建议，尽管这总是需要利用到我们从环境中知晓（或构建）的语言外特征。这些特征，从直接场景到参与者的背景故事和资历，再到直接事件背后的宏观社会政治背景，可谓包罗万象。与本书其他章节一样，本章既有详解示例，也提供了相关练习题和可供进一步讨论的主题。

2.2 直接语场与移位语场

我们在第 1 章中说过，区分话语发生的环境（已经存在的事物，包括说话人的符号学历史和场景中的显著物质特征）和由话语本身从环境中创造出来的——构建的——语境，是十分重要的。这可以从话语语场的角度来清晰地举例说明,不过在讨论语旨时也是同样重要,这一点将在第 4 章中详述。前面讲过,通常有两种类型的语场,或者更确切地说是有两种极端类型,以及兼有二者的各种混合类型。两个极端类型中最为明显的一个是当谈论的人和事在说话人的直接环境中,并且在其当时进行的活动中有直接的作用。一个很好的例子是驾驶课上学员和教练之间的交谈,因为在这种情景下,交谈几乎只涉及课程本身(McCarthy 2000),但只构成了活动的一部分,因为该课程还必须包括物质行为。另一个极端类型是谈话的主题所涉事件脱离了说话人所在的直接环境和所进行的实际活动。哈桑举了一个简单的例子,一对夫妇一边洗碗,一边讨论政治。在这种情况下,这个语场(至少话语语场)是政治,而不是洗碗。然而,这对夫妇可能会不时提及他们当下的活动,在这种情况下,语场会变为“洗碗”。然而,有些情况可能更为复杂,仅以一堂历史课为例。课堂上,老师可能先讲述历史上的某次战役。那么战役本身就是话语语场,在时间上和空间上明显地脱离了教室的物理场景以及教师和学生当下的活动。然而,从另一个层面来看,老师对战役的叙述显然是“授课”这个整体活动的一部分。在这种语境下,谈话可能会从移位事件转到直接事件,因为老师可能会打断叙述而直接针对班上某些同学讲话,或许是为了让他们理解故事的相关意义或者给他们一些指导等。请注意,这与“洗碗”的示例不同,因为在那个例子中,话题的变化代表了活动的转变(或者说注意力在两个同时进行的活动之间的转变),而在历史课中,叙述和指导都构成了子语场,作为“教授历史课”这一更广泛活动的组成部分。

在本章中,我们将看到如何使用语言来分析直接语场和移位语场,以及它们可以组合的一些不同方式。语篇 2.1 以移位语场开头,显示了话语语场与话语发生环境之间的距离可能非常远:

语篇 2.1

从前,时值隆冬,雪花飘然而落,一位皇后坐在窗边缝衣服。窗框是用黑檀木做的。她一边缝衣服,一边望着窗外的雪,突然手指被针扎破了。三滴血落在雪上。殷红的血迹在白雪之上染出一个美丽的图案,她心想:“我希望能有一个皮肤白若雪、嘴唇红似血、头发黑如乌木的孩子。"

不久，她的愿望实现了，她生了个女儿，皮肤像雪一样白，嘴唇像血一样红，头发像乌木一样黑。王后称她的女儿为白雪公主。但孩子出生后不久，王后就去世了。

一年过去了，国王娶了另一位妻子，她既美丽又傲慢，无法忍受别人在美貌上超过她。她有一面神奇的镜子。她经常对着镜子说：

"镜子，镜子，墙上的镜子，这世上谁最美丽？"

镜子会回答：

"娘娘，您是最美丽的！"

王后很满意，因为镜子总是说真话。

白雪公主很快出落成一个美丽的女孩。随着时间的推移，她变得像清晨的阳光一样美丽，甚至美过了王后本人。有一天王后问她的镜子：

"镜子，镜子，墙上的镜子，这世上谁最美丽？"

这次镜子回答说：

"除了一个人，您比所有人都美丽：

漂亮的白雪公主，像太阳一样美丽。"

这让王后心下大惊。嫉妒让她脸色煞白，憎恨让她腹心发黑。从那时起，每当她看着白雪公主，她的心便在胸中腾跃翻滚，她恨透了白雪公主。

嫉妒、傲慢和仇恨像野草淹没花朵一样吞噬着她的心灵，令她不得片刻安宁。于是她吩咐一位猎人道："把白雪公主带到森林里去，因为我再也不想见到她了。杀了她，把她的心给我带回来，作为复命的证据。"猎人是个善良而单纯的人，他谨遵懿旨，把公主带走了。当他拔出刀，就要刺向白雪公主无辜的心口时，她哭了起来，说："哦，善良的猎人，别杀我，我会逃到森林里去。我保证再不回到宫里去。"

我相信你意识到了这是格林经典童话《白雪公主和七个小矮人》（顺便说一

句,格林兄弟是著名的语言学家)的开场,你可以想象一个可能的环境——在孩子的床边,父母讲述故事,然而所构建的语场在几乎所有方面都与这种环境相去甚远。这一点从一开始就得到了强调。童话故事的一个关键特征是通过时间用语"从前",从而脱离当下。这是童话故事的标准开场白,它将事件的发生锚定在了遥远但不确定的过去。虽然时间用语并没有明确表示为遥远的过去,但我认为这是明明白白、不言而喻的,因为我们可以将短语"很久很久以前"添加到语篇里,而"几年以前"则不行!同样,故事发生地点远离讲故事的卧室,而是在宫殿里,因此,如果听到用于强调距离的常用短语"在一个遥远的地方",我们也会觉得十分自然。因此,故事的开头确定了话语语场的时间和空间场景与话语发生的环境截然不同。

在童话的时空场景中,作者进一步引入了一系列的参与者、事件和主题来作为构建中的语场的突出元素。参与者首先包括王后、国王和他们的女儿,其次是国王的第二任妻子和她的会说话的镜子——这个特征又从可能的世界和其中可能发生的事情的角度显示出了环境和语境之间的距离(见第 3 章关于过程和参与者的内容)。在此之后,作者引入了猎人,而地点转移到了"野性的森林"。因此,我们有三种不同的场景——善良的王后在她的宫殿里,邪恶的王后在她的房间里,猎人在森林里。所有这些都是距离遥远且时间久远的一个更大的魔幻语场的一部分。在每一个场景中,都发生着不同的事件,展开着不同但又相互重叠的主题,这些主题对故事至关重要:在善良的王后的宫殿里,有着美、生与死;在邪恶的王后的房间里,有着虚荣、恐惧、嫉妒和仇恨;在森林里,有着恐惧、暴力,以及普通人的同情心。

这一简单的分析揭示了几个要点:

- 在时间、空间乃至可能的世界这三个方面,话语语场可以远离话语发生的环境;
- 话语语场包括参与者、他们的行为和发生的场景;
- 不同的子语场可以组合构成一个整体语场;

- 随着语篇从一个子语场进展到下一个子语场,在参与者和/或主题方面保持着一定程度的连续性。

就第一点而言,我们可以说,在这个例子中,语篇构建了语场,也就是说,所描述的地点、人物和事件都是由语篇本身产生的,并且不会共现于环境中。与此相对,我们可以说,那些存在于环境中的要素并未被构建成与语篇相关的要素。但这个说法也并不完全正确。再看看"从前"这一开场白,这是一个常用词语,标志着说话人马上要讲一个童话故事,从而将环境中的参与者设定为特定类型叙事的讲述者和受话人,同时也设定了他们之间的某种关系。因此,这可以被看作对环境中的人们以及即将产生的语篇形式的暗示。正如前文讨论历史课时笔者所提到的,总体上构建话语语场的语篇通常会提及说话行为或讲述行为,即便是那些没有提及的语篇,人们也可以根据它们在"当下"所扮演的社会角色以及它们在说话人和受话人之间设定的关系(这也是一种构建行为)来加以解读。这一点我们将在下文作进一步的探讨。在童话故事中,这种关系通常是幼儿与父母或老师之间的关系,而在那些不是这种关系的情况下,这种典型关系的共鸣在某种程度上也是有意义的。换句话说,一个语场永远不会完全是构建性的,因为创建一个构建性语场本身就是一个实时行为。

现在我们来探讨一下截然相反的另一种极端情况——语篇与行为共同作用以开展完全或大体上被构建为在直接环境中进行的活动:

语篇 2.2 (**摘自** Ventola 1983)

A:旅行社员工,女,30—40 岁

C:顾客,男,18—25 岁

(顾客进门,走向柜台;员工中断手头的工作,开始接待顾客。)

A 1 有什么可以帮您的吗?

C 2 是的

3　我想了解,呃……去凯恩斯旅行的报价……学生优惠

A　4　高中生还是大学生?

C　5　大学生

A　6　到凯恩斯,大学生

(A 查看价格 2 秒)

7　单程 143.60 元

8　双程翻倍就行了

9　287.20 元

(1 秒)

C　10　2 点 20 分有吗?

11　好

(2 秒)

C　12　行

A　13　行吗?

C　14　非常感谢

A　15　谢谢

C　16　再见。

从语篇 2.2 的语言中,我们可以很容易地识别出这是在旅行社顾客与店员的会面中发生的活动。然而,这种语境并不完全由语言构建,因为它还需要适当的场景和参与者的各种物质行为。最明显的是这次会面是发生在一个旅行社的店面里,如果不是,我们一定会认为这个活动的变化非常显著。在这种场景下,两个参与者要扮演不同的角色:旅行社员工和她的顾客,或潜在顾客。旅行社员工的角色是满足客户的需求,这一点从一开始就体现了出来:她中断手头的活动(物质行为)和向客户致意(语言行动)。进一步标志该活动是服务会面的语言信号包括客户对其需求的陈述(3)、讨论价格(7—11)以及首先确认

成交(12—15)然后道别(16)的话轮序列。服务会面的确切性质是由所涉及的词汇所标志的:"旅行的报价……学生优惠"(3)、"大学生到凯恩斯旅行"(6)、"单程"(7)和"双程"(8)。此次会面的另一个物质行为是旅行社员工寻找所需信息(6和7中间)。我们可以看到,在这个简短的语篇中,只构建了一个语境,一次特定类型的服务会面。很自然,这就是直接语境,正如"你"和"我"二词(指代直接参与者)的大量使用所证明的那样。这一语境中包含了不同的角色——"你"和"我"有着怎样的关系——我们将在第4章中讨论这些是如何构建的。我们也可以看到在语篇2.2中的语言是其他行为的**辅助**(*ancillary*),与此次会面中不可或缺的物质行为共同作用。换句话说,这个语境并非完全由语言构建。

会面的基本要素,比如物质行为和语言行为,通常是按照严格的顺序进行的。先感谢,再告别,再提供信息,然后旅行社员工提供帮助,这种顺序是行不通的!像这样的活动结构被称为**语类结构**(*generic structures*)(Halliday and Hasan,1985,第4章;Martin,1992,第7章),是许多研究的对象,但像这样的**固定例程**(*fixed routines*)不是本书的重点。不同的活动除了语类结构的核心元素,还有可选元素,通常是与主体活动无关的**附属例程**(*side routines*)。例如,旅行社员工和客户进行一些闲聊是很稀松平常的,最有可能发生在会面之初或结束和告别之前。一个可能的话题是天气或参与者生活中最近发生的事件,这取决于他们对彼此的了解程度和服务会面的性质。因此,说话人将在构建服务会面的直接语境的同时,构建移位语境。这种社交谈话在交易中的确切功能是一个备受讨论的领域。在早期的话语分析中,它在很大程度上被认为是可有可无的,但现在大多数人都认为,它至少有助于对交易性谈话"起到促进作用"。例如,麦卡锡(McCarthy 2000:101)提供了有关一次驾驶课的以下摘录,这种服务会面的特点是几乎完全聚焦直接活动,而不像理发店里的人们那样频频闲聊:

语篇 2.3

1　I　现在天气真好,[对吧?

2　L　　　　　　　　[啊,好极了

3　(2 秒)

4　L　让你充满春天的欢乐,是吧?

5　I　的确是。

6　L　我早上通常会走过梅里恩广场

7　　　[I:是吧]所以你每天早上都能看到进展

8　　　[I:对]因为上星期番红花开了

9　　　[I:啊,当然是呀]还看得见树发芽了

10　　[I:对]樱花

11　I　是呀,这是一年中的好时光。

12　L　哦,是的,太棒了。

13　I　挂回 3 挡。

　　麦卡锡说这样的社交谈话通常只发生在很长的通畅路段上,学员不需要进行任何驾驶操作,因此这些谈话可以起到避免尴尬沉默的作用。然而,这个例子与前面一对夫妇在洗碗时谈论政治那个例子十分不同。在那个例子中,洗碗谈话打断了政治谈话,而在驾驶课上,社交谈话在整个活动中发挥着作用,因为它有助于在学员和教练之间建立更随和的关系,这种关系应该有助于课程这个直接活动①。用专业术语来讲,我们可以说闲聊有助于**重新校准**(recalibrate)学员和教练之间的人际关系。因此,正如我们在上文中看到的,移位语篇有能作用于直接语境的层面,我们也可以看到,在主要聚焦当下的事件中,常常会有一

---

① 当然,有人可能会说,洗碗谈话在政治谈话中也起到了作用,或许可以缓和紧张氛围。

段一段的移位谈话在事件中发挥着重要作用。因此,语言在其中起着辅助或必要作用的语境之间,常常有某种程度上的模糊性或是重叠性。在对整个活动进行分类时,我们必须考虑谈话的主要目的是什么。

在驾驶课为我们提供的这个活动例子中,语言基本上在构建直接语境中起辅助作用,而移位的、由语言构造的语境可能在该活动中发挥着次要功能。现在让我们来看一个相反的例子,活动的焦点主要是移位谈话,但语言也起到了辅助作用,用以安排直接场景的秩序并促进焦点活动。以下语篇来自我在圭亚那的实地调查,我在那里观察了国际发展组织 Iwokrama[1] 与以 Makushi 印第安人为主体的当地社区之间关于可持续社会发展的讨论。巴特利特(Bartlet 2012a)以一整本书的篇幅讨论了两个群体之间的互动,我将在本书中引用这项实地调查中的某些例子。在语篇 2.4 中,Iwokrama 的一名专业开发人员——莎拉[2],正在组织一场关于当地资源管理的讨论会,并任命在当地颇有声望的沃尔特担任此次讨论会的主持人。转录规则请参见辅文第 2 页:

语篇 2.4

1　S：　第二件事是:是否我们要继续谈饮用水问题,

2　　　(xxxxxxx)。现在,(xxxxx)讨论的话题,我们接下来做什么(xxx)。

3　　　你们想出来什么没? 什么是

4　　　活动接下来的阶段进程(xx)记住,这只是开始。是(? 步骤)

5　　　评估对制定管理规划的…… 嗯,T-……T-

6　　　想要做什么? …… 你们在多大程度上…… 还想让 Iwokrama 参与

7　　　这个主持的事儿。还有在…… 能力建设方面

8　　　以(xx)。((数据省略))

[1]　Iwokrama 实际上是森林的名字;该组织的全称是 Iwokrama 国际雨林保护和开发计划署。
[2]　我所引用的在圭亚那采集的数据中的所有人名都是假名。

9　S：　好，所以，你们准备把水讲完。［好。］

10　W：　　　　　　　　　　　　　　　　　［我觉得］整个重点

11　　　　（xxxx）。

12　　　　（（不清楚的背景讨论声））

13　S：　我祈愿……我希望你也许可以做这个（给教室的其他 xx）。

14　　　　这个让一个人做……这个……呃呃，我希望？（来做）

15　　　　主持人，一个人来做规划（xxxxx）。好不？

16　W：　好的。

17　S：　好，沃尔特，你准备好了没有？

18　W：　没问题.

19　S：　（或者我们可以）试一下……

20　W：　（xxxxx）。

21　S：　（xx）你想（xxx）？好，我们需要……还要两个人……瓦妮莎……尼古
　　　　拉斯

22　W：　瓦妮莎！快过来！°（xxxx）°。

23　　　　（（窸窸窣窣的脚步声））（12 秒）

24　　　　过来写点东西。

25　　　　（9 秒）

26　S：　给你，瓦妮莎，（你可以用这支钢笔）。

27　　　　（（咕哝））（50 秒）

28　　　　所以……

　　与语篇 2.2 和 2.3 一样，我们仅根据语言（Hasan 1995：228）便可以将语篇
2.4 的语境识别为一次咨询会议，或者更具体地说，是一次关于发展规划的咨询
会议。然而，在实践中，这个语境只是部分地通过语言来构建的。有助于从环
境中构建语境的重要非语言特征纯粹是物质的，例如座位的安排（将主持人座

位与会众座位区分开来），人们在这个空间中的定位和移动（标志着角色的转变），以及使用挂图做的笔记。其中一些特征可能是"静默的"，但是转录语篇中还是应该在某些地方指出这些特征（见第 22 行），其他特征可能在语篇中被提及，借助语言而变得突出。这里的情况尤其如此，因为语篇 2.3 节选自会议的开场部分，因此，其语言明显针对的是安排议程（1—11）、物理场景（12）和要扮演的角色（13—27），而不是针对会议的目的——讨论。或者更确切地说，这些物理特征与讨论的内容无关，但它们对讨论的进行方式很重要。因此，这段文字明显是起辅助作用的。但应该记住，虽然随后在讨论中所用的语言构造了移位语境，但是对使本次活动成为会议的非语言特征也是起了辅助作用的。

　　另外需要注意的一个问题是语篇 2.3 中第一和第二人称代词（我、我们、你/你们）的高频使用。通过这种方式，说话人和听众将自己构建为语境的一部分，这进一步表明该语篇的这一部分在很大程度上是辅助性的。如上所述，"我"和"你"的使用通常与特定活动中的角色有关。虽然我在语篇 2.2 中说角色是由该语篇（作为服务会面）的目的所蕴含的，但在语篇 2.4 中，我们看到这些角色不是自然产生的，而是由莎拉具体分配的（我们将在第 4 章中更详细地讨论这一点）。通过这样做，莎拉明确了她作为活动组织者的地位，而且正如我们稍后将看到的，这将对此次活动（即讨论管理计划和沃尔特在引导此次会议方面所扮演的角色）的核心焦点的功能发挥产生影响。在驾驶课的例子中，我们看到，通过引入移位语境来重新调整个人关系，从而促进了直接活动的开展。与之相反，在这个例子中我们看到了莎拉对确立规划会议背景的直接活动的处理方式，她如何重新调整了人际关系，以及这如何影响了后来的讨论（此次活动的主要目的）。

　　到目前为止，在我们已经讨论的示例中，直接语境和移位语境可以被相当清楚地区分开来，尽管其中一个可能在另一个的功能发挥中扮演着某种角色。在洗碗和驾驶课的示例中，我们看到平行语境中的主题，尽管它们在某种程度上受到了直接环境的触发，但在很大程度上与直接活动无关。在下面的例子中,直接语境和移位语境更直接地联系在一起,并且我们将看到,直接语境和移位语境之间的区别实际上并不总是那么明确。我们还将从这两个语篇中看到,不仅是个人关系可以被重新调整,话语展开的背景故事情节也可以被重新调整,这将对不同说话人的定位和权力产生影响。

在第一个例子中,莎拉解释了可持续利用区的概念(即 SUA,指森林中可以以可持续方式开发资源的区域,而不是不可开发的荒野保护区):

语篇 2.5

1　山姆刚才问我是否可以告诉你更多关于 SUA 流程的信息,以及它是如何运作的。

2　我不赞成——Iwokrama 的部门里负责管理整个 SUA 的人。

3　流程是(xxxxxxxxxx),

4　他们提出了一个方案,他们见面的地方……

5　他们组建了一个团队,

6　在这个团队里有四名 NRDDB[①] 代表,

7　政府有两名代表,来自圭亚那林业委员会,

8　这是一个政府机构,

9　圭亚那环境保护署在团队里有代表

10　都列在里面了。

11　因此,他们的意见是,他们认为他们能做的是将社区、这些政府代表和 Iwokrama 召集起来,坐下来思考如何好好地规划该地区、规划他们将在该地区开发的企业,以及如何根据 SUA,规划对土地的管理。

12　其背后的想法是,所有人将每季度会面一次,

13　在会期(xxxx)之间的两个月里,

---

① 　北鲁普努尼地区发展委员会(NRDDB)。——译者注

14　他们要做的就是坐下来讨论这个流程进展如何,

15　他们可以讨论他们的关注点和他们所认为的解决方案。

16　因此,从社区的角度来看,意见是人们希望 NRDDB 代表能够将他们认为对社区的村庄来说很重要的事项拿到会议上讨论。

17　因为,请记住,可持续利用区实际上是 Iwokrama 在保护区开发的业务。

18　这些业务将开始运营,其中

19　一个可能的业务是伐木;

20　二是生态旅游;

21　三是采收像尼比藤蔓和木薯这样的东西,用于销售,

22　他们称之为非木材森林产品。

23　所以问题是:这会对社区有何影响呢?

24　社区如何参与其中?

25　社区如何能从受保护对象中受益?

26　到目前为止,我们在 Iwokrama 讨论的是,在有 NRDDB 代表参加的这些会议的空档期,是否有可能举行一次只与社区碰头的小型会议。

在本文中,我们看到莎拉的开场白(1—2)与环境的某些关键特征共同作用,在构造语境方面起着辅助作用,因为她的开场白直接关系到会议本身的当前活动,标示了莎拉在会议场景中作为信息提供者的角色。正如我们看到的,这是讲话或报告开始时的一种常见策略。在此之后,语篇主要起了构造性作用——描述之前举行的会议以及可持续利用区的潜在商业机会。很明显,莎拉对这些话题中的第一个话题——之前的会议——的讨论构建了一个移位语境,因为这完全是通过她的谈话被再造出来的。然而,由于会议中当前的活动是关于可持续利用区的讨论,因此也可以认为本段话语帮助莎拉将本次事件构建成了会议,起到了辅助作用。这就引出了一个普遍的观点,即当直接活动严重依赖于互动者之间的谈话时,就像讨论或会议一样,构成性语言和辅助性语言之

间的界限通常是模糊的。在莎拉谈论到潜在商业机会时，这条界限变得更加模糊，这些机会在某种程度上是移位的（即脱离直接语境的——译者注），但却与社区直接相关，而社区代表共同出席讨论会，并且莎拉直接提到了社区代表。稍后我们将回到这一点。

莎拉言语中的另一个有趣之处是即使语篇在本质上是构成性的，她也会偶尔提及其在直接事件中的目的，提醒受众这段建构性谈话的辅助功能。例如，在第 11 小句和第 16 小句中，莎拉说到"意见是"；在第 12 小句中，她使用了"其背后的想法是"；在第 23 小句中，她说到"问题是"。通过这种方式，莎拉表明了这些移位事件与直接活动的相关性，以此对可持续利用区流程进行解释。第 17 小句更明确地提到了直接活动，其中莎拉直接向听众发声，要求他们"记住"可持续利用区的含义。

现在让我们来看一下语篇 2.6，取材于同一场会议上的语篇 2.5 之后不久，当地社区长者亨利叔叔①开始解释可持续利用区的含义：

语篇 2.6

1   主席先生，我现在想提出一个问题，然后发表一些评论，

2   因为看起来（xxxxxxxx）。

3   现在，我想问一个问题：

4   在座有多少人理解 SU——可持续利用……区域的含义？

5   你们如何解读它？

6   你们觉得这到底意味着什么？

7   因为这是我们讨论的核心。

8   你们都明白了吗？

9   你们很多人都不明白，

---

① 在圭亚那，"叔叔"是对年长的家庭和社区成员的一个常见的尊称。

10 这意味着你们很难理解这次会议的内容。

11 那，我们与来自不同组织的所有代表一起参加的会议：

12 我们坐在那里讨论（相对常见的）常识，

13 但我们深入讨论了可持续利用领域。

14 荒野保护区是另一个区域，

15 这就是分区的重要性所在。

16 要明确界定这个地方、区域，把可持续利用区确定下来，这就是你们的知识——我们所有人的知识能发挥作用的地方。

17 因为我们熟悉那片森林，

18 我们比住在外面的任何人都更接近森林，

19 因为我们生活在森林之中，

20 我们能给出建议。

21 我们应该这样看待这个问题。

22 因为每当你心情不好，

23 无论是谁，来的人都会再回去，

24 而我们会留在这里。

25 无论建什么、修什么，

26 我们还是会留在这里。

27 当然有的（不）会。

28 但我们在努力捍卫它，

29 因为我们大家都很担心。

30 现在，可持续利用区域指的是大家可以以可持续的方式使用自然资源的区域。

31 我们保护它……不让它衰微，

32 但如果可能的话，我们要让它不断增加

33 这样，那些东西，不管是什么，无论是藤蔓、药用植物、青蛙、蜈蚣、蛇、鱼、獭

　　狒,还是别的什么,

34　它必须留在那里

35　你一定不能去,去,耗尽。

36　让我们这一代人(xxxx)保持下去。

37　你取走了些,

38　但你必须帮助这个循环不断进行,

39　因此,资源的再生产能不断进行。

40　无论你为植树造林做什么,

41　种苗要长大。

42　如果你发现一种特殊的药用植物。

43　因为

44　如果你发现——

45　很明显,如果你找到一种非常有价值的药用植物,它可以治愈一些疾病,你
　　会占有它。

46　也就是说如果你把那里的自然资源拿出来,

47　你将让(长久以来的联系)消失殆尽。

──

　　在亨利大叔的话语中,我们看到前十行专门用来确立他在当前活动中作为信息提供者的角色(这跟前文中莎拉所做的类似),并在他就主题相关知识水平向其他与会者提出疑问时,也明确了本次会议之后的移位谈话的相关性。因此,本节中的谈话显然是构建会议语境的非语言特征的辅助。因此,本节在功能上与语篇2.5 的开场语类似。然而,即使在接下来的移位谈话中,我们也看到亨利叔叔如何不断强调那些与会者对于可持续利用区过程的参与,而莎拉只是短暂地使用了这种策略。我们还看到亨利叔叔直接向听众喊话,使用"我们"(17—29)或"你们"(30—47),教听众理解他们行动的重要性(40—47),并告诉他们应该如何行事(34、35、38)。通过这种方式,虽然亨利叔叔的语篇重构了以前会议的内容(在12

和 13 行中直接指称),因此具有构造性,但他将其作为提示来建议和指导听众,这是会议语境下的辅助行为。亨利叔叔从"我们"转变为"你们"的意义将在第 7 章中讨论,届时我们将更深入地研究这两个语篇。

语篇 2.5 和 2.6 之间的另一个值得注意的区别(我们在第 7 章中还会看到这一点),是莎拉和亨利叔叔对各自语场的构建方式非常不同,尽管两人描述的是同一个概念,即可持续利用区。莎拉突出提到了会议、组织和商业机会。然而,亨利叔叔虽然也触及了这些问题,但是更多地聚焦社区,他们的生活方式,以及他们与森林的关系。我们也可以把这称为对话语语场或故事情节的重新校准,而不是对人际关系的重新校准。这本书的一个要旨是展示话语的这两个方面是如何协同作用的,因为语场中的变化,包括直接的和移位的,都可能会导致或促进人际关系的变化,而人际关系的变化可能会加强话语语场中的变化。这些都是定位和权力所涉及的方面。现在,让我们更详细地看看,如何在话语中将直接语境、移位语境和人际关系结合起来,以达到良好的效果。①

练习 2.1

语篇 2.7 是塞巴斯蒂安·科(Sebastian Coe)在国际奥委会的讲话,他的讲话对伦敦 2012 年奥运会申办成功起到了一定作用。许多评论员都认为塞巴斯蒂安·科的参与,尤其是这次演讲,对伦敦申办成功起到了重要作用,因此这篇语篇非常值得分析,因为人们普遍认为它体现了一篇成功的话语。阅读语篇,然后回答以下问题。

语篇 2.7

1   I stand here today because of the inspiration of the Olympic Movement.
2   When I was 12, about the same age as Amber,

---

① 然而,有关效果的问题并不简单——我们必须小心区分在我们作为话语分析人士看来有效的东西和在实际实现其目标方面有效的东西。后者当然应该是应用语言学的目标,需要我们超越语篇本身,要去尝试确定受众如何回应和接受他们遇到的话语。

3　I was marched into a large school hall with my classmates.

4　We sat in front of an ancient, black and white TV

5　and watched grainy pictures from the Mexico Olympic Games.

6　Two athletes from our home town were competing.

7　John Sherwood won a bronze medal in the 400m hurdles.

8　His wife Sheila just narrowly missed gold in the long jump.

9　That day a window to a new world opened for me.

10　By the time I was back in my classroom,

11　I knew

12　what I wanted to do

13　and what I wanted to be.

14　The following week I stood in line for hours at my local track just to catch a glimpse of the medals the Sherwoods had brought home.

15　It didn't stop there.

16　Two days later I joined their club.

17　Two years later Sheila gave me my first pair of racing spikes.

18　35 years on, I stand before you with those memories still fresh.

19　My journey here to Singapore started in that school hall

20　and continues today in wonder and in gratitude. Gratitude that those flickering images of the Sherwoods, and Wolde, Gammoudi, Doubell and Hines drew me to a life in that most potent celebration of humanity Olympic sport.

21　And that gratitude drives me and my team to do whatever we can to inspire young people to choose sport.

22　Whocver they are,

23　wherever they live

24　and whatever they believe.

25　Today that task is so much harder.

26　Today's children live in a world of conflicting messages and competing distractions.

27　Their landscape is cluttered.

28　Their path to Olympic sport is often obscured.

29　But it's a world we must understand and must respond to.

30　My heroes were Olympians.

31　My children's heroes change by the month.

32 And they are the lucky ones.

33 Millions more face the obstacle of limited resources and the resulting lack of guiding role models.

34 In my travels over the last two years, speaking with many of you, I've had many conversations about how we meet this challenge.

35 And I've been reassured

36 and I've been uplifted

37 we share a common goal for the future of sport.

38 No group of leaders does more than you to engage the hearts and minds of young people.

39 But every year the challenge of bringing them to Olympic sport becomes tougher.

40 The choice of Host City is the most powerful means you have to meet this challenge.

41 But it takes more than 17 days of superb Olympic competition.

42 It takes a broader vision. And the global voice to communicate that vision over the full four years of the Olympiad.

43 Today in Britain's fourth bid in recent years we offer London's vision of inspiration and legacy.

44 Choose London today

45 and you send a clear message to the youth of the world:

46 more than ever, the Olympic Games are for you.

47 Mr President, Members of the IOC: Some might say

48 that your decision today is between five similar bids.

49 That would be to undervalue the opportunity before you.

50 In the past, you have made bold decisions: decisions which have taken the Movement forward in new and exciting directions.

51 Your decision today is critical.

52 It is a decision about which bid offers the vision and sporting legacy to best promote the Olympic cause.

53 It is a decision about which city will help us show a new generation why sport matters. In a world of many distractions, why Olympic sport matters.

54 On behalf of the youth of today, the athletes of tomorrow and the Olympians of the future, we humbly submit the bid of London 2012.

55 Mr. President, that concludes our presentation.

56 Thank you.

问题

A. 语言特征

(1) 找出语篇中(a)主要构成该语场的部分;(b)主要对本次演讲事件的非语言
特征起辅助作用的部分。

(2) 在构成的语场中,您找出了多少不同的子语场?

(3) 是否存在一个将这些子语场统合起来的总语场?

(4) 语篇中展开了哪些主题?它们与特定的子语场有关吗?

(5) 列举出让你得出 1 和 2 中的答案的语言特征。

(6) 讨论构成性特征如何也在演讲事件中发挥辅助作用。

(7) 讨论人称代词的用法。

B. 社会特征

在回答这些问题之前,你应该先了解一下塞巴斯蒂安·科,以及他作为运
动员和政治家的职业生涯与他在伦敦申办 2012 年奥运会中所扮演的角色。你
还应该对奥运会和选择主办城市的方式做一些了解,特别是要考虑到人们越来
越重视奥运会的"遗产"。掌握这些领域的背景知识将有助于你从语篇分析转
向话语分析。

(1) 讨论塞巴斯蒂安·科演讲的故事情节以及科为自己构建的不同角色。

(2) 讨论这些不同的角色如何影响塞巴斯蒂安·科在演讲中的整体"定位"。

(3) 尽管他从未提及这一点或者因为他从未提及这一点,但是你认为塞巴斯
蒂安·科作为奥运会金牌得主在哪些方面影响了他作为申办者的定位?

(4) 塞巴斯蒂安·科的演讲是以何种方式为特定受众设计的?

(5) 为了进一步进行情境分析,你可以看一看其他相关演讲,讨论你在语篇之间
观察到的任何联系,要考虑不同的作者及其不同的角色和文化资本。

2.3 衔接、指称/照应和主题的连续性

笔者在前文说过,实现语篇整体性的两种主要方法是(i)保持指称连续性(即保持照应——译者注),也就是说,重复指称相同的人和事物,尽管可能使用不同的字词来指称它们;(ii)维持和扩展某些**主题**(*motif*)(我在这里称之为motif,而非 theme 或者 topic,因为 theme 和 topic 二词在语言学中有特定的含义)。主题可以是人物、参与者或活动的类型,也可以是评价人物及其行为的方式(见第 4 章)。

2.3.1 指称/照应

指称/照应(*reference*)常常是通过代词实现的。由于代词的功能在于表示说话人预估受话人①能够识别所指的人或物(所指对象),而无需说话人明确指称,因此代词通常用来指代最后提到的人或物。不过它们在口语中也常用来指代处于同一环境中的、可以通过点头或指点来识别出的人或事。当若干次提及某个特定的所指对象,其中存在间隔时,说话人通常会使用一个以定冠词"the"开头的名词词组,因为这既让受话人能以某种方式识别出该所指对象,又表明说话人预估受话人能够通过给出的标识,从之前的谈话中找到该所指对象。当预估受话人无法识别出所指对象时,例如在第一次提及某物时,说话人将借助一个描述所指对象的名词词组,该名词词组包含一个不定冠词 a 或 an 来表示单个事物,或者包含 some 一词以表示多个事物。

有时,预期的识别可能性是由于话语双方的共有知识,或者由于所指对象处于同一直接环境中,而不是因为之前被提到过。在极少数情况下,只能通过

---

① 我所使用的"说话人"和"受话人"这两个术语,既针对口语,也针对书面语,因此在必要时这两个术语应被理解为包括作者和读者。

稍后出现的进一步标识来识别所指对象,如"他是个奇怪的人,我的兄弟"。这些不同类型的照应都有相应的专业术语。**回指照应**(*anaphoric reference*)是指可以从先前所提及的内容中找出;**下指照应**(*cataphoric reference*)是指我们需要等待片刻才能发现所指的人是谁。回指照应和下指照应都是**内指照应**(*endophoric reference*)或**语篇内照应**(*text-internal reference*)。**外指照应**(*exophoric reference*)是指我们可以从直接环境中找出所指对象。**单指照应**(*homophoric reference*)指的是共有知识足以明确所指对象,比如"我把钱包忘在厨房里了"或"首相昨天犯了一个可怕的错误"。因此,单指照应可以成为预设或构建共有知识和观念的一种好方法,这是在更广泛的环境中(通常相对于外部群体而言)定位说话人和受话人时采用的一个重要手段。

另一种表明身份可以被识别的方式是使用姓名和头衔,如"塞巴斯蒂安·科勋爵"。当说话人认为与受话人拥有共同的常识时,便可以使用头衔,因此可以用在第一次提到所指对象之时,也可用在之前通过其他方式提到过所指对象时。

有时,照应被用来辅助识别另一个不同的事物,比如"他的兄弟是个奇怪的人"。这里的**所有格形容词**(*possessive adjective*)"他的(his)"帮助我们识别一个新的参与者(他兄弟),手段是将兄弟与我们已经在谈论的人(他)联系起来。或者,当谈论同一事物的两个例子时,我们可以使用**属有代词**(*possessive pronoun*),它们各自独立出现,就像"他的车比我的旧"中的"我的(mine)"一样。通过这些方式,照应既有了连续性,也可有变化性,这是一种重要的手段,可以让说话人在推进语篇的同时保持**衔接**(*cohesion*)。

我们也可以通过空间位置来识别人或物,比如"这个人"或"那个人"。"这个(this)"在书面形式中也用于指代刚刚提到的一个想法,如"这项政策非常重要",或简单地说"这非常重要"。当单独使用时,"这个(this)"和"那个(that)"被称为**指示代词**(*demonstrative pronouns*),当在名词前使用时,它们被称为**指示形容词**(*demonstrative adjectives*)。

练习 2.2

(1)找出塞巴斯蒂安·科在演讲中使用的所有这类特征——用以表明(他预期)受话人可以通过某种方式找出所指对象的身份。答案见附录。

(2)讨论塞巴斯蒂安·科预期受话人能够识别出所指对象的方式。

(3)塞巴斯蒂安·科在第 5、20、33、39 和 40 小句中使用照应来暗示共有知识,请思考这样会产生什么额外的效果?

2.3.2 主题

主题通常是通过**语义域**(*semantic domain*)的扩展而展开的,语义域中的语篇词汇具有某种共同的意义特征,或者是相对而立。通常,单词之间的关系可以从字典中查到,这种关系被称为**同义关系**(*synonymy*)、**下义关系**(*hyponymy*)、**局部关系**(*meronymy*)和**反义关系**(*antonymy*)。这里还包括同一个词语的**重复**(*repetition*)(但是不一定指完全相同的事物)。

例如,"波斯猫"和"马恩岛猫"都是**上义词**(*superordinate*)"猫"的下义词,而"波斯猫"和"马恩岛猫"二者存在一种共下义关系。"手"和"脚"都是"身体"的**局部词**(*meronym*)(身体被称为上义词,与下义关系中一样),并且是彼此的共局部词。有时很难区分局部词和下义词,但有一个简单的测试——波斯猫和马恩岛猫都是猫(下义关系),但手和脚不是两个身体,只是身体的一部分(**局部关系** *meronymy*)。

然而,一个主题中的词汇之间的关系并不总是在字典定义中明确可得的,而是在具体的语篇中加以构建的(Brazil 1995)。

例如,在讨论政府政务举措失当时,作者可以从上义词"错误清单"开始,然后再列出此清单中所载的"糟糕的学校教育"和"医疗服务失策"来作为**依境而定**(*locally contingent*)的局部词。一个类似(但有必要加以区别)的例子是将各个具体的人称为一个范畴的**例子**(*examples*),就像把托尼·布莱尔和玛格丽特·撒切尔称为上义范畴"英国的首相们"的例子一样。不知何故,把这些人称为下义词似乎欠妥!

　　类似地,依境而定的**对比**（contrast）也可以在特定语篇中加以构建。例如,一位政治人物可能会将一个政党的成就与另一个政党的成就进行对比（尽管他们很可能会将他们所认为的成就与失败进行对比）。由于依境而定的对比和反义词（即来自词典定义的反义词）之间的界限有时很难划清,我们将在我们的语篇分析中使用对比来指称二者。

　　在展开主题中可能用到的最后一种类型的关系是词语表达的态度存在连续性或形成直接对比,比如"谋杀""独裁""人权"和"共同利益"。这些词都包含道德评价,在语篇中使用这些词会产生不同层次的**语义韵律**（semantic prosodies）（都与道德有关,两个是褒义词,两个是贬义词）,详见第 4 章。

　　在详细讨论塞巴斯蒂安·科演讲中的照应关系之后,我们将回头再来讨论主题。

2.4　塞巴斯蒂安·科向国际奥委会致辞中的照应和主题

2.4.1　塞巴斯蒂安·科致辞中的照应

　　在塞巴斯蒂安·科的演讲中,最常见的指称对象是塞巴斯蒂安·科本人（他个人或与他人一起）、国际奥委会（IOC）、当今的青年和奥运会。这种指称连续性见表 2.1。请注意表格内容的陈列方式,在一列的顶部是指称对象的一般性术语,然后在该列下面的方框内是指称上述对象的实际词汇（标型）,方框所在行标上了包含该词汇的小句对应的行号。（这使得查看表格的人更容易对照语篇进行核对）。当出现省略的情况时,我们可以在不重复指称的情况下保持照应而不需要给出指称对象,这时"省缺"的词将放在括号中。在第 5 小句中,我们看到前一句中的主语"我们"仍然暗寄其中,所以可以理解;在第 44 句中,这是因为"你们",即国际奥委会,是祈使句的隐含主语(见第 4 章)。注意,"我们的"这样的**所有格代词**(*possessive pronouns*)也包括在内。在某些小句中,同一指称对象会多次出现,所有标型都放在相应的框中。请注意,在第 29 和第 34 小句中,我认为"我们"既指称塞巴斯蒂安·科,又指称国际奥委会,因此将其放在了两个框中(见表 2.1)。

表 2.1　塞巴斯蒂安·科奥林匹克演讲中的指称/照应

Clause	Coe (+others)	IOC	Today's youth	Olympic sport
1	I			
2	I			
3	I			
4	we			
5	(we)			
6	our			
7				
8				
9	me			
10	I, my			
11	I			
12	I			
13	I			
14	I, my			
15				
16	I			
17	me, my			
18	I	you		
19	my			
20	me			Olympic sport
21	me, my, we		young people	
22			they	
23			they	
24			they	
25				
26			today's children	
27			their	
28			their	Olympic sport

续表

Clause	Coe (+others)	IOC	Today's youth	Olympic sport
29	we	we		
30	my			
31	my			
32				
33			millions more	
34	my, I, we	you,		
35	I	we		
36	I			
37	we	we		
38		you	young people	
39			them	Olympic sport
40		you		
41				Olympic competition
42				the Olympiad
43	we			
44		(you)		
45		you	youth of the world	
46		You		
47		IOC		
48		your		
49		you		
50		you		
51		your		
52				
53	us	us	a new generation	Olympic sport
54	we		the youth of today	
55	our			
56		you		

这张表格揭示了几个有趣的现象,既包括语篇中维持连续性的方式,也包括语篇展开过程中指称焦点是如何从一个参与者或群体转移到另一个参与者或群体的。

就连续性而言,我们可以看到,塞巴斯蒂安·科本人提供了一个几乎连续不断的线条,而其他每一个参与者都是从跟他的关系的角度引入的——第 18 小句中的国际奥委会,第 20 小句中的奥林匹克运动,以及第 21 小句中的今天的年轻人。被引入后,这些其他的指称对象就仿佛获得自我的生命,并且在没有塞巴斯蒂安·科的情况下相互作用,而随着演讲的展开,塞巴斯蒂安·科的存在感逐渐变得不那么强烈了。

同样值得注意的是,在整场演讲中,只有一个小句不包括这四个指称对象中的至少一个,即第 52 小句。第 52 小句中的"奥林匹克事业(*Olympic cause*)"与"奥林匹克运动(Olympic sport)"并无**同指关系**(*coreferential*),但它确实构成了一种语义联系,因为两者都是奥林匹克运动(Olympic Movement)的一部分,如下所述。

从篇章展开的角度看,在第 1—20 小句中,提到塞巴斯蒂安·科时大多是第一人称单数(I、ME 或 MY),第 21—37 小句中,混合了 I/ME/MY 和内包式 WE/OUR,以及第 38 小句中,对塞巴斯蒂安·科的指称转变为指称伦敦团队的外排式 WE/OUR,与之相对的是将国际奥委会指称为 YOU。

在表 2.1 中,同样值得注意的是,在聚焦塞巴斯蒂安·科本人之后,焦点是如何先转移到今天的年轻人,再短暂地转移到体育,然后在演讲接近尾声时转移到国际奥委会的。

练习 2.3

讨论上面描述的语篇模式以及你所观察到的任何其他特征是如何帮助该语篇成为一篇有效的演讲的。

识别语篇中的指称/照应关系,除了可以凸显出其中有趣的模式外,也是进行及物性分析的基础,后者的目的是探讨指称对象参与所描述事件的不同方式,以及他们的行为如何相互影响。及物性分析将在第 3 章中介绍。

2.4.2　塞巴斯蒂安·科演讲中的主题

表 2.2 展示了构建语场时的另一种语篇性。本表格并不旨在追溯在语篇

中重复出现的相同的指称对象,而是显示各个主题(而非具体的指称对象)是如何随着语篇的展开而引入和扩展的。我所选择的主题如下:一是塞巴斯蒂安·科从学生时代到伦敦申奥的旅程,这在我看来似乎是这篇演讲中起着统合作用的叙事;二是运动员这一类人,包括任何特定的指称对象;三是奥林匹克运动及其所有表现形式;四是问题和解决方案,作为相同主题的对立的两端。

表 2.2 首先从第一次提到这些主题开始,追踪了语篇后面出现的所有跟这些主题存在前文所述数种意义关系的概念,这些意义关系包括同义、重复、对比;部分、下义和上义;共下义、共局部、示例。在第一次提到后,识别出的标型将根据其与链中前一个标型的关系进行标记。通过这种方式,我们可以看到概念是如何分解和组合在一起的,说话人是如何以牺牲一个角度为代价而展开另一个角度的,还可看到不同的概念是如何组合在一起的。

读者会注意到,指称对象和主题之间的界限并不总是明确的。对于一个个体,比如塞巴斯蒂安·科,他作为一个特定的人的指称对象是很容易辨识的,但是对像奥林匹克运动这样一个指称对象,要在一个指称对象和一个抽象的概念之间划清界限就有点困难了——比如说,提到"铁饼"应该算是这个概念的相同指称对象,还是算作这个概念的延伸呢? 我采取的路线是尽可能地用指称一词来指提到完全相同的对象的情况;如果将其分解开来或归为一个更大的类别,那么我们可以将其视为一个主题的展开。

如上所述,同样重要的是要记住语篇中建立的许多关系都是依境而定的,也就是说,它们之间的关系取决于被构建的语场,乃至单个语篇。正如本章开头就提到,话语分析人士所感兴趣的,正是这种可以以不同方式构建一个语场的自由,因为他们想要在语境中理解语篇中所涉及的各种原因和方式。

表 2.2 揭示了一个复杂的主题组合模式,其中,塞巴斯蒂安·科的生活故事、体育、奥林匹克理想、当今年轻人面临的问题以及伦敦申办 2012 年奥运会都被建构成密切而复杂的相互关联体。实现这种效果的方式是通过展开各个主题的不同方面,使它们彼此交融,从而在论证的不同经纬之间建立各种关联。

表 2. 2 塞巴斯蒂安·科奥林匹克演讲中的主题

Clause	Coe's Journey	Athletes	The Olympic Movement	Problems and Solutions
1	I stand here today			
2			Olympic Movement	
3				inspiration
4				
5			Mexico Olympic Games (exa)	
6		Athletes		
7		John Sherwood (exa)		
8		Sheila (exa)		
9				
10				
11				
12				
13				
14		Sherwoods (rpt)		
15				
16				
17		Sheila (rpt)		
18	I stand before you (rpt)		This great movement (sup)	inspired (rpt)
19	My journey here to Singapore (sup)			

#				
20	Life in Olympic sport (mer)	Sherwoods (rpt), Wolde, Gammoudi, Doubell and Hynes (exas)	That most potent celebration of humanity Olympic sport (mer)	
21	Doing whatever we can to inspire young people to choose sport (comer)			inspire (rpt)
22				
23				
24				
25	task (syn)			task (contr)
26				Conflicting messages and competing distractions (mer)
27				Their landscape is cluttered (syn)
28			Olympic sport (rpt)	Their path to Olympic sport is often obscured (mer)
29				A world we must understand and respond to (sup)
30		My heroes (sup)	Olympians (mer)	
31				

续表

Clause	Coe's Journey	Athletes	The Olympic Movement	Problems and Solutions
32				
33				Obstacles...models (mer)
34	My travels (comer)			This challenge (sup)
35				
36				
37	common good (contr)			
38				Engage the hearts and minds of young people (syn)
39			Olympic sport (sup)	Challenge of bringing them to Olympic sport (mer)
40				This challenge (rpt)
41			Superb Olympic competition (syn)	
42			Olympiad (sup)	Broader vision (mer); global voice (mer)
43	We offer London's vision (comer)			London's vision of inspiration and legacy (exa)
44				

#			
45			Olympic Games are for you (syn)
46		Olympic Games (mer)	
47		Mr President (comer); Members of the IOC (comer)	
48			Your decision today (sup)
49			Opportunity (syn)
50		The Movement (sup)	Bold decisions (hyp); decisions which have taken ... directions (exas)
51			Your decision today (exa)
52		The Olympic cause (mer)	Decision about ... cause (syn)
53		Olympic sport (mer); Olympic ideals (comer)	Decision about ... much (syn)
54	The athletes of tomorrow (contr); Olympians of the future (mer)	London 2012 (exa)	The bid of London 2012 (mer)
55	We humbly submit the bid of London 2012 (syn)	Mr President (comer)	
56	Our presentation (syn)		

因此，许多关联都是依境而定的，通常需要思考一番才能确定这些想法是如何结合在一起的，但这往往能揭示出最为有趣的洞见。例如，我分析了第 46 小句中的"the Olympic Games are for you"，认为塞巴斯蒂安·科将之构建成了第 43 小句中"London's vision of inspiration and legacy"的同义词，因为塞巴斯蒂安·科在第 44 和第 45 小句中已经完成了将这两个概念联系起来所需的语言工作。这不仅表明了思想之间的关系是可以依境而定的，也显示了说话人如何运用他们的语言来建立这些关系。在这之后，我提出"your decison today"是"the Olympic Games are for you"的一个上义词。这似乎有点奇怪，但我们可以看到，塞巴斯蒂安·科将当前的决定定义为在五个申办城市之间的抉择，其中一个是伦敦的"vision of inspiration and legacy"，并将其重新措辞为"the Olympic Games are for you"。因此，今天的决定包括五种可能性：选择"the Olympic Games are for you"或其他四个申办口号之一！

这里需要记住的重要一点，根据话语依境而定的本质，意义关系的标记并不是一门精确的科学，而是一种思维方式，用以探讨说话人让概念所起的作用，以及说话人如何使用语言的其他方面来实现这一点的。由此看来，表 2.2 这样的表格只是完成了解读和解释之前的准备工作而已。

练习 2.4

（1）通览一遍表 2.2 中标记的意义关系。你看到笔者想要捕捉的关系了吗？你认为还有哪些语言特征可能对笔者的分析起到了帮助作用？你同意笔者的分析吗？你认为还存在什么关系？为什么？

（2）看看"问题和解决方案（Problems and Solutions）"的链条，讨论一下塞巴斯蒂安·科是如何将社会问题、伦敦申办和国际奥委会的决定联系起来的。

（3）你认为文中提到的一个个运动员在话语中的作用是什么？

（4）讨论一下各个主题如何做到时而凸显和时而隐逸的，以及你认为这是否有效。

(5)塞巴斯蒂安·科以何种方式重新调整了关乎伦敦申奥评选结果的移位的故事情节？

(6)塞巴斯蒂安·科以何种方式重新调整了他定位为申请者而国际奥委会定位为仲裁者的直接故事情节？

(7)你对第 5 和第 6 个问题的回答是如何共同作用以阐明塞巴斯蒂安·科是如何"掌控语境"的？他为什么能这么做？

2.5　总结

本章中，我们研究了直接语境和移位语境之间的区别，以及语言在构建这些语境时所起到的辅助性或构造性作用。我们思考了移位语境如何在某些直接活动中发挥某些作用，并研究了不同语境共同作用的各种方式。一方面，我们看到，我们可以在构建直接活动的同时构建移位语境，以重新校准人际关系，从而促进活动本身；另一方面，我们看到，在组织活动时，主要由移位语境构成的语言辅助性使用可以突出人际关系的某些特征，而这些特征可能会对主要活动产生影响（未完待续）。然后，我们看到了莎拉和亨利叔叔对可持续利用区过程的解释，并提出移位语境和直接语境之间的界限比我们最初所认为的更模糊（详见第 6 章）。在这些语篇中，我们还看到了不同的说话人如何通过对同一概念的不同构建来重新调整故事情节。最后，我们看了塞巴斯蒂安·科向国际奥委会发表的演讲，以了解随着语篇在直接语境中发挥作用时，如何对转变的语境的衔接模式进行管理，从而产生巨大的效果，对故事情节进行构建和重新校准，以开辟新的话语语场，这些语场涉及相关人员的不同历史和不同的权利和责任范围。这一章最为重要的观点——也是整本书的基础——是说话人会不断地重新调整为他们的话语提供背景的故事情节，以及他们自己和受话人之间的人际关系；然而，至关重要的是，这些不是独立的行为，而是相互制约的话语定位行为。本书的目标是展示一种语篇和社会分析的方法，使你能够掌握这些相互关系，并分析它们在实时话语中的作用。

在结束本章之前，我们可以参考一下布迪厄（Bourdieu 1991）和伯恩斯坦（Bernstein 1971,2000）在语场方面的研究，尤其是关于特定文化语场对来自不同文化背景的人的潜在失效效应。在这一章中，我们看到了说话人如何通过构建和重新校准语场来达到特定的目的。具体地说，在亨利叔叔的案例中，我们看到了他如何从社区参与的角度来构建可持续利用区语场，并将社区的经验作为一种有价值的知识形式加以利用。然而，这样一个过程的另一面是一些参与活动的人对这个语场感到陌生——用布迪厄的话说，当一个人的实践语场与社交领域不匹配时，他们就没有形成恰当的**规则**（*habitus*），即潜意识中对发生的事情和应对之道的一种感觉。简单地说，他们对"游戏规则"不熟悉。按照伯恩斯坦（Bernstein 2000:16-22）的说法，深谙某种文化的说话人不仅会掌握**识别规则**（*recognition rules*），让他能了解发生的事情和应对之道，也会掌握**实现规则**（*realization rules*），即以这种文化所特有的方式来行事。因此，与在自己的舒适区行事的人相比，那些在自己不习惯的语场里行事的说话人面临着双重的不利条件——任何一个试图在陌生的国家完成一项相对简单的任务（如预订房间或购买电车票）的人都熟悉这种情况。伯恩斯坦的焦点是工人阶级儿童在进入小学后遭遇（被认为是理所当然的）中产阶级的游戏规则时所面临的劣势（另见 Hasan and Cloran 1990）。布迪厄从更广阔的视角探讨了占主导地位的精英如何能够在国家机构里强行施加其规范，以便维持和复制其主导地位。虽然我们不会直接关注这些主题，但布迪厄和伯恩斯坦提出的概念显然与本书中提出的分析框架有关，你稍后会了解到他们的想法。

第 3 章 构建参与：说话人作为木偶演员

3.1 引言

在前一章中，我们从广义上研究了说话人如何在特定环境中构建话语语场。我们聚焦如何维持和展开话语领域的两种互补的手段——通过反复指称特定的人和事物，以及通过细化推进主题。在本章中，我们将更深入地研究指称对象之间所构建的关系，尤其是指称对象参与不同活动的情况，包括指称对象参与的活动类型以及指称对象在这些活动中扮演的不同角色。这将使我们能够看出谁被构建为施动者和施震者，以及谁或什么被构建为受动者和受震者！不过，请记住，构建指的是说话人利用语言资源突出某个语场的特定方面的方式，因此说话人对事件的特定构建方式既可以让我们了解说话人所谈论的人和事件，又可以让我们了解说话人本身。因此，关于说话人为什么以一种特定的方式构建一个事件的问题，可能会让我们思考和说话人所采取的立场有关的问题，以及令说话人在不同的受众面前所采取的这种立场显得合理的地位或文化资本的问题。

我们对事件参与的分析自然以动词为中心，因为动词是最典型的与行为、活动和事态相关的词汇语法资源——我们可以将所有这些统称为技术术语"**过程**"（*process*）。不过，英语中有很多动词，如果我们要考虑到它们所表达的所有意义上的差异，那么就很难捕捉到语篇内部或语篇之间的构建模式。因此，我们在将过程类型区分为形成对比的组别时,就必须确定适当的抽象程度。通过不同的方法可以做到这一点,其中一些方法取决于依境而定的对比,例如工作与玩耍的动词形成了对比,这在特定的研究主题中可能是一个需要突出的重要区别。然而,在一般层面上,语言的语法提供了过程类型之间的基本区别,这些过程类型捕捉到了不同参与者参与事件和活动的基本区别。韩礼德(Halliday and Matthiessen 2004,第 5 章)提出,所有语言都使用语法(而不是词汇)来区分**物质**(*material*)、**心理**(*menta*)和**关系**(*relational*)过程。这些范畴很可能具有普遍性,这一事实意味着,它们可能捕捉到了人类所理解的参与行为之间的基本区别,因此在话语分析中把握好这些区别是大有裨益的。除了这三个核心范畴之外,英语还有基本或最不**微妙的**(*delicate*)过程类型系统项下的**语言**(*verbal*)、**行为**(*behavioral*)和**存在**(*existential*)过程。**参与者**(*participants*)可以以不同的方式参与这些过程类型,例如,作为执行物质行为的人、打人的或被打的人。我将在第 3.1 节中深入讨论不同的过程类型和参与类型。

一旦我们考虑到语法如何区分不同的过程类型,以及作为分析者,我们如何区分说话人构建参与的方式,我们就可以观察语篇中这种构建行为的流变,并且可以看到它如何随着不同的话题和主题而变化的。在此基础上,我们可以看到一幅复杂的画面是如何编织成一个连贯的整体的,在这个整体中,不同的参与者随着主题的发展时而突出又时而隐没。在本章末,我们将思考构建参与者参与行为的语言资源可以怎样被说话人用于自我和他人的定位,以及这种定位行为如何与情景和社会环境的特征协同作用以赋予话语有效性或者力量。

3.2 及物性: 过程类型

及物性(*transitivity*)这个术语是指不同参与者在一个过程中扮演的角色之间的关系。你可能在传统语法中遇到过这个术语,它经常被用来区分带宾语的"动词"和不带宾语的"动词"。例如,抚摸是你对其他事物所做的事情,所以"抚

摸"是及物的:

1. Tom stroked the dog.

　　然而,跑步是你可以自己做的事情,所以"跑步"在日常生活中是不及物的:

2. The dog was running.

　　你可能也听说过**双及物结构**(*ditransitive constructions*),其中涉及 三个参与者,我们需要两个宾语,一个直接宾语,一个间接宾语,如:

3. I gave my aunt the teapot.

　　在这里,"茶壶"是直接宾语(它是被给予的东西),而"我的阿姨"是间接宾语(她没有被给予,但有一些东西被给了她)。

　　然而,这种对及物性的理解是很有局限性的,因为它只涵盖了三种可能的语法模式,而且它对参与者之间可以通过语法手段构建的许多不同类型的关系给出的细节太少。下面介绍的更为详细的及物性研究方法做出了更广泛的区别,可以用来分析说话人如何根据他所参与的直接事件来定位自己和他人,以及如何(正如我们所看到的那样)在直接事件中也起着关键作用的移位语场中来定位自己和他人。

　　如上所述,英语有六种宽泛的过程类型,每种类型都构建了所涉参与者之间的不同关系。不幸的是,这是一个相当复杂的语法领域,有时小句的分析十分困难。然而,作为一个推广者,笔者不可能仅仅展示这个系统的一鳞半爪。从我自身分析语篇的经验来看,无论是我自己在研究的语篇还是学生们选择的,极少语篇只依赖简单明了的及物性的例子。因此,为了避免以后产生挫败感,在进行语篇分析之前,有必要对各种过程类型进行详细的介绍。

　　及物性分析通常聚焦构成**每个小句的主要动词**的过程,但并非总是如此。我们将讨论其他的可能性。及物性分析的一个要点是我们不讨论动词是否及物,而讨论在语篇中被构建的过程是否涉及多个参与者。例如,在例 4 中,动词 JUMP 构建了一个只涉及一个参与者的过程,但在例 5 中,这个动词却构建了一个涉及两个参与者的过程:

4. Tom jumped when the television exploded.

5. The horse jumped the fence with ease.

从本书所持的角度来看,最重要的是说话人对事件的构建,以及对不同人物在这个事件中的**参与角色**(*participant roles*)的构建。因此,如果不了解某个动词在语境中的用法,就不可能说出该动词所构建的过程类型。

我们还将简要介绍及物性的另一个方面,即说话人在对行为和事态的构建中所添加的细节,通常被称为过程**周围的环境**(*circumstances*)。这包括事件发生的时间或地点、原因或影响等信息。这应能使我们能够更全面地描述所构建的语场,并从描述语篇到讨论话语的转换中,以及从讨论不同社会情境时说话人所采取的立场中,得到更多的关联点。一般而言,参与者角色构建了一个过程所涉及到的人和物,而环境则回答了为什么、何时、何地、如何等问题(包括多少、多久等复合问题)。

我将用塞巴斯蒂安·科对国际奥林匹克委员会的演讲(作为语篇 3.1)来说明不同的过程类型及其涉的参与者角色。在讨论构建的过程类型和参与者角色时,我将讨论一些关于小句分解的有趣问题:

语篇 3.1

1   I stand here today because of the inspiration of the Olympic Movement.

2   When I was 12, about the same age as Amber,

3   I was marched into a large school hall with my classmates.

4   We sat in front of an ancient, black and white TV

5   and watched grainy pictures from the Mexico Olympic Games.

6   Two athletes from our home town were competing.

7   John Sherwood won a bronze medal in the 400m hurdles.

8   His wife Sheila just narrowly missed gold in the long jump.

9   That day a window to a new world opened for me.

10   By the time I was back in my classroom,

11   I knew

12 　what I wanted to do

13 　and what I wanted to be.

14 　The following week I stood in line for hours at my local track just to catch a glimpse of the medals the Sherwoods had brought home.

15 　It didn't stop there.

16 　Two days later I joined their club.

17 　Two years later Sheila gave me my first pair of racing spikes.

18 　35 years on, I stand before you with those memories still fresh.

19 　My journey here to Singapore started in that school hall

20 　and continues today in wonder and in gratitude. Gratitude that those flickering images of the Sherwoods, and Wolde, Gammoudi, Doubell and Hines drew me to a life in that most potent celebration of humanity: Olympic sport.

21 　And that gratitude drives me and my team to do whatever we can to inspire young people to choose sport.

22 　Whoever they are,

23 　wherever they live

24 　and whatever they believe.

25 　Today that task is so much harder.

26 　Today's children live in a world of conflicting messages and competing distractions.

27 　Their landscape is cluttered.

28 　Their path to Olympic sport is often obscured.

29 　But it's a world we must understand and must respond to.

30 　My heroes were Olympians.

31 　My children's heroes change by the month.

32 　And they are the lucky ones.

33 　Millions more face the obstacle of limited resources and the resulting lack of guiding role models.

34 　In my travels over the last two years, speaking with many of you, I've had many conversations about how we meet this challenge.

35 　And I've been reassured

36 　and I've been uplifted

37 　we share a common goal for the future of sport.

38 　No group of leaders does more than you to engage the hearts and minds of young

people.

39　But every year the challenge of bringing them to Olympic sport becomes tougher.

40　The choice of Host City is the most powerful means you have to meet this challenge.

41　But it takes more than 17 days of superb Olympic competition.

42　It takes a broader vision. And the global voice to communicate that vision over the full four years of the Olympiad.

43　Today in Britain's fourth bid in recent years we offer London's vision of inspiration and legacy.

44　Choose London today

45　and you send a clear message to the youth of the world:

46　more than ever, the Olympic Games are for you.

47　Mr President, Members of the IOC: Some might say

48　that your decision today is between five similar bids.

49　That would be to undervalue the opportunity before you.

50　In the past, you have made bold decisions: decisions which have taken the Movement forward in new and exciting directions.

51　Your decision today is critical.

52　It is a decision about which bid offers the vision and sporting legacy to best promote the Olympic cause.

53　It is a decision about which city will help us show a new generation why sport matters. In a world of many distractions, why Olympic sport matters.

54　On behalf of the youth of today, the athletes of tomorrow and the Olympians of the future, we humbly submit the bid of London 2012.

55　Mr President, that concludes our presentation.

56　Thank you.

3.2.1　物质过程

最常见的,也许也是最容易分析的过程类型是**物质过程**(*material process*)。顾名思义,这些过程总是涉及物质世界中的一种行为,在这种行为中,某人或某

物做了某事,通常但不总有他人或他物作为行为的对象。这方面的一个例子出现在第 6 小句中,其中塞巴斯蒂安·科说:

6. Two athletes from our home town were competing.

　　显然,竞争是一种物质的行为,但是,仅仅分析关于小句的外观是错误的,因为许多过程都不那么清晰,这通常因为随着语言的发展,它从语法的一个领域借用了一些特征,并将这些特征应用到了新的地方,或者运用其资源来达到特殊效果。因此,有必要使用语法**检测**(*probes*)来测试过程的类型。由于过程类型是通过语法来区分的范畴,因此作为分析者,我们可以使用语法检测来区分它们,这是合乎逻辑的。仅凭印象判断被称为**意念**(*notional*)方法,虽然功能语法的一个核心原则是语法范畴与意义差异有关,但这种方法可能忽略过程类型之间看似微小但却意义重大的差异。调查涉及使用**同源小句**(*agnate clause*)来更换句子措辞,这些小句在意义上与原始小句相似,但某些方面又与之不同。物质过程的基本检测如下:

　　　　(1)这个过程可以用"*What X did*① *was*(*to*)…"的形式重新表述吗?
　　　　　　物质过程可以这样重新表述。
　　　　(2)如果一个过程现在正在进行,那么现在进行时②是用来指称这个
　　　　　　过程的最自然的形式吗 ? 物质过程行为就是这样。

　　注意,这个意义上的 DO 是一个语法词,表示一个动作,但没有具体内容,因此第一个检测和第二个检测一样都是基于"语法"的。运用这些检测,我们发现小句中的"竞争"是一个物质过程:

7. What the athletes did was (to) compete.
8. The athletes are competing right now.

---

①　或"will do""is doing"等。
②　Halliday and Matthiessen(2004:335-354)称之为"present in the present"(当下中的当下),但我应使用
　　更熟悉的术语。

我在前面说过,这些是物质过程的"基本"检测,因为这些检测为分析物质过程提供了必要但不充分的基础。正如我们将在下面看到的,另外两种过程类型也可以通过这些检测——言语过程和行为过程。这两种类型也编码了一定程度的物质性。正如韩礼德所说,我们体验和表述世界的方式并不总有明确的界限。然而,由于言语和物质过程类型编码了非常特别的行为类型,因此需要进一步检测。下面介绍的这些检测从语法上区分了言语、行为和"主流的"物质行为和活动,这是将它们视为不同过程类型的基础。

前文中对物质过程的第一个检测也让我们能够区分物质过程中的参与者角色(PRs)之一,即**动作者**(Actor)——参与竞争或涉及的任何过程的人或物。请注意,DO 在英语中有很多用法,所以检测的正确措辞很重要。例如,我们可以说"I do love you",但如果说"What I did was love you",那将是非常具有标记性的,而且可能有点轻薄无礼。请注意,英语中的行为者不一定能控制自己的动作,也不一定对自己的动作负责。在其他语言中,这种情况可能会进行语法标记,所以在这种情况下,会引入一个不同的参与者角色,或者至少是一个子范畴。例如,当塞巴斯蒂安·科在第 9 小句中说:

9. That day a window to a new world opened for me.

"Window"是动作者,是实施行为的东西(what the window did was open),尽管我们知道是奥运会使得隐喻中的窗户打开。塞巴斯蒂安·科还可以说"That day opened a new world for me",在这种情况下,"that day"就是动作者,但他并没有以这种方式来构建这一事件,而这篇语篇中令人感兴趣的正是塞巴斯蒂安·科的构建行为(欲知补充观点,请参见 Halliday 和 Matthiessen 2004:280-302 on ergativity)。

塞巴斯蒂安·科的开场白中出现了另一个令人感兴趣的地方:

10. I stand here today because of the inspiration of the Olympic Movement.

在本句中,"stand"看起来像一个物质过程,请注意这里用了一般现在时来表示现在正在发生的事情。使用这种时态（或体，视读者观点而定）暗示"stand"并不是在构建一个物质过程。在物质过程中使用一般现在时表示习惯性或重复的动作或活动，但塞巴斯蒂安·科显然指的是单次事件。把塞巴斯蒂安·科的话与下面的例子进行比较。（＊表示结构不好的例子，而? 和?? 表示存疑的例子。）

11. I stand up whenever the teacher comes in.
12. I'm standing up right now.
13. ＊ I stand up right now.

在这些例子中，"stand up"是一个物质过程，是每当老师进来时，我所习惯性做（do）的动作，或者是现在我正在做的（am doing）事情［或在过去的特定时间正在做（was doing）或在将来的特定时间我将要正在做（will be doing）的事情］。然而，在塞巴斯蒂安·科的演讲中，"站立（stand）"是一个**行为过程**（*behavioral process*），指的是他的身体姿势。下面我们将更详细地介绍行为过程，但我们可以顺便指出行为过程通常可以与物质过程区分开来，因为它们不是指**动作**（*action*），而是指状态（或介于两者之间的东西，比如呼吸），所以现在可以用一般现在时来表示。这是一个很好的例子，说明了为什么在分析过程类型时一定不能囿于意念方法。

除了将参与者构建为在做某事外，物质过程还常常将动作者构建为在对某人或物做某事。在这些情况下，动作者也有**目标**（*goal*）。更具体些，我们可以说在这样的过程中，一个动作是由一个动作者执行的，且这个动作会延续至并影响到一个目标。这一事实解释了为什么这些过程传统上被称为"及物的（transitive）"（"过渡的"——译者注）（指从动作从一个参与者过渡到另一个参与者）以及为什么目标（goal）①是动作终点的术语。有趣的是，塞巴斯蒂安·科的

---

① 　并非所有的语法方法都使用这个术语。然而，不同流派使用的术语在某种程度上反映了所采用的及物性方法更普遍的差异。因此，不同流派的术语不应混用。

演讲中几乎没有关于目标的例子,这一点稍后将再次探讨。第 20 小句中有一个例子(尽管它本身不是一个完整的小句),其中塞巴斯蒂安·科说:

14. ... those flickering images ... drew me to a life in that most potent celebration of humanity: Olympic sport. (那些闪烁不定的影像……吸引了我,让我开启了奥林匹运动的一生,奥运会是人类最伟大的赞礼。)

对过程目标的检测如下:

> 这个过程可以用"What X did to Y was..."的形式重新表述吗?如果可以,那么 Y 就是目标。

我们既可以用这个检测,也可以使用上述物质过程的第二个检测来改变塞巴斯蒂安·科的小句的措辞,如下所示:

15. What those flickering images did to me was draw me to a life in that most potent celebration of humanity: Olympic sport. (那些闪烁不定的画面对我所做的是把我吸引到了一种生活中,一种对人性刚健的讴歌。)

16. Right now those flickering images are drawing me to a life in that most potent celebration of humanity: Olympic sport. (现在,那些闪烁不定的画面正把我引向一种生活,一种对人性最刚健的讴歌。)

这些检测告诉我们,"那些画面(those flickering images)"是过程中的动作者(他们做了吸引这个动作),而塞巴斯蒂安·科[在这里通过标型"我(me)"体现]是目标(即被吸引的人,受吸引动作影响的人)。在下面虚构的小句中,情况更加一目了然。动作者后标(Ac),目标后标(Go):

17. Tom (Ac) stroked the dog (Go).
18. The dog (Ac) ate my oatcakes (Go).

在例 17 中,Tom 进行了抚摸动作,但终点是狗,受动作影响的是狗。影响也可以通过使用 GET 而不是 BE 的被动形式来检测,如"The dog got stroked"。在例 18 中,狗进行进食的动作,但终点是我的燕麦饼,燕麦饼被吃了。(这是一个真实的故事!)

注意,在被动语态中,动作者要么被省略,要么出现在单词 BY 之后,而目标被赋予了主语的地位(有关主语的更全面的描述,请参见第 4 章):

19. The dog (Go) was stroked (by Tom (Ac)).
20. My oatcakes(Go)were eaten(by the dog (Ac)).

所有物质过程都有一个动作者,要么作为明示的参与者,要么隐含在被动小句中。例如,例 21 仍然是一个物质小句,尽管缺少明确的参与者。

21. My oatcakes(Go)have been eaten.

除了动作者之外,物质小句不需要任何其他参与者。

到目前为止,这些讨论都属于相对简单的常识……但是当然存在一个陷阱——一些参与者看起来像目标,但实际不是,因为他们没有承受任何事情,他们不是终点,也没有受到影响。例如,塞巴斯蒂安·科在第 7 小句中说:

22. John Sherwood won a bronze medal in the 400m hurdles.

在这里,我们可以说“约翰·舍伍德所做的就是赢得了铜牌”,因此表明“约翰·舍伍德(John Sherwood)”被构建为动作者,你可能会认为“铜牌(bronze medal)”是赢得过程的目标。然而,如果我们进行 DO TO 检测,就会发现它不符合:

23. * What John Sherwood did to a bronze medal was win it.

所以,虽然约翰·舍伍德是这里的动作者,但没有目标。这是因为名词词组“bronze medal”描述的是他的胜利程度,它没有承受任何动作。注意,我们可以说 “The bronze medal was won by John Sherwood”,但不能说“The bronze medal got won by John Sherwood”。我们将这种类型的参与者称为过程的**范围**(scope)(Sc)①。程度不是动作的目标,第 24 小句或许能提供最明确的示例:

---

① 请注意,韩礼德早些时候对这些参与者使用了“range”一词。现在我们在分析作格性(ergativity)时使用这个术语(Halliday and Matthiessen 2004:280–303)。

24. We（Ac）ran three miles（Sc）.

　　还有另一种更为复杂、可能不那么明显和可靠的方法,可用于检测物质小句中的范围。所有物质小句都将参与者构建为在某种程度上发生着"改变",即有些事"发生(happen to)"在这些参与者身上。注意 HAPPEN 是另一个语法词。在只有一个参与者的物质过程中,有些事会发生在这位参与者身上。在有目标的过程中,有事发生的是目标。当有一个动作者和一个程度时,有事发生的是动作者。当有一个参与者、一个目标和一个范围时,有事发生的是目标。在上面的句子中,有事发生的是约翰·舍伍德,而不是奖牌:

25. ? What happened to John Sherwood at the Olympics? He won a bronze medal.

　　将其与以下小句进行比较:

26. What happened to John Sherwood in the 400m? He（Ac）won.
27. What happened to Tom Bartlett in the race yesterday? He（Ac）fell over.
28. ?? What happened to the medal? John Sherwood won it（Sc）.
29. What happened to the medal? Someone（Ac）stole it（Go）.

　　对此的一种解释是,具有范围的过程可以说只是过程的扩展形式,而不是过程和目标。用术语来讲,"赢得铜牌"是一个过程,与"获得第三名"一样。这一点也可以这样理解——范围实际上与过程存在环境关系。也就是说,它构建了某事在何处、何时或发生了多大程度的变化(有关环境因素的进一步讨论,请参见下文)。例如,在第 16 小句中,塞巴斯蒂安·科说:

30. Two days later I joined their club.

　　请注意,我们可以说"塞巴斯蒂安·科所做的就是加入他们的俱乐部",而不能说"塞巴斯蒂安·科对他们的俱乐部所做的就是加入它"。这是因为"他们的俱乐部(their club)"是这个过程中的一个范围,它没有受到影响。相同意思的另一种说法是:

31. Two days later I enrolled in their club.

在事件的这种构建中，"their club"是一个环境因素，以介词"in"为标志。然而，虽然一般来说环境因素不是过程的必要因素，但范围是固有因素。因此，范围是介于环境因素和过程中的"完全"参与者之间的。但由于它们被语法构建为补语（即小句中的必要参与者），我们说它们在语法上被体现为参与者，而我们将它们与目标区分开来，以表示它们的"边缘"状态。

范围的另一个功能是使**淡化动词**（*bleached verbs*）作为过程的一部分的意义变得完整。在例 32（第 34 小句或原文）中，塞巴斯蒂安·科说：

32. …I've had many conversations about how we meet this challenge.

在这里，动词"had"的原意"拥有"已被淡化，如果不增加"many conversations"的范围，就没有真正的意义。我们再次看到范围可能发挥使过程的意义完整的功能，而非构建目标。常见的例子有：

33. I（Ac）had a bath（Sc）.
34. John（Ac）gave Peter（Go）a kick（Sc）.

这些可以重新措辞为：（尽管例 35 的风格非常陈旧！）

35. I（Ac）bathed.
36. John（Ac）kicked Peter（Go）.

让我们比较一下例 37 和例 38：

37. John gave Peter a kick.
38. Two years later Sheila gave me my first pair of racing spikes.

从表面上看，这两个小句看起来是一样的；然而，它们之间存在**加密语法**（*cryptogrammatical*）差异。这个由沃尔夫引入的妙词，是指不能立时瞧出的语法差异（"crypto"是希腊文的"隐藏"，常常用以谈及尸体……），只有当我们对原句加以检测并深究原句**变体**（*agnates*）之后，差异才会显露出来。那么，咱们不妨试一试，稍微改动一下，将 DO TO 检测改成 DO WITH 检测。这通常会产生一种听起来更自然的变体，虽然由此可以声称这是一种不同类型的参与者，但在系统功能语言学中,相似性(而非差异)才会被视为标准的因素。

39. * What John **did to** the kick was give it to Peter.
40. * What John **did with** the kick was give it to Peter.
41. What John **did to** Peter was give him a kick.
42. What Sheila **did with** the racing spikes was give them to Seb.
43. ?? What Sheila **did to** Seb was give him his first pair of racing spikes.
44. * What Sheila **did with** Seb was give him his first pair of racing spikes.

这些检测告诉我们,在例 39 到例 41 中,"kick"显然是一个范围,其中"Peter"是目标。与此相对,在例 42 中,"racing spikes"通过了 **do with** 检测,因此可以被视为目标。我们还在例 43 和例 44 中看到,"Seb"通过这两个测试都不容易,这是因为 Seb 被构建为过程中的 **接受者**(*recipient*)(Rect),即接受完全意义上被真正"给予"东西的人(不像上文的"kick")。在例 39 到例 41 中,GIVE 的原意被淡化了,或者我们可以说这是它的隐喻用法,因此"Peter"是扩展过程+范围的目标,而不是接受者。这可以通过以下密码语法检测进行验证:

45. Sheila gave the racing spikes to Seb.
46. * John gave a kick to Peter.

真正的接受者与给予的隐喻过程中的目标不同,可以在"Give somebody something"或"Give something to somebody"两种形式中出现。这种变化也解释了为什么例 47 至少是合理的,尽管有点勉强——通过将接受者构建为补语,而不是使用介词 TO,语法将其构建得与目标更为接近,即将其构建成了被过程影响的某人或某物。这一点得到了以下同源示例的验证:

47. ?? What Sheila did to Seb was give him his first pair of racing spikes.
48. * What Sheila did to Seb was give his first pair of racing spikes to him.

因此,在"She gave the spikes to Seb"和"She gave Seb the spikes"这两种构建中,焦点略有不同:在第一种构建中,"spikes"被视作受到影响的东西,从一个人转移给另一个人;第二种构建认为"Seb"在成为新的主人时受到了影响(这肯定是塞巴斯蒂安·科想在演讲中传递的效果）。然而,系统功能语言学倾向于忽略这些不同的细微差别,所以在这两种情况下,参与者的标签是相同的：

49. Two years later Sheila（Ac）gave me（Rect）my first pair of racing spikes（Go）.
50. Two years later Sheila（Ac）gave her old racing spikes（Go）to Seb（Rect）.

注意,我不得不改变示例 50 的措辞,以使其更自然。这在决定一个想法的表达方式时有时实属必要——当考虑到及物性以外的其他特征所起作用时。

现在,我们可以对过程接受者做如下检测：

> 在给予过程中,参与者能否用"to X"的形式表达？如果能,X 就是接受者。

在物质过程中,还有另一个可选的参与者,在某种程度上与接受者类似,即委托者（client）（Cli）。不巧的是,塞巴斯蒂安·科的演讲中没有例子,所以我只能从一首老歌的歌词里找个例子：

51. If I'd known you were coming/I'd have baked you a cake.

在第二句 "I'd have baked you a cake" 中,我们可以看到"I"是动作者（我所做的是烤一个蛋糕）。但是"cake"有点难处理——我并未曾对它做什么,因为在我烘焙之前,它都不存在。然而,在韩礼德的系统功能语言学中,只是在**被转变的**（transformed）目标（有动作者对它们做了些事情）和被**创造**（created）的目标之间,做了二级区别。这两个目标都被归类为目标,但它们可以更精细地划分为子类别——Go：transformative 和 Go：creative。[1] 在系统功能语言学中,冒号用来表示如上那些比较细微的区别。但是"I'd have baked you a cake"中的"you"呢？这看起来有点像接受者,在传统语法中都被称为**间接宾语**（indirect object）,但仔细观察一下（又是加密语法）,便可得知例 51 不能用介词 TO 来重新表述,而是用介词 FOR。

---

[1]　然而,在卡迪夫语法（系统功能语言学的另一个流派）中,有一个单独的创造者和创造物类别,用于区分有效的物质过程中韩礼德所称的动作参与者和目标。

52. If I'd known you were coming I'd have baked a cake for you.

53. *If I'd known you were coming I'd have baked a cake to you.

这是针对委托者的检测:

参与者能否用"for X"的形式表达? 如果能,X就是委托者。

因此,对蛋糕这个小句的分析是:

54. I (Ac)'d have baked you (Cli) a cake (Go:cre).

在何时可以将委托者体现为补语而不用介词FOR这件事情上,不同的英语方言有不同的习惯。例如,我妻子会说:

55. Put me (Cli) one of those on the table.

在我听起来有点奇怪,但我妻子说的很多话都很奇怪。

我们在物质过程中能见到的最后一种参与者见于塞巴斯蒂安·科演讲第21小句:

56. And that gratitude drives me and my team to do whatever we can to inspire young people to choose sport.

首先来看这一句的前半部分,我们看到了一个及物性的复杂例子,在这个例子中,一些事情(感激)导致一些人(塞巴斯蒂安·科和他的团队)做一些事情(他们所能做的一切)。在这样的例子中,我们把让某人或某事做实质性事情的人或事称为**激发者**(initiator),而执行实际动作的人或物称为动作者。有各种各样的因果关系是以这种方式编码的,因此,帮助和强迫某人做某事,甚至骗某人去做某件事,都会涉及一个激发者和一个动作者(可能还有一个目标)。

过程激发者检测:

这个过程可以用"X made Y do Z"的形式来表达吗? 如果能,如果Y是物质过程的动作者,则X是激发者。

事实上,塞巴斯蒂安·科的小句比这更复杂,因为它包括第二种因果关系——激励年轻人选择运动。因此，第 21 小句构建了一个复杂的及物性链条，某事使得某人做某事，以让别人做某事——这是一个非常复杂的链条，但对下文的分析来说却十分重要。第二种因果关系稍有不同，因为选择是一种心理过程（见下文），而诱使某人进行心理过程的人或事自然地归类为**诱导者**（*inducer*）（In）。下面我们还会看到第三种因果关系，即言语因果关系。

在例 56 中，"inspire young people" 中的诱导者被理解为与前一过程（"whatever we can"）中的动作者相同，由于语篇中不可见，我们必须用方括号表示，用两个 α 表示这种关系。分析如下。注意，"whatever we can" 是一个范围，完成了"do"的含义；Sen 是**感知者**（*senser*），Phen 是**现象**（*phenomenon*），这些术语将在下一节中解释。

57. And that gratitude (In) drives me and my team (Ac α) to do whatever we can (Sc) to [α Ind] inspire young people (Sen) to choose sport (Phen).

正如本节所示，参与者参与物质过程的方式多种多样——或者更准确地说，可以将参与者参与物质过程的方式构建成各种各样的。虽然每一种这样的构建都很有趣，但本书的重点更多的是不同的参与者是如何在整个语篇（或至少是重要的语篇片段）中进行构建的。例如，在 Bartlett 2012a 中，我分析了《1977 年圭亚那印第安人法案》（以下简称《印第安人法案》），以探讨该法案为圭亚那政府和印第安人所构建的互为补充的权利和义务。语篇中的物质过程在这里非常重要，因为它们让我们洞察到，作为该法案的作者，政府将谁视为各种活动中的动作者，以及将谁视为目标：即行动者和受动者，分别对应主动者和被动者。然后，我比较了当地居民编写的语篇《NRDDB 章程》中的物质过程，该章程从当地人的角度阐述了互补的权利和义务。① 结果非常有趣，因为它们显示了政府和印第安人如何将自己和彼此定位为法律、经济和社会活动的参与

---

① 为了进行更全面的分析，我使用了及物性以外的语言特征，比如介词。例如，"on behalf of"被解读为与我们在本节中看到的由间接宾语构建的委托者角色相同。介词的这种用法在"环境成分"一节中加以讨论。

者,这些活动被视为在印第安人领地上实现良好治理和发展的核心。关于物质过程(尽管我研究了所有过程类型),在《印第安人法案》中,政府主要将自己构建为动作者和激发者,将印第安人群体构建为目标、物品和金钱的接受者以及政府代表其开展活动的委托者。总体的格局在很大程度上是政府代表基本上处于被动地位的印第安人采取行动或对后者采取行动。相比之下,《NRDDB 章程》主要将当地社区描述为代表他们自己行事,而且通常是为了政府的利益。当然,这些只是语篇分析,但如果我们认识到这两个语篇是(置于该地区社会历史情景之中的)持续的法律磋商的一部分,我们就是在进行话语分析了。

练习 3.1

在以下摘录中(马丁·路德·金著名的《我有一个梦想》演讲的开篇),我以下画线标出了所有的物质过程。分析在语篇中出现的每个过程的不同参与者角色,并思考哪些指称对象在扮演这些角色。答案见附录。然后,思考一下从物质角度构建的非裔美国人和美国政府和社会之间的关系:

语篇 3.2

1   I am happy to join with you today in what will go down in history as the greatest demonstration for freedom in the history of our nation.

2   Five score years ago, a great American, >< signed the Emancipation Proclamation. ①

3   >in whose symbolic shadow we stand today, <

4   This momentous decree came as a great beacon light of hope to millions of Negro slaves who had been seared in the flames of withering injustice.

5   It came as a joyous daybreak to end the long night of their captivity.

6   But one hundred years later, the Negro still is not free.

7   One hundred years later, the life of the Negro is still sadly crippled by the

---

①   一个完整字句出现在另一个小句中间时,符号> < 表示其在原来篇章中出现的位置,而该小句本身以 >xxx< 出现在下方。

manacles of segregation and the chains of discrimination.

8　One hundred years later, the Negro <u>lives</u> on a lonely island of poverty in the midst of a vast ocean of material prosperity.

9　One hundred years later, the Negro is still <u>languishing</u> in the corners of American society

10　and finds himself an exile in his own land.

11　So we have <u>come</u> here today to <u>dramatize</u> a shameful condition.

12　In a sense we have <u>come</u> to our nation's capital to <u>cash</u> a check.

13　When the architects of our republic <u>wrote</u> the magnificent words of the Constitution and the Declaration of Independence,

14　they were <u>signing</u> a promissory note to which every American was to fall heir.

15　This note was a promise that all men, yes, black men as well as white men, would be guaranteed the unalienable rights of life, liberty, and the pursuit of happiness.

16　It is obvious today that America has <u>defaulted</u> on this promissory note

17　insofar as her citizens of color are concerned.

18　Instead of <u>honoring</u> this sacred obligation, America has <u>given</u> the Negro people a bad check, a check which has <u>come back</u> <u>marked</u>"insufficient funds."

19　But we refuse to believe

20　that the bank of justice is bankrupt.

21　We refuse to believe

22　that there are insufficient funds in the great vaults of opportunity of this nation.

23　So we have <u>come</u> to <u>cash</u> this check—a check that will <u>give</u> us upon demand the riches of freedom and the security of justice.

24　We have also <u>come</u> to this hallowed spot to remind America of the fierce urgency of now.

3.2.2　心理过程

在上一节中,我将物质过程描述为物质世界中的构建行为。与之相反的是**心理过程**(*mental process*),它构建的过程不是动作,也不是在物质世界中发生的。相反,它们是内在状态,涉及思想、感知、情感和欲望的过程。事实上,在英语中,思考、感知、情绪和欲望的语法都有一些不同的体现方式,这给了我们四个子范畴,尽管它们都有一个共同的特点,那就是需要一个感性的参与者——能够感觉或思考的人,或被构建为能够这样做的事物,比如:

58. I decided to buy a cake.
59. The old tree had seen many a battle fought around it.

进行感知的参与者被称为感知者(Sen),如果他们所感知的被构建为一个事物,而不是另一个过程(见下文),这个事物则被称为现象(Phen)。因此,在上文讨论过并在这里重复的塞巴斯蒂安·科第 21 小句中,"young people"是感知者,而"sport"是现象。如上所述,"we"是诱导者,即被构建为导致一个心理过程的参与者:

60. And that gratitude drives me and my team to do whatever we can to ［Ind］ inspire young people (Sen) to choose sport (Phen).(这种感激之情驱使我和我的团队尽我们所能鼓励年轻人选择运动。)

这里的"选择(choose)"是一个被称为"**意愿**(*desiderative*)"的心理过程子类别的例子,因为选择是一种欲望或愿望。下面是**认知**(*cognitive*)(思考)、**感知**(*perceptive*)(用感官感知)和**情感**(*emotive*)(喜欢或不喜欢)子类别的例子。只有第一条来自塞巴斯蒂安·科的演讲:

61. ... whatever (Phen) they (Sen:cog) believe.
62. I (Sen:perc) can see the sea (Phen).
63. I (Sen:em) hate The X-Factor (Phen).

情感过程的一个有趣特征是感知者或现象都可以充当主动小句的主语:

64. I (Sen) like/hate/fear spiders (Phen).
65. Spiders (Phen) please/disgust/terrify me (Sen).

这些变体分别被称为 like-类型和 please-类型,这种互补对存在于许多语言中,好像人类经验已经引导我们将情感活动等同于感官的反应(like-类型)或现象的影响(please-类型)。说话人根据每个节点的话语需求来构建一种观点或另一种观点。

由于心理过程指的是我们头脑中发生的事情,这意味着它们不仅可以构建我们对个体事物的想法、感受、愿望或感知,还可以构建我们对完整事件或活动的想法、感受、愿望或感知。由于事件和活动在英语中通常以小句的形式出现,因此心理过程的不同子类别会以各种方式与小句结构相结合。

首先考虑**情感过程**(*emotive process*),我可以不说巧克力是我喜欢的食物,而说我喜欢的是吃巧克力的动作:

66. I like eating chocolate.

例 66 中的短语"eating chocolate"不是一个完整的小句,但它确实具有小句的某些特征,即物质过程"eating"后面跟着"chocolate"这个目标。如果我们不想说我们喜欢自己做某件事,而是想说我们喜欢别人做某件事,我们可以添加更多的小句元素:

67. I like you buying me jewellery.

小句或小句的部分在一个完整小句中作参与者的,被称为**转级小句**(*rankshifted clauses*)。在这种情况下,现象本身就是一个动作或活动,我们称之为**宏观现象**(*macrophenomcnon*)。为了标记语篇,最简单的方法是在双方括号中标记小句元素,并将整个括号中的元素标记为现象,如下所示:(这样你就不需要记住宏观现象这个术语了!)

68. I (Sen) like [[you buying me jewellery]] (Phen).

另一种复杂类型的现象是**元现象**(*metaphenomenon*),它可以通过(THE FACT/IDEA) THAT 引入的完整小句来体现。同样,我们把它们括起来就行了,并将它们标记为现象:

69. I (Sen) now regret [[that he bought me so much jewellery]] (Phen).

70. I (Sen) now regret [[the fact that he bought me so much jewellery]] (Phen).

这要是使用 like-类型的情感过程,结构会非常自然。当然,也可以使用 please-类型的过程,但结构通常不太自然:

71. [[The fact that he bought me the necklace]] (Phen) surprised me (Sen) greatly.

塞巴斯蒂安·科演讲的第 35 小句包含了一个 please-型心理过程的例子,其中感知者充当被动小句的主语:

72. And I've been reassured
73. and I've been uplifted
74. we share a common goal for the future of sport.

我们可以在例 75 这个并列句中添加"by the fact that",以表明我们句中存在元现象:

75. And I've been reassured and I (Sen)'ve been uplifted by [[the fact that we share a common for the future of sport]] (Phen).

不过,这句话可不像表面上看来那么简单,我稍后会再谈这个问题。

英语中的介词在 that-小句之前会省略,这可能使元现象难以识别。因此,如下所示,例 76 代表一种心理过程和元现象,尽管例 77 不符合语法:

76. I was angered that he should have acted that way.
77. *I was angered the fact that he should have acted that way.
78. I was angered by the fact that he should have acted that way.

感知过程(*perceptive processes*)可以以类似于情感过程的方式将宏观现象作为补语:

79. I (Sen) saw [[you crossing the road]] (Phen).

然而,在感知过程中,可以区分是感知到某人某物是正在做某事(如例 79),还是感知到完整的动作或事件(如例 80)。例 81 中的结构在情感过程中

是不可能的:

80. I (Sen) saw [[you cross the road]] (Phen).
81. *I (Sen) like [[you cross the road]] (Phen)

　　这里有一个重要的语义区别——例 80 中的**有界**(*bounded*)小句意味着您完成了过马路,并且我看到了整个过程,而例 81 中的**无界**(*unbounded*)小句没有这样的内涵。这似乎是一个很小的区别,但在分析法律话语时,这可能很重要,例如,在区分什么样的事件被部分或全部看到,或者什么样的目击者被构建为看到全部或部分事件的时候。

　　由于感知过程的现象是整个事件(宏观现象),而不是事实或想法(元现象),它们不能由 THE FACT THAT 结构引入:

82. *I saw [[the fact of you crossing the road]].
83. *I saw [[the fact of you cross the road]].

　　感知过程的另一个显著特征是,当它们指的是正在进行的状态时,它们通常使用情态动词 CAN(或其过去式 COULD):

84. I (Sen) can smell gas (Phen)!
85. I was always happy as long as I (Sen) could see the sea (Phen).
86. I (Sen) can feel a stone (Phen) in my shoe.

　　当我们谈论一种感知的开始时,我们通常不使用 CAN 一词:

87. I was excited when I (Sen) saw the sea (Phen).
88. Dick (Sen) suddenly felt [[a sharp object being pushed into his back]] (Phen).

　　请注意,对于感知过程,可以将整个事件构建为一种事物,在这种情况下,它只是一个简单的现象:

89. The old tree (Sen:perc) had seen many a battle (Phen).

　　当**认知过程**(*cognitive processes*)与动作和事件相关时,它们会将其**投射**

(*project*)为完整的小句,可以选择由 that-小句引入。尽管它们与观念有关,但心理投射与其他元现象不同,因为它们指的是感知者头脑中的观念,而其他元现象则被构建为预先存在的观念或预设事实(这是哲学和法律话语中的一个非常重要的范畴)。我将使用双斜线//来标记投射:

90. I（Sen）think //（that）it will rain tomorrow.
91. ＊I think the fact that it will rain tomorrow.

然而,如果它是一个问题而不是一个陈述,那么我们就不用 THAT,而是用 IF 或 WHETHER 来引导 yes-no 问题,或者用 wh-单词来引导 wh-问题。塞巴斯蒂安·科演讲第 10 小句中出现了此类示例:

92. By the time I was back in the classroom I（Sen）knew //what I wanted to do and what I wanted to be.

在这里,这个小句可以看作对未被问到的问题"你想成为什么样的人"的回应。这个小句还包含了最后一种认知过程——意愿过程,即表达愿望或希望的过程。当这些过程指的是我们希望整个事件或行动发生时,它们会投射出一个略为缩减的带有 TO 的不定式小句:

93. England（Sen）expects //every man to do his duty.

请注意,EXPECT 也可以用作认知意义,意思大致与 THINK 而不是 WANT 相同。这种区别体现在语法中,如例 94:

94. I（Sen）expect //that it will rain tomorrow.

当所希望的事件或行动由感知者自己执行时,投射小句中没有主语:

95. I（Sen）wanted// to be a runner. ①

我们在前文看到,LIKE 通常会体现一个情感过程。然而,在下面的例子

---

① 第 4 章中给出了将例 95 等小句解释为具有情态的单一小句的另一种解释。

中,半预制的短语 WOULD LIKE 和 WOULD HATE 表达的是一种意愿意义(你可以用 WANT 或 NOT WANT 来改变这些小句的措辞),而这也反映在语法上:

96. Would you (Sen:desid) like //to go to Spain this year?
97. I (Sen:desid) would hate //to be all alone.

例96和例97与下列(语法构建的)情感用法进行比较:

98. Do you think you (Sen:em) would like [[living in Spain]] (Phen)?
99. She always said she would hate [[us saying goodbye]] (Phen).

由于心理过程是状态而不是活动,因此这四种子类型即便在描述"现在"时都采用一般现在时:

100. At the present moment I (Sen) think //it was a mistake.

这不同于:

101. At the present moment I'm thinking about my holidays.

同样,心理过程不是你"做"的事情,因此无法通过 DO 检测,而行为过程则可以通过:

102. * What I did was think it was going to rain.
103. What I'm doing is thinking about my holidays.

心理过程检测:

(1)这个过程中的一个参与者一定是有感知能力的吗? 该过程的措辞是否可以修改为(i)将另一个事件投射为一个小句,或者(ii)接一个转级小句作为参与者? 心理过程就是这样的。

(2)表达现在发生的事情的最自然的形式是一般现在时吗? 心理过程就是这样的。

(3)该过程是否未通过 DO 测试? 心理过程不能通过。

假设心理过程的一般检测已经通过之后,可以用以下检测来区分心理过程

的类型:

(1)是否可以修改该小句的措辞而使现象成为一个转级小句(对于无
    界事件使用-ing,对于有界事件使用不定式)? 如果可以,那么这
    个过程是感知的。

104. I (Sen:perc) saw your brother (Phen).

105. I (Sen:perc) saw [[your brother buying sweets at the corner shop]] (Phen).

106. I (Sen:perc) saw [[your brother buy some sweets at the corner shop]]
     (Phen).

(2)是否可以修改该小句的措辞使该现象可以用以下两种方式表达:
    (i)仅使用-ing 形式的级转移小句,或者(ii)一个以 THE FACT 引
    导的完整小句? 如果是这样的话,这个过程就是情感性的。

107. I (Sen:em) like your brother (Phen).

108. I (Sen:em) like [[tickling your brother]] (Phen).

109. * I like [[tickle your brother]].

110. I (Sen:em) like [[your brother tickling me]] (Phen).

111. I (Sen:em) now regret my actions (Phen).

112. I (Sen:em) now regret [[(the fact) that your brother ever tickled me]]
     (Phen).

请注意,情感小句可以采用带有 TO+不定式的级转移小句(与感知小句所
接的省 TO 不定式相反):

113. I like to tickle your brother.

114. * I saw to tickle your brother.

二者形成对照,因为-ing 形式暗含对活动本身的喜欢或不喜欢,而 TO 形式
则意味着对它的发生感到满意或不满意:

115. I like to do my homework as soon as possible because I hate doing it!

(3)这个过程能否(在不可能包含 THE FACT 的情况下)在现象的位置

上投射一个可能由 THAT-、IF-或是 WH-词引导的一个完整的小句？ 如果能, 这个过程就是认知性的。

116. She（Sen : cog）doesn't even know my name（Phen）.
117. She（Sen : cog）knows //（that）I am called Tom.
118. * She knows the fact that I am called Tom.
119. I（Sen : cog）wonder // if it will rain.
120. I（Sen : cog）can't imagine // why you would do that.

　　（4）这个过程能否投射一个包含一个 TO 不定式的小句来代替一个现象, 但是不能投射一个-ing 小句？ 如果是这样的话, 这个过程就是意愿性的。

121. Do you（Sen : desid）want an apple（Phen）?
122. Do you（Sen : desid）want//to eat an apple?
123. Or do you（Sen : desid）want//me to eat it?
124. I（Sen : desid）decided//to go.
125. * I want going.
126. * I decided going.

　　心理过程可以用来构建不同的参与者, 表现为思考、情感体验、感知事物或渴望事物。这可能是一个重要的区别, 尤其是不同阶层的人经常被构建成有不同的心理反应, 或者他们会在心理上做出反应而不是在物质过程中行动。然而, 这又是一种语篇上的区别, 我们必须在更广泛的环境中考虑任何语篇分析, 以讨论说话人将男性或女性构建为行动型或深思熟虑型、情感型或敏感型的人的相关性, 以及这是否在每个节点上从积极的角度来构建他们。顺便提一下第 4 章才会讲到的两个术语, 在术语 THINKING 和 FEELING 中并没有内在地包含正面或负面的态度, 尽管可能会有某些态度被激发出来。同样, 我们在权衡不同参与者想要某事发生的力度时, 必须要考虑权力关系。

3.2.3　言语过程

言语过程（*verbal processes*）与认知过程非常相似，不同之处在于言语过程将主意或想法构建为用语言表达出来的东西，而不是停留在某人的头脑中的东西，例如，当塞巴斯蒂安·科在第 47—48 小句中陈述道：

127. ... Some might say that your decision today is between five similar bids.

言语过程总是涉及**讲话人**（*Sayer*），即传递信息的人或物，以及以某种形式传递的信息。在例 127 中，讲话人是假想的"some"，塞巴斯蒂安·科想象他们所讲的话在小句"your decision today is between five similar bids"中被投射出来。与认知心理过程一样，THAT 可用在投射中，但 THE FACT THAT 不能使用：

128. ... Some might say your decision today is between five similar bids.
129. ... ＊Some might say the fact that your decision today is between five similar bids.

言语过程也可以包括**受话人**（*Receiver*）（Recr），即接收信息的人，但这并不是必要的，如例 128 所示。塞巴斯蒂安·科也可以加上一个受话人：

130. ... Some（Sayer）might say to you（Recr）//that your decision today is between five similar bids.

请注意，在言语过程中是受话人必须有感知能力，而非讲话人：

131. The sign（Sayer）announced to passers-by（Recr）//that this was private land.

受话人可以体现为补语或在介词 TO 之后体现。然而，许多过程让它们可以采取的形式有限制：

132. He（Sayer）swore to me（Recr）// that he was innocent.
133. ＊He swore me that he was innocent.
134. He（Sayer）told me（Recr）// that he was innocent.

135. ＊ He told to me that he was innocent.

和心理过程一样,如果投射的不是一个陈述句,而是一个问句,那么我们用
IF 或 WHETHER,而不是用 THAT 来表示 yes-no 问题,同时用 wh-单词来表示
wh-问题。

136. He (Sayer) asked me (Recr)//whether I liked it or not.
137. May I (Sayer) enquire//when you are leaving?

请注意,INQUIRE 一词很少接受话人,如果接,那么听起来是相当正式的:

138. Might I (Sayer) enquire of you (Recr) when you are leaving?

当投射一个命令时,小句中要包含一个带 TO 的不定式,与意愿心理过程类
似(因为两者都传达了某人想要某人做某事的想法):

139. The boss (Sayer) ordered me (Recr)//to clear my desk immediately.

你会发现,我们经常使用不同的动词,如 INFORM, ENQUIRE 或者
ORDER,这取决于我们是在投射一个陈述、一个问题还是一个命令。TELL 的不
同寻常之处在于它可以用于这三种情况,且每种用法都符合语法:

140. He [Sayer] told me [Recr]//that he was called John.
141. [Sayer] Tell me (Recr)//if you want it or not.
142. I (Sayer) told him (Rccr)//to get lost.
143. I was hoping you (Sayer) could tell me (Recr)//why you did that?
144. The dying cowboy (Sayer) told me (Recr)//what he was called.

请注意,在例 141 中,**投射过程**(*projecting process*)“tell”是一个祈使式,讲话
人被理解为“you”,因此我们必须将“Sayer”写在方括号中。

另一个可能的例子是在塞巴斯蒂安·科的演讲中有一个受话人。这已在
我们上面看到的并列句中出现过:

145. And I've been reassured
146. and I've been uplifted

147. we share a common goal for the future of sport.

鉴于前面的例句提到的是对话，我认为塞巴斯蒂安·科此处使用"reassure"是将其作为一个言语过程的：

148. People (Sayer) have reassured me (Recr) //that we share a common goal for the future of sport.

然而，"令人放心/踏实（reassure）"也包含情感反应的概念，塞巴斯蒂安·科用了"令人感到鼓舞（uplift）"的概念，这是一个 please-类型的情感过程，不可能是一个言语过程。然而，由于二者都能接表面上相似的 that-结构，这种过程类型的差异在塞巴斯蒂安·科最后的那句话语中变得模糊。因此，在笔者读来，"that we share a common goal for the future of sport"这句话同时发挥着两种功能，一是投射"放心/踏实"（reassured），二是充当"鼓舞（uplifted）"的现象。因此，其全部含义是：

149. And (Recr) I've been reassured//that we share a common goal for the future of sport and I(Sen)'ve been uplifted by [[the fact that we share a common goal for the future of sport]] (Phen). [我们对体育的未来有着共同的目标，这令我感到放心/踏实，而我也因此（我们对体育的未来有着共同的目标）感到振奋。]

这种模棱两可的情况在自然语言中经常发生！对于分析人员来说，这是不幸，也是万幸。

有时，所说内容可以浓缩成一个名词词组，称为**讲话内容**（*verbiage*）（Vb）：

150. The dying cowboy (Sayer) told me (Recr) his name (Vb).

讲话内容还包括信息单位，如：

151. [Sayer] Tell me (Recr) a story (Vb).
152. He (Sayer) barely said a word (Vb) all night.

对言语过程的基本检测如下：

> 该过程能否将单独的事件作为一个小句进行投射?① 过程中是否有一个必须具有感知能力的受话人？如果两者都是肯定的，那么这个过程就是言语性的。

在另一种完全不同的言语过程中，会在言语中对评估**目标**(*Target*)(Tg)进行评价：

153. ... activities (Tg) which have been highly praised by the Government (Sayer).

有目标的语言过程之后通常会有一个环境因素来解释评价的原因：

154. The Goverrment (Sayer) praised the activities (Tg) as daring and innovative.
155. Everybody (Sayer) blamed her (Tg) for the accident.
156. I (Sayer) can't thank you (Tg) enough for what you have done.

目标检测如下：

> 这个过程是否同时构建了一个动作或言语和一些评价性内容？该过程是否涉及两个参与者，其中一个(X)负责进行评价，另一个(Y)实体是被评价的？如果是这样的话，X 是讲话人，Y 是目标。

还要注意的是，与表示非物质状态的心理过程相比，言语过程作为思想的物质表现，既可通过 DO 测试，又通常采用进行时态来表达"现在"：

157. What's he doing? He (Sayer)'s telling them (Receiver) the time (Vb).

所有的言语过程都构建了某种信息的传递，要么传递给整个世界（在这种情况下不会将接受者表达出来），要么传递给特定的接受者。这将产生两个重大后果。首先，尽管我们把这些过程称为言语过程，但它们并不总是通过语言手段来构建信息的传递。其次，并不是所有的说话行为都被构建为言语过程。

---

① 在这里，UTTER 可能是一个例外，因为它似乎只用于信息单位类型的讲话内容。

可以将过程类型的名称用作标签,但有时它们可能会产生误导,这也是我们之所以依靠语法检测而不是凭直觉来给它们分类的另一个原因。也许**信息过程**(*informative processes*)是一个更好的术语。

在塞巴斯蒂安·科演讲的第 53 小句中,有一个非语言的言语过程的例子(!):

158. ... which city will help us (Sayer) show a new generation (Recr)//why sport matters.

这里也可以重新措辞,用讲话内容代替投射:

159. ... which city① will help us (Sayer) show a new generation (Recr) the importance of sport (Vb).

虽然"show"一词在这里被用来表示通过物质手段传递信息,但它仍然是一个言语过程。至于非言语过程的谈话行为,将在下一节行为过程中介绍。

言语过程在分析地位和权力时很有用,原因有三:第一,也是最明显的,它们将某些人构建为说话而不是做、思考或感觉(如上所述,在给定环境中,每种过程的相对优点是依境而定的话语事件);第二,它们可以暗示谁的话值得被重复;第三个(与第二个原因相关的)原因是,它们可以被用作一种对一个特定的想法进行褒贬的手段(见第 4 章关于归因的讨论)。

3.2.4 行为过程

塞巴斯蒂安·科在其演讲的第 34 小句中说:

160. In my travels over the last two years, speaking with many of you, I've had many conversations about how we meet this challenge.

---

① "哪个城市(which city)"是一个言语过程的激发者,但不幸的是,没有专门的术语来描述这个问题——也许"prompt"可以。

虽然这里有两个谈话的例子，"说话"和"交谈"，但在这两种情况下都不表述信息传递本身。显然，这种转移一定是发生了，但作为语篇分析者，令我们更感兴趣的并非现实世界中的行动，而是对事件在特定语境中的构建方式、写作者如何聚焦和解读其所表述的事件的特定方面和细节。在本例中，塞巴斯蒂安·科将他的谈话表述为一种活动形式，而不是信息交流。如上文"how we meet this challenge"一句中所述，我们可以聚焦谈话的主题，并在构建中加入对话者，但由于没有表述谈话的实际内容，所以根据上一节论述的定义和标准，这些过程不能归类为言语过程。相反，它们是一种**行为过程**（*behavioural processes*）①，韩礼德和马蒂森（Halliday and Matthiessen 2004：248）将其描述为"生理和心理行为（通常是人类）的过程"，且通常是心理过程的物质表现。从这个意义上讲，"交谈"和"聊天"都是行为过程，侧重于说话的活动，而不是将说话的动作构建为信息传递的言语过程。回到上面的例子，我们可以指出，塞巴斯蒂安·科在这里强调的是他一直在大量参与谈话活动，暗示着进行了双向信息交流，但没有提到所说内容的具体细节。

顺着这个思路，我们可以从整体上讨论不同小句表述不同程度的信息传递。

161. Gerard (Beh) was talking.
162. He (Beh) was talking to his colleague (Recr).
163. He (Beh) was talking about football (Circ：matter).
164. He (Sayer) was slagging the game (Tg) off.
165. He (Sayer) told me (Recr) the score (Vb).
166. He (Sayer) told me (Recr) // that the score was five-nil.

在例 161 中，杰拉德被构建为参与了一个行为过程，从进化的角度来看，比物质过程高了一级，但没有传递任何具体的信息。在例 162 中，我们有一个受话人，但仍然没有传递信息。例 163 引入了一个话题，但这个话题仍然模糊，不

---

① 　如果我们把例 160 的淡化动词和范围当作一个词项。

构成信息传递。例 164 构建了信息的传递,但用的是相当模糊的语言——我们知道杰拉德说了一些关于游戏的坏话,但我们不知道他到底说了什么。在例165 中,我们得到了更详细的信息,但直到在例 166 中,我们才了解杰拉德构建的确切信息。因此,在这些小句中,我们看到被构建的信息交换的程度逐渐增加,但从例 164 开始才有言语过程类型,因为这意味着这个过程将信息传递编码为其意义的一部分。这些差异表明,整个小句的意义构建是各种元素的组合——过程本身的性质,以及参与者和环境(见下文)的性质,它们也是及物性系统的一部分。

其他行为过程更接近认知心理过程。在这些情况下,它们所指的不是我们的希望和信念,而是我们暂时的关注点:

167. I (Beh) was just thinking about my holidays.

同样,也有一些行为过程与我们主动聚焦我们的感知有关:

168. What are you (Beh) looking at?

涉及说话、思考和感知的行为过程几乎总是只编码一个参与者,即人类**行为者**(*behaver*)(Beh)。当关注点是行为时,通常要通过介词引入,如上文例 167 和例 168,以及塞巴斯蒂安·科演讲的第 34 小句所言("had conversations about")。韩礼德(Halliday and Matthiessen 2004:251)将 WATCH 一词看作例外,因为 WATCH 编码了两个参与者,即行为者和现象。塞巴斯蒂安·科演讲的第 5 小句就是一个例子:

169. and ［we (Beh)］ watched grainy pictures from the Mexico Olympic Games (Phen).

尽管韩礼德声称 WATCH 在这里是个例外,但 SMELL、FEEL 和 TASTE 的动作意义似乎也属于这一类:

170. I got my nose stung when I (Beh) was smelling the flower (Phen).

　　另一种行为过程是指呼吸、咳嗽或放屁等生理过程。进化得更高级一点的是反映意识状态的过程，比如大笑、微笑和皱眉。有趣的是，这些过程可以用在直接引语后作引证词：

171. "I feel a little queasy", she frowned.（"我觉得有点恶心，"她皱眉道）。

　　如上所述，涉及身体姿势的过程被归为行为过程：

172. I（Beh）stand here today.

　　鉴于行为过程含义广泛，且有时与心理和言语过程相似，从语篇分析的角度最好区分出行为——心理（或更精确一点，如行为：认知等），行为：言语，以及其他行为过程。从这个角度来看，我们可以分析上面的例 167：

173. I（Beh：cog）was just thinking about my holidays.

　　由于行为过程是各种形式的活动，所以在提到"现在"时，它们采用进行时：

174. Shut up, will you? I'm（Beh：cog）thinking.

　　正如你所见，行为过程有点儿像个杂物筐，只有一个共同的特征可以检测，即对有感知能力的参与者的需求（即使在这点上，这种检测本身也无法将行为过程与认知过程等区别开来。）

　　行为过程检测如下：

　　　　这个过程是否编码了一个必须具有感知能力的参与者？

　　然而，由于行为过程被视为有感知能力的人的活动，它们通常用进行时来表示此时此刻。当然也有例外，尽管听起来有些过时或过于正式：

175. I（Beh）stand here today.
176. She（Beh）breathes！
177. Why do you（Beh）laugh？

　　DO 测试也可能提供不太令人信服的结果：

178. ?? What he did next was breathe.

韩礼德和马蒂森(Halliday and Matthiessen 2004:248)承认行为过程是"六种过程类型中最不明确的一种",一些分析者根本不认为需要这样一个类别(参见 Banks 即将推出的新作或其他学者的论述)。然而,从话语分析的角度来看,我认为有必要做一些区分,比如,信息的传递,作为一种活动的交谈,以及大笑和打嗝这样的非言语人类行为。

练习 3.2

看看下面这篇语篇,内容为托尼·布莱尔在 2005 年 7 月 7 日伦敦爆炸案后的发言,我将其中的物质、心理、言语和行为过程用下画线勾了出来。找出参与这些过程的不同参与者以及任何投射的小句,然后讨论托尼·布莱尔的发言在思想和行动方面是如何展开的,以及为什么这种修辞策略可能比较有效。

为了深入了解布莱尔的讲话的语境,你应该查阅这些事件的有关资料,对托尼·布莱尔及其与选民的关系做一些背景阅读,同时读一读与美国所说的"反恐战争"这个更为广泛的话题的相关资料。这些信息将有助于我们以后更详细地分析作为话语的语篇。看看新闻评论员当时是如何评价布莱尔的演讲的,看看他们的评价是否与及物性分析和后面章节中的其他分析所获得的语言学见解相匹配,这也会很有趣。

语篇 3.3

1   I am just going to make a short statement to you [[on the terrible events that have happened in London earlier today]],

2   and I hope

3   you understand

4   that at the present time we are still trying to establish exactly [[what has happened]],

5　and there is a limit to 〔〔what information I can give you〕〕,

6　and I will simply try and tell you the information as best I can at the moment.

7　It is reasonably clear that there have been a series of terrorist attacks in London.

8　There are obviously casualties, both people 〔〔that have died〕〕 and people seriously injured,

9　and our thoughts and prayers of course are with the victims and their families.

10　It is my intention to leave the G8 within the next couple of hours and go down to London and get a report, face-to-face, with the police, and the emergency services and the Ministers 〔〔that have been dealing with this〕〕, and then to return later this evening.

11　It is the will of all the leaders at the G8 however that the meeting should continue in my absence, that we should continue to discuss the issues that we were going to discuss, and reach the conclusions which we were going to reach.

12　Each of the countries round that table have some experience of the effects of terrorism

13　and all the leaders><share our complete resolution to defeat this terrorism.

14　>as they will indicate a little bit later<

15　It is particularly barbaric that this has happened on a day 〔〔when people are meeting to try to help the problems of poverty in Africa, and the long term problems of climate change and the environment〕〕

16　Just as it is reasonably clear that this is a terrorist attack, or a series of terrorist attacks,

17　it is also reasonably clear that it is designed and aimed to coincide with the opening of the G8.

18　There will be time to talk later about this.

19 It is important however that those engaged in terrorism <u>realise</u>

20 that our determination to <u>defend</u> our values and our way of life is greater than their determination to <u>cause</u> death and destruction to innocent people in a desire to <u>impose</u> extremism on the world.

21 Whatever they <u>do</u>,

22 it is our determination that they will never succeed in <u>destroying</u> what we hold dear in this country and in other civilised nations throughout the world.

你可能已经注意到,在第 7—11 小句的开头,以及第 20—22 小句中,还有一些与知识、希望和愿望有关的词语。我在这里没有分析它们,因为它们在小句中的功能不是作为过程。然而,它们在托尼·布莱尔的发言中发展的思想和行为的相互作用中发挥着非常重要的作用,我们将在第 5 章详细讨论。

3.2.5　关系过程

到目前为止,我们已经研究了说话人如何构建他人的内在和外在经验。在塞巴斯蒂安·科演讲的第 25 小句中有另一类过程的例证:

179. Today that task is so much harder.

这是一个**关系过程**(*relational processes*)的示例。这些过程根据指称对象和概念之间的逻辑关系将他们联系起来。在这里,塞巴斯蒂安·科并不是说"that task"涉及任何活动,他是根据它的一个属性或定义特征来描述它,这比以前更困难。因为关系过程所构建的是状态而不是活动,它们甚至会使用一般现在时来表示"此时此刻",如例 179 的变体例 180 所示:

180. Right now that task is so much harder.

几个小句之后,塞巴斯蒂安·科进一步阐述了自己的想法,描述了当今儿童的生活,解释了为什么现在任务难度更大:

181. Their landscape is cluttered. ①
182. Their path to Olympic sport is often obscured.

在每个例子中,我们都有一个被描述的参与者和一个描述他们的术语,我们可以将他们称为**载体**(*carrier*)(Ca)和他们具有的**属性**(*attribute*)(At):

183. Today that task (Ca) is so much harder (At).

顺便说一句,值得注意的是,用"参与者"一词来指称上述关系过程中的属性,似乎有点不符常理,因为它是在特定的语法意义上使用的。在下面的例子中,它听起来更为自然。

如上所述,属性通常指的是特点,但它们也可以指类别,正如塞巴斯蒂安·科演讲中两个小句之后的这句所示:

184. My heroes (Ca) were Olympians (At).

这是用以描述某人谋生手段最常用的一种结构,就像例 185 一样,不过也可以用于其他目的:

185. My grandfather (Ca) was a doctor (At).
186. You're (Ca) a bloody idiot (At)!

如上所述,除了属性(通过形容词体现)或类别(通过名词词组体现),还有属性表达的时间、地点、方式和原因等关系,这些通常是通过环境体现的概念。在塞巴斯蒂安·科的演讲中有一个例子,其中他描述了自己的位置:

187. By the time I (Ca) was back in my classroom (At:Circ).

有关主题和原因的例句有:

188. This book (Ca) is about text analysis (At:Circ).
189. The delay (Ca) was because of leaves on the track (At:Circ).

---

① 表面上看起来这像一个被动用法。然而,时间序列意味着被动将是"their landscape has been cluttered"。

如下文所述,归属过程通常涉及动词 BE,然而,有时时间和地点等概念是包含在过程本身中的:

190. The voyage from Oban to Castlebay（Ca）takes about five hours（At）.

一个非常类似的例子出现在塞巴斯蒂安·科演讲的第 41 小句中:

191. But it（Ca）takes more than 17 days of superb Olympic competition（At）.

在英语中,年龄也是一个属性,如塞巴斯蒂安·科演讲的第 2 小句:

192. When I（Ca）was 12（At）.

关系过程可能还额外包括了一种变化的概念,在这种情况下,是可以用进行时的:

193. He's（Ca）growing old（At）.

及物性指的是参与者之间的关系,像 193 这样的例子仍然是关系性的,尽管从概念上来说,变老可能被认为是一个物质过程。类似地,关系过程可以包含感知的元素。在这些情况下,它们仍然编码了载体和属性之间的关系:

194. This all（Ca）seems/looks/sounds quite complicated（At）.

在这些情况下,可以将感知添加为子分类符。

195. This all（Ca）looks（relational:perc）quite complicated（At）.

当存在一定的可控性时,归属过程可以采用进行时态。在这种情况下,它们通常也能通过 DO 测试:

196. He's（Ca）just being silly（At）!

197. When they are frightened what some animals（Ca）do is play dead（At）.

归属过程有时会影响委托者:

198. He'll（Ca）make someone（Cli）a good husband（At）one day.

在许多其他语言中，年龄是用一个动词来表达的，这个动词的一般意思是"拥有"，情感和恐惧也是如此。在英语中，"to have"用来表示一种不同类型的归属关系，即占有关系：

199. My friends（Ca：pos）have all got Porsches（At：pos）.

在塞巴斯蒂安·科演讲的第 37 小句中有一个所有式归属的例子：①

200. … we（Ca）share a common goal for the future of sport（At：pos）…

归属小句可能涉及一个额外的参与者——负责归属的参与者，称为归属者（Attr），如：

201. Why did you（Attr）call me（Ca）stupid（At）？
202. You（Attr）could always paint them（Ca）green（At）.

在类似结构中属性偶尔出现在物质过程后：

203. They（Ac）built the wall（Go）too high（At）.

我们刚才看到**的归属小句**（*attributive clauses*）是关系小句的一种类型，另一种类型是**识别小句**（*identifying clauses*）。归属小句从特征的角度来描述某人或某事，而识别小句则用来说明两件事物在某种程度上是同一件事物。所以，举一个相当简单的例子，让我们看看塞巴斯蒂安·科演讲的第 32 小句，他说：

204. And they are the lucky ones.

这里说的幸运儿是指塞巴斯蒂安·科的孩子们。注意，塞巴斯蒂安·科并不是简单地说他们是幸运的，而是说他们组成了一个群体"the lucky ones"，他说的"millions more"组成了另一个不幸的群体。按照科的说法，"the lucky ones"和"my children"是同一回事，我们用哪种方式表达这种关系并不重要：

---

① 虽然这可能是一个所有式识别小句（后来引入的），因为有一些同源小句是可逆的。

205. My children are the lucky ones.
206. The lucky ones are my children.

识别过程的另一个例子出现在第 40 小句中,塞巴斯蒂安·科在委员会面前讨论了挑战的性质后,转而指出如何应对挑战才最好:

207. The choice of Host City is the most powerful means you have to meet this challenge.

同样,这一小句可以"颠倒":

208. The most powerful means you have to meet this challenge is the choice of Host City.

这种"可逆性"的特点不适用于归属过程。例 209 与前面的例 185 相反,是一种非常突兀的用法:

209. *A doctor (At) was my grandfather (Ca).

与之相反,正如我们所看到的,动词为"be"的识别小句逆转非常容易。然而,并不是所有的识别小句都是由 BE 体现的,每当使用不同的动词时,可逆性就需要使用被动形式。想象一下,我正在用厨房桌子上的任何可用的东西描述一场战斗。我可以说:

210. The salt cellar is the HQ.
211. The HQ is the salt cellar.
212. The salt cellar represents the HQ.
213. The HQ is represented by the salt cellar.

因此,我们可以区分识别小句中的参与者,尽管他们被构建为同一件事物!代表其他事物的参与者被称为**标记**(*token*)(Tk),由某种东西代表的参与者被称为**价值**(*value*)(Val)。我们甚至可以通过使用 REPRESENT 一词来改变原本使用 BE 的小句的措辞来实现这一点。虽然这听起来有些不自然,但总是可以理解的。记住,标记代表价值。据此,我们可做以下分析:

214. My children (Tk) are the lucky ones (Val).
215. The lucky ones (Val) are my children (Tk).
216. My children (Tk) represent the lucky ones (Val).
217. The lucky ones (Val) are represented by my children (Tk).
218. The salt cellar (Tk) is the HQ (Val).
219. The HQ (Val) is the salt cellar (Tk).
220. The salt cellar (Tk) represents the HQ (Val).
221. The HQ (Val) is represented by the salt cellar (Tk).

与归属过程一样，识别过程中也可能包含一个环境因素。以下示例包括了持续时间的含义：

222. The meeting (Tk) takes up the whole afternoon (Val).
223. The whole afternoon (Val) is taken up by the meeting (Tk).

在这些小句中，整个下午和会议被视为**共延关系**（*coextensive*），这里的语法表达了这种等同关系。共延关系既可能与时间有关，也可能与空间有关，例如：

224. Trees (Tk) line the road (Val).
225. The road (Val) is lined by trees (Tk).

在这里，树木不仅是道路的特征，也是道路边界的标志——道路极限的标记。将其与更具描述性的归属变体进行比较：

226. The road (Ca) is lined with trees (At).

识别过程可能很难分析，因为它们通常是通过其他过程类型的隐喻扩展来实现的，尤其是言语过程。例如，上文将 SHOW[①] 描述为一个非言语过程可能会造成混淆，但可能让读者更为不解的是，在下面的示例中，"show" 是一个识别过程：

227. The arrows (Tk) showed where we should walk (Val).

---

① SHOW 还可以构建物质过程，如 "He showed us the book"。

例 227 的逆转非常自然,这与 SHOW 的口头用法不同:

228. Where we should walk (Val) was shown by the arrows (Tk).
229. The teacher showed us why he was wrong.
230. ?? Why he was wrong was shown (to us) by the teacher.

还要注意的是,作为描述状态的关系小句的一个子类,识别小句采用一般时态,而动词过程往往采用进行时来表示"此时此刻":

231. * Trees (Tk) are lining the road (Val).
232. The teacher (Sayer) was showing us (Recr)//why he was wrong.

识别过程可以将宏观现象作为标记或价值:

233. [[(The fact) that he's stupid]] (Val) is shown by his behaviour (Tk).
234. His behaviour shows (Tk) [[(the fact) that he's stupid]] (Val).

识别小句也可能涉及负责识别的参与者,称为**分配者**(*assigner*)(Assr),如:

235. Why on earth did they (Assr) elect you (Tk) as the president (Val)?

如本例所示,价值可以由介词 AS 表示(此处为可选)。

顺便提一下,还有一种所有式识别小句(正如它们的可逆性所示),但我必须承认我还没有弄清楚这个类别的语义:

236. George Washington once owned these false teeth.
237. These false teeth were once owned by George Washington.

关系过程的检测:

(1)如果过程的无标记形式的"right now"测试是一般现在时,并且该过程无法投射,那么它就是关系过程。如果这个过程不能逆转,那么它是归属过程,其主语是载体;如果这个过程是可逆的,那么它是识别过程,并且标记是主动形式的主语。

(2)当存在变化或控制的成分时,归属关系过程可以采用进行时。

3.2.6　存在过程

我们将研究的最后一种过程类型是**存在过程**(*existential process*),它以 THERE 为主语(或者可以将其插入而不会有意义变化)和一个动词,整个结构后面跟着一个参与者,被称为**存在物**(*existent*)(Ex)。

注意要区分存在主语 THERE 和指示代词 THERE。前者可以用短元音发音,而后者不能。存在过程通常与位置环境一起使用,将新参与者引入语篇。比较一下例 238 中的存在过程和例 239 中的关系过程:

238. There was a strange-looking man (Ex) on the corner.
239. The strange looking man (Ca) was there (At:Circ).

从它们的名字可以看出,它们也被用来构建某物在不特定或特定地点的存在:

240. Is there any sugar (Ex)?
241. Is there a God (Ex)?
242. There are no chocolates (Ex) in the chocolate box.

不过要小心,动词 EXIST 构建了一个参与者的关系过程! 环境可以置于存在结构之前。在这种情况下,这个存在过程就先于存在者。相比之下,当指示代词 THERE 放置在句首时,过程是跟在载体后面的:

243. In the room there was a cat (Ex).
244. There (At:cicr) the cat (Ca) is!

体现存在过程的动词通常是 BE。当环境因素出现在句首时,可以使用 BE 以外的动词。可以使用其他关系过程、表示移动或出现的不及物物质过程,偶尔也可以使用无施事的被动句,在这种情况下,这个过程被认为是存在过程:①

---

① 在这种情况下,也许可以为过程类型提供一个双标签。这与其他将存在小句视为人际变异的观点是一致的。

245. In the room (there) stood a single bookshelf (Ex).
246. Over the mountain (there) flew an eagle (Ex).
247. Into the room (there) ran a small boy (Ex).
248. Out of the dark (there) appeared a grim figure (Ex).
249. Onto my lap (there) was placed a small child (Ex).

当环境放在存在结构之前时,可以省略 THERE,但它始终可以作为插入语(正如括号所示),而这是对存在过程的检测。

存在过程总是第三人称的,即使存在者是你或我。用代词时总是单数的,即使这些代词本身是复数:

250. There's me (Ex) and there's you (Ex).
251. There's them (Ex) and there's us (Ex).

BE 的缩略单数形式也经常用于存在结构中,即使存在者是复数:

252. There's no chocolates (Ex) in my chocolate box.

存在过程检测:

 (1)如果有主语 THERE 或可以插入 THERE 而不改变过程意义,那么该过程就是存在过程。

 (2)存在过程在"right now"测试中用一般现在时。

练习 3.3

我已经在托尼·布莱尔的演讲中画出了所有的关系和存在过程。找出不同的过程类型和参与者(答案见附录)并讨论这是如何增强你之前对语篇的理解的。

1 I am just going to make a short statement to you on the terrible events that have happened in London earlier today,

2 and I hope

3 you understand

4 that at the present time we are still trying to establish exactly what has happened,

5 and there is a limit to what information I can give you,

6　and I will simply try and tell you the information as best I can at the moment.

7　It is reasonably clear that there have been a series of terrorist attacks in London.

8　There are obviously casualties, both people that have died and people seriously injured,

9　and our thoughts and prayers of course are with the victims and their families.

10　It is my intention to leave the G8 within the next couple of hours and go down to London and get a report, face-to-face, with the police, and the emergency services and the Ministers that have been dealing with this, and then to return later this evening.

11　It is the will of all the leaders at the G8 however that the meeting should continue in my absence, that we should continue to discuss the issues that we were going to discuss, and reach the conclusions which we were going to reach.

12　Each of the countries round that table have some experience of the effects of terrorism

13　and all the leaders><share our complete resolution to defeat this terrorism.

14　>as they will indicate a little bit later<

15　It is particularly barbaric that this has happened on a day when people are meeting to try to help the problems of poverty in Africa, and the long term problems of climate change and the environment

16　Just as it is reasonably clear that this is a terrorist attack, or a series of terrorist attacks,

17　it is also reasonably clear that it is① designed and aimed to coincide with the opening of the G8.

18　There will be time to talk later about this.

19　It is important however that those engaged in terrorism realise

20　that our determination to defend our values and our way of life is greater than their determination to cause death and destruction to innocent people in a desire to impose extremism on the world.

21　Whatever they do,

22　it is our determination that they will never succeed in destroying what we hold dear in this country and in other civilised nations throughout the world.

---

①　现在时态的使用表明这是一种归属关系用法,而不是被动用法。

3.2.7 检测概述

表 3.1 总结了不同过程类型的检测(或潜在的语法模式)——试一下吧!

表 3.1 检测汇总表

	DO-test	Projection or macrophenomenon?	THERE as Subject	Right now-test	Receiver	Recipient	Client
Material	√	X	X	cont.	X	√	√
Mental	X	Cognitive and desiderative——projection;Perceptive and emotive——macrophenomenon	X	simple	X	X	X
Verbal	√	Projection	X	usually cont.	√	X	X
Behavioural	?	Only after preposition except for WATCH and FEEL	X	usually cont.	√	X	X
Relational:attributive	For control or change only	X	X	simple except for change or control	X	X	Rare
Relational:identifying	X	Macrophenomenon only	X	simple	X	X	X
Existential	X	X	√	simple	X	X	X

3.3 及物性: 环境成分

如前所述,及物性不仅涉及构成所述事件**核心**(nucleus)或必要元素的过程
类型和参与者,还涉及提供额外可选细节的环境成分。例如,在下面的例子中,
"slowly"这个词可以省略,而该小句的其他成分都是完整描述事件所必需的:

253. The coachman slowly rang the doorbell.

那么,在示例 253 中,该过程是"rang"的,参与"rang"过程的参与者是"the coachman(车夫)"和"the doorbell(门铃)"。因此,这三个成分都是表述事件所必需的。相比之下,"slowly"是一个可选的额外选项,告诉我们他是如何按铃的[①]。因此,它被称为方式环境成分。在英语中,方式环境成分通常以-ly 结尾的副词来体现。限于篇幅,这里对环境成分不作深入讨论,但表 3.2 总结了九种基本类型,因为读者至少需要对它们略知一二。在分析语篇如何展开时,对环境的分析尤其重要,因此我们将在第 5 章中再次对其进行探讨。它们也是完整的及物性分析的一部分,我们现在将借由塞巴斯蒂安·科的演讲进行完整的及物性分析,内容见表 3.3。(如果想要更全面地了解对环境的论述,请参见 Martin, Matthiessen and Painter 1997:127-130 和 Halliday and Matthiessen 2004:259-279)。

表 3.2　环境成分类型

类型	子类型	回答的问题	示例
Extent	Distance	How far?	He jumped three metres.
	Duration	How long?	The film lasted (for) three hours.
	Frequency	How often?	She comes every second Thursday
Location	Place	Where?	I stroked the dog on the ear/in the park.
	Time	When?	He got promoted last year.
Manner	Means	By what means? /How?	He blew it up with dynamite.
	Quality	How?	He rang the bell slowly.
	Comparison	Like what?	She ran like the wind.
	Degree	How much?	Tom loves Mary more than anything.
Cause	Reason	Why?	She ran because she was scared.
	Purpose	For what purpose? /To what end?	She ran to raise money
	Behalf	On whose behalf? /Who for?	She died for the cause.
Contingency	Condition	Under what conditions?	In the event of fire leave the building.
	Default	Under what negative conditions?	Without an agreement the plan will fail.

---

① 必要的要素被称为小句的核心,额外可选成分被称为附加语。

续表

类型	子类型	回答的问题	示例
	Concession	With what concessions? / Despite what?	Despite my advice the plan failed.
Accompaniment	Comitative	(Along) with who/what?	I saw him walking with Jane.
	Additive	Who/what else?	I like my gin with tonic.
Role	Guise	What as?	He came as a pumpkin.
	Product	What into?	She turned him into a mouse.
Matter	Matter	What about?	We were talking about the game.
Angle	Source	According to whom?	According to the papers the game was fixed.
	Viewpoint	In whose view?	To me it's all a load of rubbish.

3.4 完整语篇的及物性分析

在本节中,我将完整地呈现并讨论对塞巴斯蒂安·科演讲的分析。这里需要注意的一点是,我是围绕第 2 章中所说的最重要的指称对象进行及物性分析的。另一种方法是分析每个小句的主要动词,两种方法各有优点。分析每个分句的主要动词可以告诉我们很多关于各个语篇的风格和语言体裁的信息,但这种方法忽略了很多动作,这些动作通常出现在嵌入的小句中。借由指称对象的分析,我们可以看到说话人是如何构建这个人或事物的,这对讨论话语中定位和权力是如何体现的是很有意义的。当按指称对象进行分析时,无论其在小句中的功能如何,我们都会观察指称对象所涉及的每一个过程。这意味着有时有的小句会没有相关的过程,反之,在有的小句中我们会分析几个相关过程。我们还将额外分析指称对象作为人称代词出现的情况(如在"their lives"中),以及指称对象出现在小句的环境中而不是在核心部分的情况。这些补充信息提供了额外的分析角度。我为那些不那么明了的例子提供了注释(至少有一次,我合理地"随心所欲"了一番!)。一起仔细阅读语篇和表3.3,然后进行后面的讨论。

表 3.3　塞巴斯蒂安・科奥林匹克演讲的及物性分析

Clause	Process	Coe (and others)	Athletes	Olympic Games/sport	Community	IOC
1	stand	Beh		Circ:cause		
1	inspiration①	(Sen②)		Phen		
2	be12	Ca				
3	march	Go				
4	sit	Ac				
5	watch	Beh:perc		Phen		
6	compete		Ac			
7	win		Ac	Circ:loc		
8	miss		Ac	Circ:loc		
9	open	Cli				
10	be back in classroom	Ca				
11	know	Sen:cog				
12	want	Sen:desid				
12	do	Ac				
13	be	Ca				
13		Sen:desid				
14	stand	Ac				
14	catch a glimpse of	Cog:perc				
14	bring		Ac			
16	join	Ac				
17	give	Rect	Ac			
18	stand	Beh				

续表

Clause	Process	Coe (and others)	Athletes	Olympic Games/sport	Community	IOC
18	inspire	Sen		Phen		
19	started	my journey Ac				
20	continues	my journey Ac				
20	draw	Go	Ac	Circ:loc		
21	do	Ac				
21	inspire	Ind		Phen		
22	be				Sen	
23	live				Ca	
24	believe				Ca[3]	
26	live				Sen:cog	
27	be				Ca	
28	be			Circ:loc	their landscapes Ca	
29	understand	Sen:cog			their path Ca	
29	respond	Ac			their world Phen	
30	be Olympians		At		their world Circ:cause	
31	change				My children's heroes Ac	
32	be the lucky ones				Tk	
33	face	Ac⑤			Sen:perc④	
34	my travels	Ac⑤				
34	speak	Beh:verbal				Recr
34	have conversations	Beh:verbal				
34	meet	Ac⑥				Ac

No.	Process				
35	reassure	Recr			
36	uplift	Sen	Ind		
37	share	Ca⑦	Ca		
38	do		Ac		
38	engage	The hearts and minds of young people Go	Ac		
39	bring	Go	Rect		
40	have		Ca:pos		
40	meet		Ac		
41	take	At			
42	take	Global voice At			
42		Global voice Sayer	Rect		
43	offer	Ac	circ:temp	Rect	Common goal for the future of sport At:pos
44	choose		Sen:desid		
45	send a message	Recr	Beh:vbl		
46	be	Ca	Circ:Cli		
48	be	Your decision Ca/			
50	make bold decisions	Sen:desid⑧ Beh:desid			
50	take forward	Go			
51	be	Your decision Ca/			
52	promote	Tg/Go⑨	Sen:desid		

(Sayer)

续表

53	be		Your decision At/ Sen:desid Sayer
53	show	Sayer⑩	Recr
53	matters	Ca①	
53	matters	Ca	
54	submit	Ac	3xCirc:behalf
55	Conclude	Our presentation	
	Go/Sayer		

注释：

①虽然从语法的角度来看，"inspiration"并不是一个过程，而且在前面已列为Circ:cause，我还是将其添加了进来，因为它构建了塞巴斯蒂安·科利和奥林匹克之间的关系。

②塞巴斯蒂安·科作为感知者是隐含的。

③"Live"在这里的意思是"居住"，后面必不可少地接上了处所的wh-词；无标记的时态是一般现在时，所以我将之分析为关系过程。

④"Face"可以比喻 "the fact that they have limited resources" 或者 "having limited resources" 作为补语。

⑤这个是比喻短语，意思是"旅行之时"，所以我将之视作心理过程，因为这对分析的角色作动作者，因为塞巴斯蒂安·科称作行动者。如果我们所讨论的是构建方法而不是内容的话，也许应进行不同的分析。

⑥"Face"一词类似，但不能接那个小句做补语。这里还有"解决"之意，而且其进行时态也很自然，所以我将其进行时态是可逆的。

⑦这与33小句中所有式识别小句（后来引入的），因为有一些同源小句是可逆的。

⑧虽然这可能是一个所有后面几个小句，我分析了这些例子，因为确定国际奥委会和/或塞巴斯蒂安·科的角色，以及整个名词词组"your decision"[这是目标（target）]，另一方面增加这项事业的知名度"your decision"或"our presentation"。实际上，可能二者兼而有之。

⑨我认为这是一个带无标记一般现在时的例子，一方面赞颂奥林匹克事业[这是目标（goal）]，另一方面增加这项事业的知名度，以及塞巴斯蒂安·科的角色，以确定国际奥委会和/或塞巴斯蒂安·科的角色，以及整个名词词组"your decision"或"our presentation"。

⑩请参考本章对"show"的讨论。

⑪一个带无标记一般现在时的关系过程，意为"重要"。

3.5　分析讨论

及物性分析为我们在第 2 章中看到的关于指称/照应和主题的连续性和变化的篇章性增加了另一个维度。对于较长的语篇,最恰当或者最可行的方法是考虑语篇的整体**展开方法**(*method of development*)(参见第 5 章),手段是通过找到语篇中一些较长节段中哪些参与者关系的具体结构占主导地位,然后观察这些结构如何随着语篇的发展而变化。在较短的语篇中,研究问题更为集中,可能有必要研究较小范围的变动。我们在这里的分析角度是观察塞巴斯蒂安·科为了在国际奥委会面前增强伦敦申奥的合理性,是如何在直接语境中为自己构建不同定位的,以及他构建和重新调整故事情节(包括他自己在其中的角色)的方式。因此,我们可以更仔细地关注这些构建行为是如何以及在哪里发生的,而不是更宽泛的模式。

让我们先看看塞巴斯蒂安·科为自己构建的各种定位。在开场白中,我们看到他将自己置于眼前的环境中,考虑到赛事的惯例,我们知道他的立场是作为一个恳求者代表伦敦申奥,但是他给出的理由是"the inspiration of the Olympic Movement"。因此,从一开始,我们就看到塞巴斯蒂安·科以两种不同的方式定位于奥运会:作为国际奥委会面前的恳求者和受奥林匹克运动启发的人。

然后,塞巴斯蒂安·科通过他童年时的奥运会经历的移位语境,拓展了第二次定位——首先是作为一名观察者,然后是作为一名了解自己未来的人,最后是根据自己的经验采取行动的人。这种由奥运会给予塞巴斯蒂安·科灵感,然后塞巴斯蒂安·科根据灵感采取行动的模式,在物质方面反映在他对奥运会运动员之一希拉·舍伍德的构建行为中,包括希拉·舍伍德给了他第一双跑鞋,以及他加入了舍伍德夫妇的俱乐部。有趣的是,虽然在塞巴斯蒂安·科的演讲中,运动员几乎完全被构建为动作者,但这很少涉及(作为受影响的参与者的)目标;相反,运动员的行动改变了他们自己(见上)。不过也有例外之处值得注意,包括舍伍德夫妇将奖牌带回了家乡,希拉·舍伍德将她的跑鞋交给了年轻的赛巴——这两种行为都象征着他们将成功传递给下一代(请记住,留下"遗产"是当前申办奥运会的一个重要标准)。在本节中,我们将塞巴斯蒂安·科视为真正的"受启发者",首先是作为灵感(一种心理反应)的感知者,然后是一名动作者,他受到奥运会的感召而从事跑步的物质活动。在第18小句中,塞巴斯蒂安·科用一个简单的短语"35年过去了"回到了直接语境中,但每个听到的人都会知道,在这35年里,塞巴斯蒂安·科成为双金牌得主和奥运会历史上最伟大的运动员之一。塞巴斯蒂安·科作为奥运会运动员的**具身资本**(*embodied capital*)在这里是如此之巨大,乃至他可以在不提及它的情况下调用它! 塞巴斯蒂安·科以第19和第20小句结束了演讲的这一**阶段**(*phase*)。因此,塞巴斯蒂安·科在开场白中引入灵感的概念之后,他已经确立了他的定位——作为一个深受奥运感召的光辉榜样,因而是一位可敬的恳求者。从定位之星的角度而言,我们可以说在重新调整故事情节的过程中,作为伦敦申奥这个直接事件的一份子,塞巴斯蒂安·科在这些特定的受众面前增加了他话语的符号资本。这样一来,我们可以看到定位之星的各个点位如何既可以被视为具有约束性,又可以被视为具有功能可供性。

在第21小句中,塞巴斯蒂安·科再次使用了"inspire"一词,但现在轮到他去激励今天的年轻人,以回报他所获得的灵感和受到激励之后而开启的生活。这一策略使塞巴斯蒂安·科能够将故事情节从他自己的少年时代成功转移到今天的年轻人和他们麻烦更多的生活上。在此处,塞巴斯蒂安·科还为自己构建了一个作为父母的定位,一个能够应对当今年轻人问题的人。

从第34小句开始,塞巴斯蒂安·科为自己构建了另一种定位——一个与国际奥委会分享了谈话和经验的提供者(Beh:言语)和接受者(复杂小句中的接受者和感知者)。因此,他和国际奥委会被构建为共襄盛举之人——心怀"a common goal for the future of the sport",也被隐含地构建为当今年轻人的激励者。因此,通过在第39小句中赞扬国际奥委会的工作,塞巴斯蒂安·科也提升了他自己(以及伦敦的)的愿景。塞巴斯蒂安·科现在有一系列令人钦佩的定位——恳求者、受到激励而胸怀大志的孩子、父亲,以及与国际奥委会同怀美好愿景的共事者。

塞巴斯蒂安·科接着引入了一个新的故事情节(之前也曾暗示过),他说奥林匹克运动的挑战是持久的,将延续到奥运会之外。这一点在第 41—43 小句中得到了体现——塞巴斯蒂安·科回到了直接语境和他作为恳求者的角色,首次明确提到"legacy"的概念,作为他所代表的伦敦申奥愿景的一部分。然后,他以这一主题为基础展开,将伦敦申奥重新调整为为当今年轻人(第 45、46 小句)申奥,并将国际奥委会定位为负责实现这一愿景的机构,并且以此构建为基础展开,直到第 53 小句。记住,他已经把国际奥委会和他自己构建为有相同的愿景。可以说,他使用"offer"这个词与希拉·舍伍德给赛巴第一双跑鞋以作激励的手段相类似。塞巴斯蒂安·科在结束时回到了直接语境和手头的工作,将伦敦申奥构建成"on behalf of the youth of today, the athletes of tomorrow and the Olympians of the future"——也就是说,代表那些今天受到鼓舞、明天将变得伟大的人,就像塞巴斯蒂安·科当年一样。因此,在整个演讲中,塞巴斯蒂安·科重新成功调整了申办奥运会的故事情节,从"17 days of superb Olympic competition"转变为当今年轻人的愿景,让他们像塞巴斯蒂安·科和他之前的运动员一样行动起来,改变自己。考虑到这一故事情节,塞巴斯蒂安·科自我构建的深受鼓舞的年轻人、伟大的奥运健儿、家长以及与国际奥委会心怀相同愿景的共事者,这一切都有助于提升他在直接语境里的定位的说服力——无论是作为向国际奥委会伦敦申奥(被他构建为"灵感与遗产"的盛会)的恳求者,还是作为代表当今处境不利的年轻人的倡导者。

尽管塞巴斯蒂安·科在通过描述各个移位语境来重新调整故事情节时,为自己构建了数个定位,但是他作为国际奥委会面前的恳求者这一直接定位未曾改变,这一直接定位因为他把多个定位整合成一个整体而得以巩固。在后面的章节中,我们将研究更复杂的情况,其中说话人在直接语境中扮演多重**角色**

(*roles*)。这些不同的角色可以构成单一**角色集合**(*role set*)的一部分,比如医生在诊断师和咨询师的角色之间切换,或者与演讲者同时持有的不同社会定位或**地位相关**(*statuses*)。

在下一章中,我们将不再讨论经验意义和对语场和参与者角色的构建,转而探讨人际意义和语境的语旨。我们还将思考人际关系和经验意义(尽管在语言学理论上是互相独立的)在社会实践中有着怎样不可分割的联系。

第4章 人际意义:语篇中的互动与协调

4.1 引言

在前一章中,我们看到写作者和说话人如何在小句或以下层面上利用及物性的词汇句法资源,在语篇中表述不同参与者的活动类型和程度。有人认为这是一种构建行为,是事件的众多可能表述形式中的一种,特定作者对事件的构建方式需要根据语篇产生的语境/环境来加以解读。然而,虽然这些表述是特定说话人针对特定目的选择的,但或多或少可以根据它们与真实或想象事件的对应程度进行评价。也就是说,经验意义在很大程度上与客观真理(或谬误)有关(不过这种说法当然过于简单化而具有误导性)。因此,经验意义是早期语言学研究的唯一对象,属于真值条件的哲学研究范畴。一般来说,现代语言学理论认为经验意义只是几种意义中的一种,我们在第 1 章中已讲过这一点。而在本章中,我们将研究韩礼德所说的**人际意义**(*interpersonal meanings*),在这个范畴下语言是用以构造身份和建立关系的资源,而这些概念存在很大程度上的主观性,因此不能据真值来判断它们。

在话语中,通过语言来构建人际意义有多种相互关联的方式,在本章中,我们将探讨:

- 不同说话人所扮演的言语角色(例如,讲述者、询问者、命令者);

- 说话人为自己的主张表达的肯定程度和提供的证据基础;

- 说话人对事件表达的可能性或必要性程度;

- 讲话者在评价人、事和行为时所使用的不同评价标准。

　　读者肯定注意到了,这些范畴的确与真或假有些关系,但它们主要关涉说话人自己的主观评估,而这些评估的真假是无法得到客观验证的。也就是说,如果我宣布"月亮是奶酪做的",你可以证明或反驳这个说法;但你无法证明我是否相信这个说法。如果我问你是否在下雨,或者让你给我买一杯啤酒,你如何能测试这问题或命令的真假呢? 出于这个原因,语言哲学家们开始探讨**言语行为**(*speech acts*)的**适切条件**(*felicity conditions*),即令这些行为有效而非真实的必要条件。大家也一定要记住,正如定位之星所示,这是本书的核心主题,只不过所聚焦的是整个语篇,而不是只言片语。韩礼德(Halliday 1978:117)将人际意义称为语言的**干预者功能**(*intruder function*),因为这个领域明确地允许说话人的个人判断对语篇进行干预。然而,大家也不能忘记,正如前几章所讨论的,对事件的任何表述已经都是说话人个人所构建的,因此人际意义绝不是说话人可以干预语篇的唯一途径。

　　在我们单独研究了体现人际意义(而不涉其他意义)的语法资源(这不过是一个方便的理论抽象)后,我们将开始思考这些特征是如何与我们在前面两章中所讨论的语场变量相互作用的,以及不同的组合与说话人(针对不同受众,基于所控制的不同符号资本)所采取的不同定位之间的关系。

　　在第 2 章中,我区分了直接事件和移位事件,我们看到了移位事件可以如何在直接环境中使用。相比之下,人际意义总是与说话人在当前话语事件中的定位有关(但是可能对长远也有所着眼)。因此,它是表明构成性语篇在直接事件中所起作用的手段之一。因此,正如下文所述,在确定语言所构建的活动类型时,人际意义与经验意义同样重要。

4.2　语气与言语功能

现在让我们再看看管理规划研讨会的语篇(这里复制英文版为语篇 4.1),
并考虑一些有助于人际意义的基本形式—功能关系:

语篇 4.1

1　　S: The second thing is is whether or not we want to continue with drinking water,

2　　(xxxxxxx). Now (xxxxx) topic of discussion, where do we go from here? (xxx).

3　　What = what is, what kind of thing you've put together so ↑far and what is the

4　　future … next steps of activity? (xx) remember, this is just the beginning, it's a

5　　(? step) assessment. Of (x) developing a management plan … erm, what does T- …

6　　what does T-want to do … and to what extent would you like to … continue to

7　　have Iwokrama involved in … in … in facilitating it? And in … in building

8　　capacity to to (xx)? ((data omitted))

9　　S: Okay, so you're prepared to finish off the water? [Okay.]

10　W: 　　　　　　　　　　　　　　　　[I feel] the whole point (xxxx).

11　　((unclear background discussion))

12　S: I wish … I was hoping that maybe you could (xx) do it (to the other xx room).

13　　Just kind of get one person to do what er … what … er er I was hoping (? to be)

14　　facilitator and one (person xx) to do the planning (xxxxx). Yeah?

15　W: Okay.

16	S:	Right, Walter, you in shape for this?
17	W:	A'right.
18	S:	(Or we could) try …
19	W:	(xxxxx).
20	S:	(xx) did you want (xxx)? So we need … two other people … Vanessa … Nicholas …
21	W:	VANESSA! COME NOW! ∘(xxxx)∘.
22		((shuffling)) (12s)
23		Come here and do some writing.
24		(9s)
25	S:	Here, Vanessa, (you could do with this pen).
26		((mumbling)) (50s)
27		So …

正如我们在第 2 章中看到的,这段文字的语言的作用是辅助其他活动来对参与者和环境进行组织安排,以将该语境确立为会议。因此,在活动的这一阶段有着不同的说话人在提供和检查组织上的细节、让其他人为他们做事情、同时也主动提出自己承担某些事情。这些不同的活动对应韩礼德和马蒂森(Halliday and Matthiessen 2004:107-108)所说的四种基本言语功能,即说话人所扮演的话语角色。这些可以列在一个表格中,以突出它们之间的语义相似性和差异(见表 4.1)。

表 4.1　言语角色

	信息（说）	物品和服务（做）
给予	陈述	提供
求取	提问	请求

陈述（*statement*）、**提供**（*offer*）、**提问**（*question*）和**请求**（*request*）这四个术语只不过是宽泛的名称,它们涵盖了许多种类的相关言语行为。例如,命令、强制命令和劝诫都是对各种类型的物品和服务的求取(禁令也是如此,只是所要求的

是不做某事)。有些学者已经做出了各种尝试来更详细地定义和区分言语行为(例如,Hasan 1996),但在本书中,我们将坚持这一基本的四类区别。这意味着在哈桑的论述中,例如,"提问"这个词比笔者在这里给出的含义更为具体——所以请务必留心! 读者在自己的研究中,可能希望使用更细微的描述——这都涉及关于你的地图的详细程度的问题:取决于你是想从家里走到超市,还是从奥斯陆飞到柏林?

注意,陈述、提供、提问和请求都是语义范畴,我们通过语调和词汇语法特征的组合来识别它们。在一个非常基本的描述层面上,我们可以区分英语中的疑问句和陈述句,因为**主语**(*subject*)(S)和**限定成分**(*finite*)(F)在每个句子中出现的顺序不同。下面的例子改编自 16 小句莎拉所说的"You in shape for this?"(稍后我们将讨论她的原话):

1. Are (F) you (S) in shape for this?
2. You (S) are (F) in shape for this.

从语法上讲,这些结构被称为**疑问语气**(*interrogative mood*)和**陈述语气**(*declarative mood*),它们分别是疑问句和陈述句的**一致性**(*congruent*)体现(下文将详细介绍)。

限定成分和主语最好结合在一起描述。主语是与我们所作陈述相关的人或物,限定成分是动词中表征时态(或可能性,见下文)的部分,在英语和许多其他语言中它要与主语一致。共同作用之下,它们在(假设的)空间和时间中锚定了话语,合称为**语气成分**(*mood element*)。所以,在例 1 和例 2 中,"are"表示现在时(比较"were")",而且与主语"you"一致(比较"He is"),这表明行为的空间是以"you"为中心的。一般来说,除了第三人称单数(I go,you go,he/she/it goes,we go,they go),英语中没有多少表示主谓一致的标记,但它仍然是一个相关因素。英语中的另一个使问题复杂化的现象是限定成分经常与**主要动词**(*main verb*)(描述过程的词)**融合**(*fused*)在一起,如规则的"He walked"和不规则的"He went"。这里的单词"walked"和"went"既包括主要动词"walk"和"go"

的语义,也包括标示时间的限定成分。在这两个例子中,限定成分都是标示过去时态。在疑问和其他一些形式中,这两个成分是分开的,比如"Did he walk?"和"Did he go?"。这里的"did"是助动词 DO 的限定形式,在这里用来标记过去时态。但请注意,在这两个例子中,主语和限定成分的顺序仍然是疑问句的 F^S(其中^表示必要顺序)。

因此,语气成分发挥着多种功能。它标示时间、我们所作的陈述与谁或与什么相关、小句的言语功能,以及我们将在下面讨论的其他类型的意义。这些都是人际意义的要素(说话人如何根据所交换的经验意义来确定自己和他人的定位),因此,分析不同小句的语气成分对于描述语篇的人际意义以及它们在话语中与说话人定位的有何关系至关重要。

然而,这里面有一个复杂化的因素,即提问分为两大类,并通过不同的结构加以体现。首先是所谓的**两极疑问句**(*polar interrogatives*),通常寻求是/非的答案来验证一个想法是否正确。我们一直在说的那句话"Are you in shape for this?"就是两极疑问句的一个例子。但也有一些寻求细节的问题,叫作 *wh-*疑**问句**,这些疑问句不是询问某个想法的真假,而是要求提供更具体的信息。语篇4.1 中有几个例子:

3. What is the future?
4. ... to what extent would you like to continue to have Iwokrama involved in facilitating it? (……您希望 Iwokrama 在多大程度上继续参与推动这项工作?)

wh-疑问句包括一个 wh-疑问词(where、why、what、when、who、who 以及 how!),通常位于小句的开头,但有时在前面可加一个介词(如例4)。当 wh-疑问词是小句的主语时,语序是 S^F,而不是两极疑问句的 F^S,如:

5. What(S)is(F)the future?

然而,请注意,这仍然被称为疑问句。

当 wh-疑问词不是主语时,其顺序与两极疑问句相同:

6. ... to what extent would you like to continue to have Iwokrama involved in facilitating it?

请注意,在例 6 中,限定成分不是指时间,而是指可能性的程度,这是一种情态,很快我们将在下文做相关介绍。简言之,限定成分可以在时间或可能的世界中定位话语。

到目前为止,我们已经看到了三种语气类型——陈述式、两极疑问式和 wh-疑问式。还有一种主要类型,①**祈使语气**(*imperative*,此词来自意为"命令"的拉丁词根,与 emperor(皇帝)一词同源)。语篇 4.1 第 23 小句有一个双重祈使语气的例子,沃尔特对瓦妮莎说:

7. Come here and do some writing.

这里的祈使语气由主要动词体现,而没有明显的语气成分。在某些情况下,可以加入主语,如:

8. You (S) come here!

或者限定成分,如:

9. Do (F) come here ...

我们最好将这些变体视为额外的资源,而不是规则的例外情况——毕竟它们确实产生了不同的含义。在例 8 中,"you"意味着额外的强调意味,可能会产生一种对比意义,暗示"因为**我不会!**"。在例 9 中,"do"表示出于某种原因增加了额外的坚持程度。

当我们遇到否定祈使句时,否定助词 DON'T 被加为限定成分,就像 DO 被加在一些疑问句中一样:

10. Don't (F) come here.

一般来说,祈使的对象只是我们的**对话者**(*interlocutors*),所以我们可以把

---

① 也有少见的感叹语气,比如"What an ass I am!"

他们称为第二人称祈使。然而,由于这一类别包括绝大多数情况,我们通常就称之为祈使。但祈使也可以指向包含说话人的一个群体。我们随后将在马丁·路德·金著名的《我有一个梦想》演讲中看到一个例子:

11. Let us not wallow in the valley of despair.

通常由结构 LET'S 和不定式实现的话语功能有几个名字,例如弱祈使、劝勉祈使和建议祈使等,我们将该结构本身称为第一人称复数祈使。注意要将这些与动词 LET 的第二人称祈使区别开来:

12. Please let us stay up late tonight, mum!

还有第三人称祈使,虽然极为少见:

13. Just let him try!!!
14. Let them eat cake.

在更正式的语言中,可以用 MAY 一词:

15. May he rest in peace.

在本书中,我们可以将这些形式在语篇中的出现标记为 1plimp、3simp 和 3plimp(第一人称复数祈使、第三人称单数祈使和第三人称复数祈使),而不去考虑是否用了 LET 或 MAY。第二人称祈使只会标记为 imp。

不同的语气类型可以是肯定的,也可以是否定的,这种区别被称为极性或者**归一性**(*polarity*)。这样,示例 11 表示为负 1plimp。由于肯定极性远比否定极性更常见,所以只把示例 2 标记为 decl,而将示例 13 标记为 imp。

正如你现在可能已经意识到的,上面讨论的都是相当理想化的情况,所以现在是时候解释什么是**一致性**(*congruence*)了。例如,当我们说疑问语气是通过疑问结构一致地体现时,我们的意思是这是无标记形式(也就是说,不加任何额外内容的形式)。无标记形式通常是实现功能的最常见和最简单的结构,通常是最早进入语言并被儿童学习的形式。就我们的目的而言,最重要的一点是

有标记形式的产生往往需要更多麻烦,也承载着额外的意义。所以,当莎拉说:

16. I was hoping you could do it to [in?] the other room.

她似乎是在提出建议,间接要求其他参与者采取一些行动,而不仅仅是让他们知道她当时的心理状态。间接性通常意味着有额外的意义在起作用(例如,对其他可能性的考虑、含糊其词、礼貌和各种面子功夫),这反映在(与使用一致式祈使形式相比)额外的语言活动上(Brown and Levinson 1987):

17. Do it in the other room.

有时很难精确地描述实时话语中进行的言语行为(这也许就是为什么言语哲学家要创造出例子和语境的原因),然而,到底一段文字的功能主要是提供信息,要求采取行动,或者是这些内容的混合,却通常是很清楚的。同样,这些言语行为是直接地还是间接地进行(即语法结构是否具有一致性),这一点通常也很清楚。更复杂的问题是在什么语境下,使用标记形式是未被标记的行为(Watts 2003)。语篇中还有两种对物品和服务的间接求取:

18. Could we try ... and
19. So we need two other people.

正如你将看到的,这些间接体现形式包含着一些可能性或必然性的概念,并通过动词"could"(CAN 的一种形式)和"need"来体现的。有一组动词被称为情态动词,它们会编码诸如可能性和必要性之类的概念,通常与语气上的选择相互作用,以体现不同的言语行为。因此,在语言用法的描述中,语气和情态通常一起加以讨论,我们将在下一节作更深入的探讨。

有观察力(但不是那么强)的读者会注意到,我没有讨论表 4.1 中的第四个言语功能:"提供"。这是因为英语没有实现"提供"的一致化结构(不像西班牙语和法语,它们使用一般现在时)。最常见的提供方式是将疑问语气与情态助词 SHALL(尤其是在英式英语中)或 WILL 结合起来,如:

20. Shall I open the window?
21. I'll do that for you.

然而,别的情态动词也经常被用来表示提供:

22. Can I help you?

在下一节中,我们将深入了解情态。不过现在,我们来快速地看一看语篇 4.1 中的另外两个示例。第一个来自第 9 小句:

23. Okay, so you're prepared to finish off the water? Okay.

完整的句子是陈述式的,然而,莎拉使用升调(在文本中用问号表示),这是要求信息而不是提供信息的一致语调模式。其效果是,莎拉既在做一个陈述,又在询问其是否属实,这种言语行为有时被称为**核对**(*check*)。为了表达这种混合性,陈述式结构和升调的组合通常被称为**疑问陈述句**(*queclarative*)形式。然而,就本书而言,将结构标记为陈述句且将语音功能标记为要求信息就足够了。这将标志着形式和功能的匹配不一致。全面观察第 23 例,我们看到莎拉用了第二个"Okay",但没有升调,这表明缺乏回应可以被视为确认。这证实了将她第一句话视为信息需求而非陈述的分析。查看周围的语篇通常会为分析者提供这样的线索。

遗憾的是,由于篇幅所限,我们无法在此详细讨论语调模式。关于英语语调的完整描述(你可能已经猜到,它比这里暗示的要复杂得多),请参见 Halliday and Greaves(2008)、Tench(1996)或 O'Grady(2010)。

莎拉还在第 16 小句中使用了以下"句子"(上文讨论了其经由操纵的变体版本):

24. Right, Walter, you in shape for this?

这里省略了限定成分,因此不可能严格地确定它是陈述句还是疑问句,所以我们必须依靠直觉来测试语境中两种可能的完整形式的合理性。这种"遗漏"单词的现象被称为**省略**(*ellipsis*)。我认为,在此语境中,"Are you in shape for this?"比"You're in shape for this?"更为合适,可能是因为之前没有关于沃尔特是否准备好讨论会促使莎拉使用核对形式。有时识别完整形式会更容易些,比如在非正式用语中:

25. You go to the shops yesterday?

　　由于省略是指单词的缺漏,而不改变它们的形式(你得相信我的话……),所以我们排除了"went"的可能性,那么在通常情况下,疑问句"Did you go to the shops yesterday?"与带有高度标记的陈述句"You did go to the shops yesterday?"相比,更可能是实际的完整句型,因为后者中的"did"暗含本句中所具有的确定性,而升调则意味着不确定性。这种句型将按照其完整、无省略的形式标记为陈述式或疑问式,不过请记住,这里的话语是非正式的。

练习 4.1

在语篇 4.1 中,我们看到莎拉如何通过她所扮演的话语角色来控制直接语境。在第 2 章中,有人提出,莎拉在这种直接语境下为自己构建的立场可能会对后来的管理规划研讨会产生影响。在 Bartlett 2012a 一书中,我对整个话语进行了深入分析,情况似乎是这样的——会议控制权尽管已被正式让渡给了沃尔特(这是作为这项活动的中心目的),最后却逐渐又回归到了莎拉身上。我认为这是因为她作为活动组织者的角色(在活动的设置安排过程中得到了强调),再加上她作为专业开发工作者的资本,那么当出现问题时,她几乎不可避免地会从主持人转变为组织者,从而从沃尔特手中接管了控制权。在语篇 4.2 中,我们可以看到,实际情况的确如此,因为这时莎拉重新牢牢地掌控了局面。阅读语篇并回答以下问题。

语篇 4.2

1　S：Okay, so... so the activity... is ... to do what?

2   >To get a reservoir ... set up ... in the village? < Right?

3   That's the activity?

4 N?: Yeah.

5 S: Right.

6   And then ... how does that fit with ... . with all these other things in terms of

7   of agricultu:re, health, and all of those ... is the next thing you're talking about?

8   Makes it more accessible, makes it easier ... maybe healthier, those kind of stuff,

9   right?

10   So ... so, let's just back up.

11   So, you wanna do ... three.

12   (15s)

13   And remember this from yesterday ... the various points we've built, right?

14   (5s)

15   Right?

16   And re ... re ... and so ... that's one, it is "How does it fit with other things in the

17   village?",

18   and you're saying it makes it more accessible an' easier.

19   So ...

20   (6s)

21   Any other ... things [to go with]

22 N: [Safer], it was safer.

23 S: Sa:fer. ((writing it down?))

24　W：　(xxx) safer (xxx).

25　S：　(xxx).

26　　　(9s)

27　S：　Because drinking water is such a straightforward thing, these two collapse into

28　　　one basically.

29　　　I mean 'cause it's not like you're talking about lo:gging or ... or cutting

30　　　down trees to do agriculture, right?

31　　　So 1 and 2 would ...

32　N：　Less time taken to ... t= =for your water.

33　S：　Yeah. 1 and 2. Less time taken to acquire (our) water.

34　　　So, less labour, right?

35　?：　((grunt of assent))

36　　　(14s)

37　S：　Mm-hmm. Anything else?

38　　　(6s)

39　W：　Encourage agr ... kitchen gardens.

40　S：　Encourage agriculture, right?

41　　　(20s)

42　　　Anything else?

43　W：　Is it okay that hoping they erm ... a flush toilet system (xxxxx)?

44　S：　In the future?

45　W：　Mm-hmm.

46　S：　But that's not meant to be activity right now?

47　　　(Eh,) the activity right now is to find somebody to fund ... the reservoir. and the...

48　　　　pipes ... to certain points, right?

49　　　　So, potential future ... so that's potential.

50　N：　I think maybe we should put that part.

51　　　　((W and N mutter a while)) (12s)

52　S：　We have ... you talked about this yesterday, activity (xx), How it's going to each

53　　　　home and ... and ...

54　N：　We could have taken it from under ... easier access, (xxx).

55　　　　(12s)

56　S：　(What about other) sanitation, Walter?

57　　　　Flush toilet system, (? sanitary towel) system. (This is to put under) positive =

58　N：　= We don't see water in the home as something that should be automatic.

59　　　　((mumbling from floor)) (16s)

60　S：　They would get what?

61　　　　(((further mumbling, with N's voice suddenly becoming prominent.)) (6s)

62　N：　... not a necessity,

63　　　　you could collect (more than) water from outside.

64　　　　I mean, which can happen,

65　S：　[Could everyone]

66　W：　[When we] talked about the flush toilet, it was the ... around the nearby

67　　　　well ... (xxxxx). Nearby homes to the wells, because of er ... (away then

68　　　　from) the shit-juice bringing into the wells and the water stream.

69　S：　Right.

70　　　　So it links (xxxx).

71		Sanitation, right?
72	W:	Right.
73	S:	We also talked yesterday about ecotourist things … having better water supply.
74		So that if we collapse … in here we could do one and two together, kind of
75		collapse it in … okay?
76		So …
77		((mumbling leading to laughing, especially from N)) (23s)

问题

(1) Identify both the mood and speech function of all the utterances in Text 4.2 that are not declaratives functioning as statements. Mark where short utterances like "right" or nominal groups check or confirm an idea.

(2) Identify those utterances where Sara is genuinely seeking information that is unknown to her and those where she already knows the answer.

(3) Provide more delicate labels, such as suggestion, for some of the utterances and say what features of the statement and/or the cotext led you to choose the name.

(4) Can you find any examples where Sara *reformulates* the answers given to her?

(5) How would you describe the overall *tenor* of the text as relationships construed between the participants and the way Sara engages the community—does it remind you of any other contexts?

(6) Relate your answers in 1 to 5 to the Positioning Star, taking the semantic features of Sara's talk as aspects of the acts she is performing.

4.3 情态、归因和言据性

前文说过,人际意义与真值条件无关,而真值条件曾是语言哲学中句子语义学研究的焦点。然而,这种说法并不完全正确(不过我们将在这里探讨的方法与哲学家的方法有着截然不同的侧重点)。在本节中,我们将不考虑说话人话语中与"客观现实世界事实"相关的经验的真实性或其他方面,而是讨论说话人自己对出现在实时话语中的各种想法的真实性或其他方面的判断。这是将语篇分析作为话语分析的桥梁的一种非常重要的手段,因为它揭示说话人不仅可以根据构建中的故事情节的具体方面来定位自己,还可以根据其他说话人作为真理仲裁者的权利和能力来定位自己。这与不同说话人的相对文化资本有着明显的联系,不仅体现在他们在特定观众面前所持有的知识或权威定位,而且还体现在他们试图为自己**争取**(*appropriate*)的新定位。围绕真相和充当仲裁者的权利这两个方面的磋商是权力斗争的关键战场,而且不仅仅是语言权力(Bourdieu 1991)。这里既有短期考虑,也有长期考虑,因为在关于"真相"的斗争中取得成功,就可以在未来的讨论中增加说话人的文化资本,尽管正如我们即将看到的那样,这不一定会产生积极的影响。我一直在这里使用"真相"这个词,但请允许我进一步加以阐述,并将其与上文讨论的语气和言语角色以及本节的重点——情态联系起来。让我们考虑下面的话语:

26. Vanessa is writing.

这是一种通过陈述语气实现的陈述。我们可以说,这是一个作为"真相"提出的**命题**(*proposition*),没有任何争议,也不涉及其他可能性。将其与通过疑问语气实现的两极问题进行比较:

27. Is Vanessa writing?

我们可以说,这句话的功能是核对所提出的命题是否属实。因此,这些问题引入了其他可能的真相,并有助于让其他人参与对真相的构建中。还有其他方法来处理其他可能的真相,比如以"if"引导的小句引入假设性陈述。这里没有足够的篇幅将"engagement(参与、介入等义)"作为一个语义范畴来处理,但它是马丁、怀特和罗斯等人阐述的**话语语义学**(*discourse semantics*)的核心系统之一,他们(Martin and White 2005, Martin and Rose 2003)对此做了极好的概

述。祈使句或命令与真值的关系略有不同。请思考下面的例子:

28. Do some writing, Vanessa.

在这里,我们可以说,说话人要求瓦妮莎完成提议的活动(或提议)。在"提供"的情况下,说话人表示自愿实现提议的活动:

29. I'll do the writing.

命题的真实性和提议的真实性之间的区别也适用于**情态**(*modality*)。比较以下两个例子:

30. You must be home by ten.
31. He must be home, the light's on upstairs.

在例 30 中,说话人要求受话人履行义务,使提议成为现实;在例 31 中,说话人提供了他自己对命题的评估,认为该命题很可能是真的。因此,这两个例子代表了两种不同**类型**(*types*)的情态,在文献中有多个不同的名称。对于涉及假设性提议的可取性或必要性的话语,学者们称之为**道义情态**(*deontic modality*)、**事件情态**(*event modality*)、**意态化**(*modulation*)等术语。我们将在本书中使用道义情态这个术语。对涉及命题是否真实的话语,有**认知情态**(*epistemic modality*)、**命题情态**(*propositional modality*)和**情态化**(*modalisation*)这三个术语。我们将在本书中使用认知情态这个术语。还需要注意,一些情态助词,如 MUST,可以同时用于道义意义和认知意义,而在其他情况下,可以使用不同的助词来区分这些概念。让我们再看看几个例子:

32. You should be home by ten.
33. He might be at home, I suppose.

在这里,我们再次看到道义情态和认知情态这两种类型的区别,但在这两种情况下,说话人的话语强度都不如例 30 和 31。也就是说,说话人对例 32 的提议实现的必要性没那么坚持,对例 33 的提议的真实性也显示出了较少的信心。正如我们将要看到的,我们通常可以将这种肯定程度或值分为高、中和低三等,这意味着我们现在有六个子类别的情态(三种值×两种类型)。

然而,应该注意,认知情态和道义情态有时不易区分,比如:

34. Taxis from Cardiff Central should cost no more than £ 5.

这里说话人是在评估自己的提议的真实性程度,还是在表达他们对一个提议实现的可取性或必要性的看法?这种情态意义的**混合**(*blending*)是相当普遍的,它揭示了我们的一些社会事实以及人们往往认为经常发生的(即很有可能为真的)事情也是可取的倾向。比如说,"他不正常"这句话就包含了极重的评价性负荷,"你不能那样做"这句话也常常用作控制行为的手段。

情态的另一个非常重要的方面是它反映了说话人对正在进行的话语中的命题或提议的定位,因此它总是在直接语境中体现言语行为。例如,当一位说话人说"你必须在十点之前到家"时,事件本身可能在未来发生,但义务的施加发生在说话人说话的时候。同样,对过去事件进行当前情态评估也是可能的,其中需要使用不定式的完成式来表示事件的"过去性":

35. He must have fallen down a hole.

在本例中,说话人正在对过去事件发生的可能性进行当前评估。这一点对构建移位语境的语篇来说是很重要的,比如期刊文章,其中的语言绝大多数都是构成性的。情态在这些语篇中的使用表明了作者在提供信息的行为方面——这是文章的直接语境——的定位,尽管它不是实时发生的。

注意情态也可以出现在疑问句中:

36. Could he have come back in through the window?

在这里,说话人使用"could"一词来构建命题在一定程度上的可能性,同时让受话人作为合作伙伴参与这种构建。注意,当我们使用情态助动词时,它充当限定成分,所以它在疑问句中位于主语之前。因此,限定成分可以标记时态

（如上所述）或情态，这取决于说话人是想锚定事件的时间，还是想评估事件发生的概率、可取性或可能性。因此，情态是人际意义的另一个方面，体现在小句的语气成分中。

到目前为止，我们只研究了情态动词和两种主要的情态类型，但事情变得更复杂了。想想我刚才说的一句话：

37. We can generally grade this commitment as high, median or low.

"Generally"这个词在这里的功能是什么？它表明这个命题并不总是为真的。因此，我们有不同但相关的认知情态类型，它们可以被标记为**通常性**（*usuality*），如例 37 所示，和**可能性**（*probability*），如例 35 所示。同样，对于道义情态，我们可以区分**倾向性**（*inclination*），如例 38（情态助动词 WILL 历史上与形容词 WILLING 有关）和**义务**（*obligation*），如例 39。

38. I'll do that for you.
39. Thou shalt not steal.

因此，我们现在有十二个类别的情态（四种类型×三个值），而且还不只如此，如例 37 所示，情态也可以通过副词来表达。这意味着情态是语义学而不是语法本身的一个领域，因为它可以通过各种语法手段实现（Halliday and Matthiessen 2004：613-625）。然而，由于语法有自己的意义类型（Halliday 2002：291-322），因此被表达的情态类型和使用的语法形式有一定的对应关系。关于这点，容我稍后再谈！

现在让我们来看一个语篇例子，观察一下话语中的情态。

语篇 4.3

1　　G：　Added to that, then, there's the whole question of (who owns) agriculture,

2　　　　we talked about (xx) and (xx) … Another one was the land, the whole question

3		of the relationship between Toka and the Government and what land was
4		available for use … and that's tied in with（xxx）, tied in with long-term
5		security … ？
6	N：	That's … that should be tied in to ownership of other resources like water,
7		（xxx）…
8	G：	Ownership and use of management（product）. Management（rights xx）.
9		（p）
10		The target（h）as communication we've got in … which I think comes into
11		the first thing, that's called mechanisms how … ＞ how your views can be
12		reflected both ＜ with the government, with UNDP,① with Iwokrama, with
13		everybody.
14		（p）（（some mumbling））
15		Another big one … we've seen … that seems to affect a lot of things is creek,
16		your ideas of creek management …（detay）reforestation.
17	N：	I think it's a whole restoration process.
18	G：	Restoration（xxxx）？
19	N：	Not only that. But the（xxxx）. Because of cultural restoration. Maybe
20		you couldn't finance that, you know？ Because what we find there's
21		disadvantage when we've been government, erm, driven programmes, they've
22		been … financially supported properly … and our erm programmes are not,
23		traditional ways are not supported so. They have an advantage right away
24		there（xx）find that … they actually killing … government is（xx）not knowing

---

① 联合国开发计划署是在圭亚那开展活动的几个联合国组织之一，在北鲁普努尼工作历时已久。

25		（they）erm killing culture.
26	S：	°Not knowing?°
27	?：	°（xx）°
28		（p）
29	G：	I'm not sure if this doesn't（xxxx）my interpretation.
30	N：	（What your interpretation is?）
31		（（Interference, pauses and muttering.））
32		I think one of the things we have to do（actually）is we have to be …
33		（adventure,
34		you know）with a（pi xx）. When we develop plans that erm … the government
35		na① see it as being, you know, complementary … complementary with the
36		present development strategies of the government, so … we're not supported,
37		but
38		it should be supported,（na?）
39	G：	But this comes back again to this whole question of whether or not anybody's
40		listening to what you're saying. Which doesn't appear to be the
41		case. At all levels. Sometimes because before in our communities they don't
42		know how to listen. Sometimes they're just not terribly interested in listening.

　　该语篇与语篇 4.1 都摘取自同一场管理规划研讨会，但时间较 4.1 早了一天，是规模较小的小组讨论。这里的说话人是尼古拉斯（Nicholas）、戈登（Gordon）和莎拉（Sara），他们在各自的社区和机构中都享有很高的地位。尼古拉斯是当地社区著名的长者，戈登和莎拉分别是 Iwokrama 的科学家和社会科学家。不同的说话人对彼此地位的了解和评估是话语非物质环境的一部分，因为

---

① “Na”在圭亚那英语中是一个普遍的否定标记。

他们可能会在说话人着手管理语境的方式中提供约束和可供性功能,即重新调整故事情节、各自的定位和符号资本。讨论的主题是当地发展,以及地方社区、政府和其他组织在促进当地发展一事中的参与。因此,当地发展是由语言构成的移位语场。然而,由于本次会议也是当地发展进程的一部分,而且发言者都是这一领域的重要参与者,因此出现了一种情况,即直接语场和移位语场重合。这意味着辅助性语言和构成性语言相互作用,以复杂的方式构建、制定和重新调整各群体参与当地发展的历史(故事情节)和该语场内的地位关系。我们先看看语篇中的几个情态示例后再进一步讨论这个问题。

在第 6 行,尼古拉斯说:

40. That's … that should be tied in to ownership of other resources like water …

在这里,我们使用"should"来表示尼古拉斯认为的必要性。因此,它是义务的一个例子,是道义情态的一种类型。与"must"或"could"相比,"should"在这里表示中值,不过尼古拉斯倒可以在同样语境中分别使用高值或低值的词。然而,我要说的是,虽然**中值义务**(*median obligation*)表明了情态系统中的系统性对比,但它并没有表达出"should"在此处的完整概念,此词于该处似乎也包含"恰当"之意。这向我们展示了情态动词在语言系统中的相互关系以及它们在语言使用中的具体用途之间的区别。有时,像"合适"这样的进一步解释,有助于以一种高/中/低区分所不能的方式捕捉到语言的用法。我们会在可能性情态中再次看到这一点。然而,在概括划分整个篇章中使用的情态类型及它们对整个话语的影响——而非特定的局部意义——时,高、中、低这三个术语让我们可以将情态用语集中起来进行概括比较。

情态的下一个用法为我们的讨论提供了另一个角度,以及另一组用于区分说话人所掌握的情态的特征。记得我在之前说过,情态是一个语义领域,可以通过语法的不同部分来实现。如第 10、11 行所示,戈登说:

41. The target(h)as communication we've got in … which I think comes into the

first thing, that's called mechanisms …

戈登的"I think"在这里是用作了**模棱语**（*hedge*），淡化了他话语的绝对性，将其构建为可能真实，而不是像"I know"那样会将其构建成绝对真实。因此，虽然"I think"在语法上显然是及物性的一个例子，但它在这里的功能却是在情态的语义域内表达中值可能性，并被归类为**伪情态**（*pseudomodal*）。然而，"I think"等伪情态的使用与情态助词本身在意义上有显著区别。如果戈登说"it could come into the first things, called mechanisms"，这将是一种主观主张，一种他个人观点的表达（见下文），但主张的主观性质将是**隐含的**（*implicit*）（也就是说，没有明确说明）；通过使用"I think"，他用"I"来**明确**（*explicit*）其主张的主观性质。正如上面所说，我们在这里看到了形式上的语法差异是如何由于动机驱使而产生重要的语义差异的。这就在等式中引入了一个新的变量，因此我们现在有二十四种情态（加油！）：三种值×四种类型×两种**裹覆程度**（*investment*）①（此处"裹覆程度"一词为作者自创的术语，用以刻画情态是明示的还是暗示的——译者注）。

请注意，几行之后，尼古拉斯用了与戈登的相同的语言：

42. I think it's a whole restoration process.

这很有趣，因为事实上尼古拉斯与戈登所说的意见相左，但他对情态协调地使用有助于保持人际关系的相对平稳——尽管明确使用"I"可能会增加一点个人色彩。在这些例子中，我们可以看到说话人如何像玩猫捉老鼠的游戏一般，相互提供事件的替代性构建方式，同时出于对彼此身份的尊重而淡化自己的建议。这里涉及很多相互定位。

尼古拉斯在第 32、33 行的话语中也提供了情态形式有趣互动的示例。我对这个例子进行了一点规范化，以便在不改变情态意义的情况下使读者更容易

---

① 这是笔者自创的术语。韩礼德和马蒂森将此作为一个特征或取向。

理解下面的要点:

43. I think one of the things we have to do, actually, is we have to be adventurous, you know ...

在这里,尼古拉斯对"have to"的使用表明了高值义务,但在这个意义上,它与 MUST 形成了对比,因为它少了尼古拉斯陈述自己主观观点的想法,更多的是他将这种必要性陈述为客观事实的想法。考虑下面差异最小的一对话语,并说说哪一句更有可能是由同学而不是老师说出:

44. You must hand your work in by the 15th.
45. You have to hand your homework in by the 15th.

例 44 如果是由某位同学说出,会具有很强的标记性。正如我们在上面简要讨论的那样,情态助词在直接语境中实现言语行为,因此例 44 是对义务的规定,而相比之下,例 45 只是引述一些未命名的其他人强加的义务。为进一步探讨这一点,让我们看一看这两种形式与过去相关的用法:

46. You must have passed your driving test to apply for this job.
47. He had to leave his job immediately ...

在第一种情况下,虽然通过驾驶考试是过去的事了,但这项义务是在声明本身中所规定的。MUST 没有过去式,与之相对,在例 47 中,我们看到 HAS TO 可以用于过去来表示以前的必要性。因此,虽然 HAVE TO 涉及义务的语义领域,但它不是真正的情态用语,通常被称为**半情态用语**(*semi-modal*)。这也反映在这样一个事实上——它不是小句的限定成分(除了在越来越少的英语方言中,但是这是出于不同的语言原因),如例 48 所示:

48. Do we have to go to the shops?

有趣的是,NEED 有完全情态和半情态两种形式:

49. Need I say more?
50. Do you need to do that?

也许这使它成为四分之三情态词？MUST 和 HAVE TO 的区别在于一个是**主观取向**（*subjective orientation*），一个是**客观取向**（*objective orientation*）。然而，这两种情况又颇为相似，因为没有明确说明义务的来源。我们已经看到了"I think"与 MUST 不同，那是一个显式主观情态的例子，以下是一个显式客观情态的示例：

51. It was necessary for us to leave the following day.

在这种情况下，情态的客观性质用"it"清楚地表示出来，这与第一人称"I"或"we"在显式主观形式中的使用形成对比。这就让情态类型总数达到了四十八种之多：三种值×四种类型×两种裹覆程度×两种取向。我很高兴地告诉你，这就是所有的种类了。通常，在比较语篇时，我们所感兴趣的只是其中的几个参数的对比。除了伪情态形式的显式主观取向，我们还可以明确表达说话人以外的其他人的观点：

52. John thinks it's a good idea.

这是**归因**（*attribution*）的 一个例子。在这种情况下，说话人将命题归因于第三方，并表达了不同程度的确定性。因此，归因与情态密切相关：

53. John's adamant that it's a good idea.
54. John suggests it might be a good idea.

有关归因涉及的许多变量的更全面讨论，请参见 Bednarek（2006）。就本书的目的而言，我们将只考虑命题或提议是否被归因，以及归因于特定类型的人将如何影响说话人自身的定位。

注意，对于隐式主观情态的疑问形式，其中涉及的是受话人的主观性，而不是说话人的：

55. Must we go?

在例 55 中，说话人问的是受话人强加的义务。

在语篇 4.3 中,有另一个(与概率有关的)显式主观情态的例子,戈登说:

56. I'm not sure if this doesn't (xxxx) my interpretation.

在这里,我们将"not sure"标记为低概率,因为否定本身就逆转了"sure"的高情态。

语篇中还有一个隐式客观评价中值通常性的例子:

57. Sometimes they're just not terribly interested in listening.

这里的"sometimes"被称为**情态附加语**(*modal adjunct*)。这些词的行为很像副词或副词短语,但与它们有着重要的区别。首先,与真正的副词短语如"during meetings"不同,"sometimes"不能用来回答"他们什么时候对听不感兴趣?",除非话语中包含至少一定程度讽刺性的文字游戏。其次,真正的副词或副词短语有时不能出现在主语和限定成分之间,而情态附加语可以。当限定成分被强调时尤其如此:

58. He sometimes does eat like a bit of a pig, I agree.
59. He at every meal does eat like a bit of a pig.

当你在分析中对类似副词的单词或短语的功能有疑问时,这是一个很好的测试,它再次显示了语义和语法之间的重要联系。在这种情况下,"sometimes"可以介于主语和限定成分之间,因此位于语气成分中,因为它带有人际意义,而不是经验意义。回到语篇 4.3,还有一两个情态的例子:

60. ... how your views can be reflected both with the government, with UNDP, with Iwokrama, with everybody.

在这里,戈登使用"can"来考虑当地社区的观点被其他群体反映的可能性。在其他情况下,CAN 的核心含义是能力,比如在"I can swim"中,它具有边界情态含义,因为能力是一种可能性,但它不能像情态通常那样反映说话人的评价。当我们讨论**评价**(*appraisal*)时,我们将再次探讨 CAN 的核心含义。

CAN 偶尔被用来表示中值通常性,如"linguistics can be fascinating"。过去时态可以用来表示较低的可能性,正如尼古拉斯所说:

61. Maybe you couldn't finance that, you know?

例 61 这个句子的这种形式有点不寻常,尼古拉斯似乎认为这个命题的概率很低(因为它是否定的)。或者可以说,这是在能力意义上 CAN 的示例(COULD 是 CAN 的假设形式,是英语中唯一一个特殊假设形式)。我们并非总能做出明确的判断,因为正如上文 SHOULD 一词所示,一种情态常常与另一种情态融合在一起——高明的说话人偶尔会有意无意地对这种情态很好地加以使用。

COULD 的肯定极性表示概率较低,如:

62. It could rain tonight.

类似的含义也可构建为:

63. It might rain tonight.

这两个情态动词都表示概率较低,但在某种情况下,有微妙的区别,如以下例子所示:

64. It could rain tonight, but it won't.
65. ?? It might rain tonight, but it won't.

例 64 是讲得通的,因为这里的"could"表示假设的可能性,所以说话人是在说可以设想一下下雨的可能性,但在说话人看来不会。而例 65 非常奇怪,因为"might"是一个主观评估,其概率大约为百分之五十,所以在它后面跟着概率为零的一个主观评估,这就产生了矛盾!当考虑说话人的陈述对语篇的影响时,将它们都归类为中值情态就够了,但当我们仔细观察语篇的短小节段时,就需要进行更微妙的区分。

表 4.2 列出了我们一直在探讨的不同情态类型。有关更全面的讨论,请参

见 Halliday and Matthiessen 2004:613-625。请注意,并不是所有的单元格都有内容,而且有些示例比其他示例听起来更自然。你可能还注意到通常有三种以上的值,例如"She's desperate/determined/keen/willing to do it"。

表 4.2　情态概述

		Explicit subjective	Implicit subjective	Implicit objective	Explicit objetive
Deontic:obligation	High	I order you to leavel; I insist you leave.	You must leave.	You have to leave; you're required to leave.	It's essential you leave.
	Median	I suggest you leave; I want you to leave.	You should leave.	You're supposed to leave.	It's advisable you leave.
	Low	I don't mind if you leave.	You can leave now.	You're allowed to leave.	It's okay for you to leave.
Deontic:willingness	High			Mick's desperate to do it.	I's our determination that they will not defeat us.
	Median		Mick'll do it.	Mick's keen to do it.	It's our wish that they win.
	Low			Mick doesn't mind doing it.	It's okay with Mick to do it.
Epistemic:probability	High	I know he'll be home by now.	He must be home by now.	He's definitely home by now.	It's certain he'll be home by now.
	Median	I think he'll be home by now.	He'll be home by now.	He's probably home by now.	It's probable he'll be home by now.
	Low	I guess he could be home by now.	He might be home by now.	He's possibly home by now.	It's possible he'll be home by now.
Epistemic:usuality	High	I expect it to rain in July.	On sunny days my folks will just sit ouside and snooze.	It always rains in July.	It's inevitable that it rains in July.

续表

	Explicit subjective	Implicit subjective	Implicit objective	Explicit objetive
Median		It can rain in	It usually rains in July.	It's normal for July.
Low			It sometimes rains in July.	It's rare for it to rain in July.

除了情态,语篇 4.3 还包含**言据性**(*evidentiality*)这个相关资源的示例,其中戈登说:

66. Which doesn't appear to be the case.

戈登是在现有证据的基础上做出陈述的。言据性与情态的相似之处在于它与说话人对命题真实性的评估有关。然而,情态与确定性水平等有关,但言据性指的是支持命题的证据的性质。这可能是非常模糊的,比如在例 66 中,戈登暗示他的说法是基于现有证据,但没有非常明确地说明具体是哪种类型的证据。动词 SEEM 也用于表示非特定证据:

67. She seems very nice.

然而,我们可以更具体地说明我们是如何发现证据的,如例 68 中的证据所示:

68. She sounded like she was very upset.

在例 66 中,戈登的主张具有隐含主观性。把它和下面的例子进行对比:

69. I can see that this isn't the case. (显式主观言据性)
70. Apparently this isn't the case. (隐式客观言据性)
71. It appears that this isn't the case. (显式客观言据性)

还有另一种形式可用于将对证据的感知归因于一些未命名的其他人:

72. He was seen to place the Buddha on the mantelpiece.
　　及

73. He was heard to have called her a liar.

请注意,例 72 和例 73 中的心理过程的主动形式不接小品词"to",但是其被动形式要接。这暗示着这些被动形式是特殊的言据性结构(Fawcett 2007:935-938)。

74. ∗ We saw him to place the Buddha on the mantelpiece.
75. ∗ He was seen place the Buddha on the mantelpiece.

这再一次说明了语法的重构是如何产生不同的意义的。

最后,可以援引某个特定的感知到证据的人。例 76 是这种归因言据性的一个例子,类似的例子是新闻报道和法庭案件的主要内容:

76. His neighbour heard him fire three shots.

在这里,真实性的责任被转移到了第三方身上。与归因的其他用法一样,通常要援引一个可靠的来源,用于支持说话人的命题,例如:

77. Three police officers witnessed the defendant speeding.

语篇 4.3 中有一个归因言据性的例子,尼古拉斯在第 33、34 行中说:

78. The government na see it as being complementary.

然而,在这里,尼古拉斯的归因言据性似乎是为了降低政府的可信度,而不是为给予这一命题以权威性。

应该指出的是,语篇中很少使用情态、归因或言据性,从分析者的角度来看,这比较遗憾。然而,说话人还可以使用其他资源来评估个人行为、人和事(而不是表达命题或提议的整个小句的真值),而且这些资源使用更为普遍。我们将在下面讨论评价(appraisal)时再对此详加探究。

如前所述,语旨(tenor)指的是语境中的人际方面:语篇中所呈现的个人定位以及他们之间的关系。请注意,由于语旨是语境而不是环境的一个方面,[①]它不涉及说话人之间可能存在的任何其他关系——尽管说话人对这些社会关系的理解将影响所构建的可能语旨,了解这些特征将有助于分析人员将语篇作为话语进行详细地解读,尤其是当话语中的预期关系和实际构建的语旨之间存在紧张关系时。

间接言语行为可以用来缓解可能伤害对方面子的言语行为的力度(Brown and Levinson 1987)或者他们可以被那些意识到他们的定位将使他们的提议很可能被接受并付诸实施的说话人使用。这意味着不拘礼节且平等的语旨不一定意味着话语中的权力平衡。同样,虽然我们可以在说话人的话语中区分主观和客观情态,但即使使用客观情态,我们也必须问说话人将义务陈述为不言而喻的事实意味着什么,是什么样的社会定位赋予了他们这样做的权利,或者他们在这样做的过程中占据了什么样的定位。

练习 4.2

(1)从话语的整体语旨、人际感觉的角度对语篇 4.3 进行讨论,找出语气、情态和言语角色以及你认为相关的任何其他特征。

(2)根据你对说话人的了解,你认为这篇作为话语的语篇中正发生着什么?

4.4　评价

正如我们到目前为止所讨论的,情态、归因和言据性与评估整个小句的真实性有关。然而,这些资源的侧重点可能仅限于参与者或过程,如:

---

① 　然而,许多系统功能语言学文献在这一点上都不甚确然。

79. a visibly inferior team
80. the probable cause of the accident
81. the alleged culprit
82. a man described as inspirational by his students

与其他形式的评估一样，这些评估可以归因于某个特定的人，如例 82 所示，或者（由于各种话语原因）不透露来源，如例 79—例 81 所示。

这些评估在小句层面上都有对应的评估（言据性例 79，情态例 80，归因例 81 和例 82）。理解这些意义是如何在语篇中重复、强化和分布的是**评价**（*appraisal*）的重点，这是一个最初由彼得·怀特和吉姆·马丁提出的（例如，Martin and White 2005）文本分析框架。它是现今系统功能语言学理论中，尤其是**语类理论**（*genre theory*）研究中非常重要的方法。这里我们只讨论一些最基本的区别，但强烈建议你对评价这一主题进行更广泛的阅读，以补充本书中概述的分析方法。

虽然评价通常是整个框架的名称，但评价实际上只是该理论涵盖的评估性语言的一个类别，其他类别包括**介入**（*engagement*）和**分级**（*graduation*）。介入包括前文介绍过的归因。在本节中，我们将重点介绍评价的类别及其项下的三个子类别——**情感**（*affect*）、**判定**（*judgement*）和**鉴别**（*appreciation*）。

情感与情绪反应有关，与小句层面的**情感过程**（*emotive process*）有关；判定涉及对行为的评估，与小句层面的情态有关；鉴别关注各种现象在美学、连贯性、价值或有效性方面的价值（Martin and White 2005:57）:

83. Sometimes they're just not terribly interested in listening.（情感）
84. They don't really want to listen.
85. They have an advantage right away there（xx）find that … they actually killing … government is（xx）not knowing（they）erm killing culture.（判定）
86. the government is behaving in ways that it <u>shouldn't</u>
87. When we develop plans that erm … the government na see it as being, you know, complementary … complementary with the present development strategies

of the government …　（鉴别）

88. the strategies don't <u>look</u> good to the government/the government doesn't think these strategies will be <u>effective</u>

　　上述每个范畴都可以在一个更细微的层次上划分。在这本书中，我们对情感将再增加一个细分层次，对判定和鉴别增加两个细分层次，因为我发现这些区分大有裨益且最具实践性（见图 4.1）。

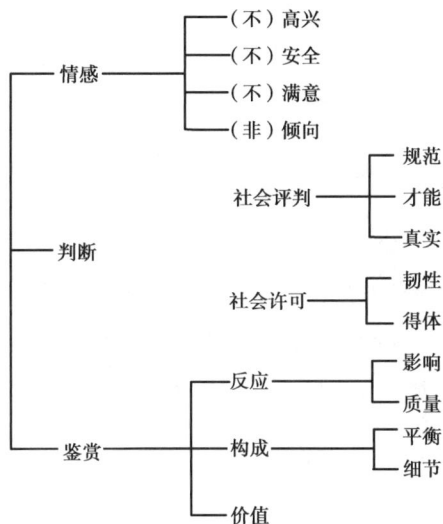

```
情感 ─┬─ （不）高兴
      ├─ （不）安全
      ├─ （不）满意
      └─ （非）倾向

判断 ─┬─ 社会评判 ─┬─ 规范
      │            ├─ 才能
      │            └─ 真实
      └─ 社会许可 ─┬─ 韧性
                   └─ 得体

鉴赏 ─┬─ 反应 ─┬─ 影响
      │        └─ 质量
      ├─ 构成 ─┬─ 平衡
      │        └─ 细节
      └─ 价值
```

图 4.1　评价类别

　　情感和判定项下的标签是不言而喻的，但鉴别项下的标签则需要作一些说明。**反应**（*reaction*）指的是某人或某事引起情感反应的性质，要么是因为它以某种方式"抓住（grab）"你（Martin and White 2005：57），要么是因为它无法抓住你（+/-影响），要么是因为你喜欢或不喜欢它（+/-质量）。这与情感形成了对比，情感指的是人类感知者感受到的情感，而不是现象的性质。因此，"interesting"或"delightful"分别是（+鉴别：反应：影响）和（+鉴别：反应：质量），而"interested"或"delighted"分别是（+情感：满足）和（+情感：愉悦）。**构成**（*composition*）由不言而喻的范畴"**平衡**（*balance*）"（事物的整体性如何）和"**复杂性**（*complexity*）"组成。**评估**（*valuation*）是一个涵盖更广、更为主观的范畴，指的是我们经过思考后,所持关于某样东西的某些方面是否有价值的意见。正如马丁和怀特所言(Martin and White 2005:57):"在这些变量中,评估对语场尤其敏感,因为事物的价值在很大程度上取决于我们的制度焦点。"

每个类别都可以取正或取负,笔者在分析中对极性做了标记,如:

89. a weak government（-判定:社会尊重:能力）
90. an honest man（+判定:社会许可:诚实）
91. dangerous times（-情感:安全性）

与情态一样,评价也可以通过使用附加语来表达:

92. Thankfully, no one was hurt.（+情感:愉悦）
93. Disgracefully, he voted against the proposal.（-判定:社会许可:得体性）

这样的附加语表达了说话人对整个命题的评价,被称为**评论附加语**（*comment adjunct*）。"Hopefully"这个词经常被用作一个评论附加语,这让不太懂语法的学究们很恼火。他们指摘这样的句子:

94. Hopefully Man City will lose tonight.

理由是曼城不太可能"以充满希望的方式"输掉比赛。然而,他们并没有按照同样的逻辑挑剔这句话,

95. Admittedly, Man Utd have as good as won the title.

毕竟曼联不太可能以"in admitted fashion"赢得比赛! 另一个反对这些迂腐之人的理由是评论附加语在小句中的定位十分灵活:

96. Man City will hopefully lose tonight.
97. Man City hopefully will lose tonight.

这种灵活性对方式副词来说是不可能的,这清楚地表明了该词的功能。有关评论附加语及其子分类的更完整的讨论,请参见 Halliday and Matthiessen 2004:608-612。

与情态一样,评价有时可以用"it's 小句"来表达,使其听起来更客观,或者预设有共同的协意,如例 98(有关这方面的更多信息,请参阅第 5 章):

98. It's great news that you can come.

练习 4.3

请再次阅读以下语篇——托尼·布莱尔在 2005 年 7 月 7 日伦敦爆炸案后的讲话,并回答以下问题。

语篇 4.4

1　I am just going to make a short statement to you on the terrible events that have happened in London earlier today,

2　and I hope

3　you understand

4　that at the present time we are still trying to establish exactly what has happened,

5　and there is a limit to what information I can give you,

6　and I will simply try and tell you the information as best I can at the moment.

7　It is reasonably clear that there have been a series of terrorist attacks in London.

8　There are obviously casualties, both people that have died and people seriously injured,

9　and our thoughts and prayers of course are with the victims and their families.

10　It is my intention to leave the G8 within the next couple of hours and go down to London and get a report, face-to-face, with the police, and the emergency services and the Ministers that have been dealing with this, and then to return later this evening.

11　It is the will of all the leaders at the G8 however that the meeting should continue in my absence, that we should continue to discuss the issues that we were going to discuss, and reach the conclusions which we were going to reach.

12　Each of the countries round that table have some experience of the effects of terrorism

13 and all the leaders> < share our complete resolution to defeat this terrorism.

14 >as they will indicate a little bit later<

15 It is particularly barbaric that this has happened on a day when people are meeting to try to help the problems of poverty in Africa, and the long term problems of climate change and the environment.

16 Just as it is reasonably clear that this is a terrorist attack, or a series of terrorist attacks,

17 it is also reasonably clear that it is designed and aimed to coincide with the opening of the G8.

18 There will be time to talk later about this.

19 It is important however that those engaged in terrorism realise

20 that our determination to defend our values and our way of life is greater than their determination to cause death and destruction to innocent people in a desire to impose extremism on the world.

21 Whatever they do,

22 it is our determination that they will never succeed in destroying what we hold dear in this country and in other civilised nations throughout the world.

问题

(1)根据我们讨论过的不同子类别,对情态和评价的例子进行识别并标注。答案见附录。

(2)讨论隐式/客观和主观/客观情态的使用——鉴于爆炸发生时的社会环境和托尼·布莱尔所面对的各种受众,你认为这对布莱尔的定位有什么影响(你可能想与布什的"Bring Them On"演讲进行比较,见第 183、184 页)。

回到语篇 4.3,在为评价做标记时,我们还要做一个更为重要的区分。请考虑以下尼古拉斯的话:

99. Because what we find there's disadvantage when we've been government, erm, driven programmes, they've been … financially supported properly … and our erm programmes are not, traditional ways are not supported so.

你认为尼古拉斯在这里使用的"traditional"这个词是评价性的吗? 为什么? 词典会在"traditional"的定义中包含这样的评价吗? 我个人的观点是,尼古拉斯打算用这个词来进行正面评价,其中"真实"和"虚假"是正负两极的有用术语。然而,这种积极的评价只有在语境中使用这个词时才会被**唤起**(*evoked*),而不是**载明**(*inscribed*)为词典意义的核心部分。这样,我们就有了四十八个不同的评价标签:十二个评价类型的子类别×两个极性×载明/唤起。然而,唤起范畴是一个模糊的领域,分析者必须小心地解释唤起的评估可以合理地假设达到什么效果,而不是依赖于他们自己的直觉。奥哈洛兰和科芬的两篇优秀文章(O'Halloran and Coffin 2004;Coffin and O'Halloran 2006)对相关风险作了充分说明。在其中一篇文章(Coffin and O'Halloran 2006)中,他们对费尔克劳夫(Fairclough)的一项分析提出异议,因为费氏在分析中称动词"flock"带有负面含义。科芬和奥哈洛兰使用语料库证据证明,"flock"在大多数情况下不带有负面含义,因此在没有进一步证据的情况下,不能不假思索地认为该词将唤起负面评价。同时,他们从一个完全不同的角度证明"东欧人"一词虽然表面上是中性的,但是会给《太阳报》的读者带来负面联想,因为在采自该报的语料库中,"东欧人"几乎总是与极端负面的词搭配。但这又让我们想到了另一点:如果一个词,比如"flock",出现在一个与东欧人相关的子语料库中,在这个子语料库中,东欧人受到了压倒性的负面评价,或者出现在一个负面评价**饱和**(*saturated*)的语篇(Martin and White 2005:19)中,那么我们可以假设"flock"本身会在该语篇中带有负面评价。因此,作为唤起评价的子类别,我们就有了基于语料库、基于子语料库和基于语篇的唤起。饱和是**语义韵律**(*semantic prosody*)的一个极端情况。有些作者使用韵律一词来指单个单词的唤起性负载,[1]但是对于韩礼德和其他人来说,它更多指的是整个语篇或一段语篇的评价性感觉:

　　意义的人际成分是说话人对言语情境的持续不断的干预。这是他(原

---

① 如约翰·辛克莱和比尔·卢的论述中。

文如此)对交流的看法,他分配和扮演的言语角色。人际意义不能轻易地表达为离散成分的构型……语义系统这一部分的意义潜势的本质是,大多数选项都与整个意义行为相关联……这种人际意义……作为一个连续的色彩主题贯穿在整个小句中……其效果是累积的……我们称这种类型的体现是"韵律的",因为意义像韵律一样分布在连续的话语中。

(Halliday 1979:66-67)

这意味着,在一篇包含许多潜在的唤起性评价实例的语篇中,此类意义的饱和使得负面解读彼此强化。

练习4.4

看下面关于查韦斯的维基百科条目的语篇,然后回答下面的问题。

语篇4.5

1　Chavs have been noted to often don designer sportswear.

2　Brands such as Adidas, Burberry, Puma, Umbro, Ecko, Carbrini and Kappa are very popular,

3　with many chavs often wearing a full tracksuit or tracksuit bottoms, with a hoodie or polyester jacket, baseball cap and oversized trainers.

4　Clothing attire is usually navy, white, black, red or grey for the chav male,

5　and pink and white are very common with the "chavette", particularly jogging bottoms, velour tracksuits or shell suits.

6　Stereotypical attire might be accompanied by some form of bling, such as oversized gold hoop earrings and necklaces, bracelets and rings, and an abundance of tattoos.

7　Several stereotypical traits are associated with chavs;

8　smoking, drinking and taking drugs in gangs on street corners and outside shops, petty thievery and violence, vandalism and graffiti, an exaggerated "tough" gangster-like voice and lingo and foul, aggressive language (with common expressions such as "Am I bovvered" or "Warru on about"), council house/flat accommodation, unemployment and state benefits scrounging

9　(and despite this still appearing to have money for show),

10　teenage girls being sexually promiscuous and smoking whilst pregnant,

11　driving a highly modified and chromed up Vauxhall Nova (in particular), Vauxhall Cavalier, Ford Sierra, Ford Escort or Austin Metro,

12　usually souped up with alloys, stickers, oversized spoiler, side panels, exhaust pipe and engine

13　painted white or in some flamboyant colour,

14　enhanced speakers blasting hip-hop, R&B, garage, drum and bass or rave/jungle music

15　and chewing whilst being spoken to.

16　Stereotypical chavs tend to sport skinheads, or very short hair with short back and sides and fringe, usually gelled down.

17　In northern British cities such as Manchester, it is fashionable for some chavs to sport longer hair and sides in the Mod fashion.

18　Chavettes' stereotypically wear their hair tightly scraped back into a ponytail or bun,

19　known as the "Council house face lift"

20　Burberry is a clothing company

21　whose products became associated with the "chav" stereotype.

22　Burberry's appeal to "chav" fashion sense is a sociological example of prole drift, where an up-market product begins to be consumed *en masse* by a lower socio-economic group.

23　Burberry has argued that the brand's popular association with "chav" fashion sense is linked to counterfeit versions of the clothing.

24　"They're yesterday's news", stated Stacey Cartwright, the CEO of Burberry.

25　"It was mostly counterfeit, and Britain accounts for less than 10% of our sales anyway."

26　The company has taken a number of steps to distance itself from the stereotype

27　It ceased production of its own branded baseball cap in 2004

28　and has scaled back the use of its trademarked checkered/tartan design to such an extent

29　that it now only appears on the inner linings and other very low-key positions of their clothing

30 It has also taken legal action against high-profile infringements of the brand.

31 The large supermarket chain Asda has attempted to trademark the word "chav" for a new line of confectionery

32 A spokeswoman said: "With slogans from characters in shows such as *Little Britain* and *The Catherine Tate Show* providing us with more and more contemporary slang,

33 our Whatever sweets—now nicknamed chav hearts—have become very popular with kids and grown-ups alike

34 We thought we needed to give them some respect and have decided to trademark our sweets

35 A BBC TV documentary suggested that "chav" culture is an evolution of previous working-class youth subcultures associated with particular commercial clothing styles, such as mods, skinheads and casuals.

36 The widespread use of the "chav" stereotype

37 has come in for some criticism

38 Some argue that it amounts to simple snobbery and elitism

39 Critics of the term have argued that its users are "neo-snobs",

40 and that its increasing popularity raises questions about how British society deals with social mobility and class

41 In a February 2005 article in *The Times*, Julie Burchill argued that use of the word is a form of "social racism", and that such "sneering" reveals more about the shortcomings of the "chav-haters" than those of their supposed victims

42 The writer John Harris argued along similar lines in a 2007 article in the *Guardian*

43 The Welsh rap group, Goldie Lookin Chain, have been described as both embodying

44 and satirising the "chav" aesthetic

45 though the group themselves deny any such agenda,

46 simply making a mockery of the subject

47 In the BBC TV series *Doctor Who*, Episode *New Earth*, 15 April 2006, the character Lady Cassandra is transplanted into Rose Tyler's body (Billie Piper)

48 When Cassandra sees herself in a mirror,

49 she exclaims "Oh my God ... I'm a chav!"

50 Characters described as "chavs" have occurred in a number of British televi-

sion programmes.

51　The character, clothing, attitude and musical interests of Lauren Cooper and her friends in the BBC comedy series *The Catherine Tate Show* have been associated with the chav stereotype.

52　The comedy series *Little Britain* features a character with some similarities, Vicky Pollard.

问题

(1) Indicate as many examples of inscribed Appraisal in the text as you can and assign each to the appropriate subcategory.

(2) Indicate as many examples of evoked Appraisal in the text and assign each to the appropriate subcategory.

(3) Check some of these words in a corpus and see if they generally carry negative, positive or neutral evaluations.

(4) Discuss the text in terms of saturation and text-based evocation.

(5) Read Wikipedia's policy on neutrality, below, and discuss how linguistic resources such as modality and attribution are used in an attempt to make the entry comply with this policy. How successful do you think this strategy is?

　　Editing from a **neutral point of view** (**NPOV**) means representing fairly, proportionately, and as far as possible without bias, all significant views that have been published by reliable sources. All Wikipedia articles and other encyclopedic content must be written from a neutral point of view. NPOV is a fundamental principle of Wikipedia and of other Wikimedia projects. This policy is nonnegotiable and all editors and articles must follow it.

　　"Neutral point of view" is one of Wikipedia's three core content policies. The other two are "Verifiability" and "No original research". These three core policies jointly determine the type and quality of material that is acceptable in Wikipedia articles. Because these policies work in harmony, they should not be interpreted in isolation from one another, and editors should try to familiarize themselves with all three. The principles upon which this policy is based cannot be superseded by other policies or guidelines, or by editors' consensus.

(6) Consider the repeated use of the words "stereotypical" and "stereotypically" in

terms of both modality and evaluation and discuss their usage here.

(7) Look at the current entry for Chavs to see what changes have been made to make it comply better with NPOV.

Bartlett 2012b 一书就维基百科上存在的唤起性及载明性评价问题作了更加全面的讨论，Jones 2012 对反查维斯主义作了深入的讨论，两书可资参考。

本文向我们展示了看似中性的词汇如何在特定语篇中传递评价性的含义。当词汇可以在整个语言系统中转换类别时，类似的过程会在更广泛、更显著的范围内发生。先思考一下"左撇子"一词。这个词可以被认为是－社会尊严：规范，因为主体人群中的大多数人都是右撇子。然后，请思考一下不同语言中的左右两个单词，并考虑这些单词或相关单词的弦外之音和它们所属的评价类别：

右：dexter（拉丁语）、droite（法语）、derecho（西班牙语）、rechts（德语）

左：sinister（拉丁语）、gauche（法语）

你从中了解到了历史上人们对通常性的态度是什么了吗？（请与将"You don't do that"作为禁令的情况加以比较。）另外，在苏格兰盖尔语的一些方言中，左手被称为"错手"，这十分有趣。

近年来，评价分析被广泛使用。例如，对闲聊中表达的观点的分析被用来建议客户和服务提供商如何在促进商业交易的过程中让他们的评价立场保持一致（参见第 2 章）。更典型的例子是比较同一国家或不同国家的政党、宗教团体或报纸之间的评价依据。例如，一个令人感兴趣的研究问题是，不同政党之间或是政治传统大体相似的世俗国家之间，对事物运行的状况（鉴别）和从道德角度对事物加以评判（判定）所赋予二者的相对权重。从一个更复杂的角度来看，评估分析可以显示语篇中从一个类别到另一个类别的转换是如何自然进行的，还可以探讨评价领域的这种混乱与语篇产生的环境有何相关性。

练习 4.5

作为本章对人际意义和语旨的讨论的总结,我们将详细探讨马丁·路德·金 1963 年的《我有一个梦想》。请阅读该演讲以及当时的美国民权运动的相关资料。然后阅读语篇并回答以下问题。

语篇 4.6

1　I am happy to join with you today in what will go down in history as the greatest demonstration for freedom in the history of our nation.

2　Five score years ago, a great American, > < signed the Emancipation Proclamation.

3　>in whose symbolic shadow we stand today, <

4　This momentous decree came as a great beacon light of hope to millions of Negro slaves who had been seared in the flames of withering injustice.

5　But one hundred years later, the Negro still is not free.

6　One hundred years later, the life of the Negro is still sadly crippled by the manacles of segregation and the chains of discrimination.

7　One hundred years later, the Negro lives on a lonely island of poverty in the midst of a vast ocean of material prosperity.

8　One hundred years later, the Negro is still languishing in the corners of American society

9　and finds himself an exile in his own land.

10　So we have come here today to dramatize a shameful condition.

11　In a sense we have come to our nation's capital to cash a check.

12　When the architects of our republic wrote the magnificent words of the Constitution and the Declaration of Independence,

13　they were signing a promissory note to which every American was to fall heir.

14　This note was a promise that all men, yes, black men as well as white men, would be guaranteed the unalienable rights of life, liberty, and the pursuit of happiness.

15　It is obvious today that America has defaulted on this promissory note

16　insofar as her citizens of color are concerned.

17　Instead of honoring this sacred obligation, America has given the Negro people a bad check, a check which has come back marked "insufficient funds."

18　But we refuse to believe

19　that the bank of justice is bankrupt.

20　We refuse to believe

21　that there are insufficient funds in the great vaults of opportunity of this nation.

22　So we have come to cash this check-a check that will give us upon demand the riches of freedom and the security of justice.

23　We have also come to this hallowed spot to remind America of the fierce urgency of now.

24　This is no time to engage in the luxury of cooling off or to take the tranquilizing drug of gradualism.

25　Now is the time to make real the promises of democracy.

26　Now is the time to rise from the dark and desolate valley of segregation to the sunlit path of racial justice.

27　Now is the time to lift our nation from the quick sands of racial injustice to the solid rock of brotherhood.

28　Now is the time to make justice a reality for all of God's children.

29　It would be fatal for the nation to overlook the urgency of the moment.

30　This sweltering summer of the Negro's legitimate discontent will not pass

31　until there is an invigorating autumn of freedom and equality.

32　Nineteen sixty-three is not an end, but a beginning.

33　Those who hope that the Negro needed to blow off steam and will now be content will have a rude awakening

34　if the nation returns to business as usual.

35　There will be neither rest nor tranquility in America

36　until the Negro is granted his citizenship rights.

37　The whirlwinds of revolt will continue to shake the foundations of our nation

38　until the bright day of justice emerges.

39　But there is something that I must say to my people who stand on the warm threshold which leads into the palace of justice.

40　In the process of gaining our rightful place we must not be guilty of wrongful deeds.

41　Let us not seek to satisfy our thirst for freedom by drinking from the cup of bitterness and hatred.

42　We must forever conduct our struggle on the high plane of dignity and discipline.

43　We must not allow our creative protest to degenerate into physical violence.

44　Again and again we must rise to the majestic heights of meeting physical force with soul force.

45　The marvelous new militancy which has engulfed the Negro community must not lead us to a distrust of all white people,

46　for many of our white brothers, >< have come to realize

47　>as evidenced by their presence here today,<

48　that their destiny is tied up with our destiny.

49　They have come to realize

50　that their freedom is inextricably bound to our freedom.

51　We cannot walk alone.

52　As we walk,

53　we must make the pledge

54　that we shall always march ahead.

55　We cannot turn back.

56　There are those who are asking the devotees of civil rights,

57　"When will you be satisfied?"

58　We can never be satisfied

59　as long as the Negro is the victim of the unspeakable horrors of police brutality.

60　We can never be satisfied,

61　as long as our bodies, heavy with the fatigue of travel, cannot gain lodging in the motels of the highways and the hotels of the cities.

62　We cannot be satisfied

63　as long as the Negro's basic mobility is from a smaller ghetto to a larger one.

64　We can never be satisfied

65　as long as our children are stripped of their selfhood

66　and robbed of their dignity by signs stating "For Whites Only".

67　We cannot be satisfied

68　as long as a Negro in Mississippi cannot vote

69　and a Negro in New York believes

70　he has nothing for which to vote.

71　No, no, we are not satisfied,

72　and we will not be satisfied

73　until justice rolls down like waters

74　and righteousness like a mighty stream.

75　I am not unmindful

76　that some of you have come here out of great trials and tribulations.

77　Some of you have come fresh from narrow jail cells.

78　Some of you have come from areas where your quest for freedom left you battered by the storms of persecution and staggered by the winds of police brutality.

79　You have been the veterans of creative suffering.

80　Continue to work with the faith that unearned suffering is redemptive.

81　Go back to Mississippi,

82　go back to Alabama,

83　go back to South Carolina,

84　go back to Georgia,

85　go back to Louisiana,

86　go back to the slums and ghettos of our northern cities, knowing that some-how this situation can and will be changed.

87　Let us not wallow in the valley of despair.

88　I say to you today, my friends,

89　so even though we face the difficulties of today and tomorrow,

90　I still have a dream.

91　It is a dream deeply rooted in the American dream.

92　I have a dream

93　that one day this nation will rise up

94　and live out the true meaning of its creed:

95　"We hold these truths to be self-evident:

96　that all men are created equal. "

97　I have a dream

98　that one day on the red hills of Georgia the sons of former slaves and the sons of former slave owners will be able to sit down together at the table of brotherhood.

99　I have a dream

100　that one day even the state of Mississippi, a state sweltering with the heat of injustice, sweltering with the heat of oppression, will be transformed into an oasis of freedom and justice.

101　I have a dream

102　that my four little children will one day live in a nation where they will not be judged by the color of their skin but by the content of their character.

103 I have a dream today.

104 I have a dream

105 that one day, down in Alabama, with its vicious racists, with its governor having his lips dripping with the words of interposition and nullification; one day right there in Alabama, little black boys and black girls will be able to join hands with little white boys and white girls as sisters and brothers.

106 I have a dream today.

107 I have a dream

108 that one day every valley shall be exalted,

109 every hill and mountain shall be made low,

110 the rough places will be made plain,

111 and the crooked places will be made straight,

112 and the glory of the Lord shall be revealed,

113 and all flesh shall see it together.

114 This is our hope.

115 This is the faith that I go back to the South with.

116 With this faith we will be able to hew out of the mountain of despair a stone of hope.

117 With this faith we will be able to transform the jangling discords of our nation into a beautiful symphony of brotherhood.

118 With this faith we will be able to work together,

119 to pray together,

120 to struggle together,

121 to go to jail together,

122 to stand up for freedom together, knowing that we will be free one day.

123 This will be the day when all of God's children will be able to sing with a new meaning,

124 "My country,'tis of thee, sweet land of liberty, of thee I sing.

125 Land where my fathers died, land of the pilgrim's pride, from every mountainside, let freedom ring."

126 And if America is to be a great nation

127 this must become true.

128 So let freedom ring from the prodigious hilltops of New Hampshire.

129 Let freedom ring from the mighty mountains of New York.

130 Let freedom ring from the heightening Alleghenies of Pennsylvania!

131   Let freedom ring from the snowcapped Rockies of Colorado!

132   Let freedom ring from the curvaceous slopes of California!

133   But not only that; let freedom ring from Stone Mountain of Georgia!

134   Let freedom ring from Lookout Mountain of Tennessee!

135   Let freedom ring from every hill and molehill of Mississippi.

136   From every mountainside, let freedom ring.

137   And when this happens,

138   when we allow freedom to ring,

139   when we let it ring from every village and every hamlet, from every state and every city,

140   we will be able to speed up that day when all of God's children, black men and white men, Jews and Gentiles, Protestants and Catholics, will be able to join hands and sing in the words of the old Negro spiritual,

141   "Free at last! free at last! thank God Almighty, we are free at last!"

问题

(1) Can you identify stretches of text which are characterised by particular features of mood and/or modality? How would you characterise these stretches in terms of their rhetorical effect?

(2) Can you identify stretches of text which are characterised by particular configurations of evaluative language?

(3) How do mood, modality and evaluation interact with shifts in field, including transitivity relations?

(4) What different positions do you think Martin Luther King is construing for himself and for his audience?

(5) How does King recalibrate the storyline at different points?

(6) Do you recognise styles of rhetoric from different traditions in the speech?

(7) Do you think the positions adopted by King all belong to a single role set appropriate to a single social status or is there a mixing here of different roles belonging to different role sets?

(8) Relate the positions taken up by King to the historical context and King's status(es) and discuss why you think this speech is generally regarded as of great historical significance.

(9) Relate your answers in 1-8 to the Positioning Star, remembering that all aspects

of the language used are part of the act, but that they affect and are affected by
the other points of the Star.

4.5　结论

在本章中，我们研究了说话人可以利用的相关资源，用以显示和确立他们
在持续互动中的角色，并对讨论的主题进行主观评估和评价。然后，这些特征
共同构建了话语的语旨、说话人作为说话人的个人投入，以及他们通过持续的
谈话建立和重新校准的社会关系。从定位之星的角度来看，语言的人际特征与
经验特征一样，是话语行为的一部分，它们构建了说话人定位的一个方面。正
如我们在以上例子中所看到的，人际定位的确立涉及权力和文化资本的问题，
而这些问题又以不同的方式与故事情节联系在一起。因此，我们可以看到，虽
然为了便于分析，我们可以将人际意义和经验意义分开，但说到底，这两种意义
以及我们稍后将看到的语篇意义都不能孤立地考虑。这个问题我将在第 6 章
和第 7 章中详细探讨。

第5章 语篇意义:说话人作为编织者

5.1 引言

在前几章中,我们已经研究了个别小句的描述意义和交换价值,以及它们在语篇中的分布方式;在本章中,我们将开始研究说话人和作者如何控制意义和衔接手段的分布,从而产生连贯一致的语篇。这就是韩礼德所说的**语篇意义**(*textual meaning*),他将其描述为"**使能元功能**(*enabling metafunction*)",因为它是组织语篇的手段,用以让人际意义和经验意义更有效地发挥作用。然而,术语语篇意义(或语篇元功能)可能有点令人困惑。正如我上面所说的,人际意义和经验意义的各种结合模式将口语和写作转化为语篇,因此它们显然有助于语篇的"语篇性"。然而,我们所说的语篇元功能是指语言所产生的这种资源——它们明确地表明语篇的不同要素之间互相联系的方式或者与其产生的时间和地点之间的联系方式。在本章中,我们将重点关注这么一种主要的资源——它用来表明作为语篇块的小句是如何结合在一起的,即小句的主位组织结构,以及随着语篇的展开这些主位成分是如何展开的。如果经验成分和人际成分是语篇中的丝线,那么我们可以说语篇元功能是指将这些成分编织在一起形成图案的方式。

5.2 主位与述位

让我们再来看看丘吉尔"On the Beaches"的演讲中最著名的片段,这篇演讲闻名遐迩的名字就源于此段:

> … we shall not flag or fail. We shall go on to the end. We shall fight in France,
>
> we shall fight on the seas and oceans,
>
> we shall fight with growing confidence and growing strength in the air, we shall defend our island,
>
> whatever the cost may be. We shall fight on the beaches,
>
> we shall fight on the landing grounds,
>
> we shall fight in the fields and in the streets, we shall fight in the hills;
>
> we shall never surrender

这一节最明显的特点之一是,丘吉尔在列举他承诺将采取的各种行动以保卫国家免受纳粹入侵时,每一个小句都以"we"这个词开头。从演讲语篇组织的角度来看,丘吉尔所做的是在这一节点上把语篇锚定在"we, the British people"上,并以多种方式逐一展开这一理念。在功能术语中,我们将小句或一系列小句的锚称作**主位**(*Theme*),而将小句的其余部分,即与主位相关的内容,称为**述位**(*Rheme*)。在英语中,主位出现在小句的开头,但其他语言不一定如此。

更具体地说,我们可以将**经验主位**(*experiential Theme*)①视为具有经验意义的小句中的第一个成分,即指称参与者、过程或环境的成分。马丁·路德·金演讲中的以下小句分别以参与者和环境为主位。稍后我们会看看将过程作为主位的例子。

---

① 其他作者使用"主题主位"一词,这可能更好地体现了这一成分在语篇展开中的作用。但是,我将使用"经验主题"一词,因为这抓住了与人际主位和语篇主位的对比,这将在本章后面讨论。

1. Some of you have come from narrow jail cells
2. One hundred years later, the Negro lives on a lonely island of poverty ...

经验主位可以被看作发挥着一种副标题功能,即引入一个稍后展开的角度或主题。由于主位信息的主要功能是表明说话人在语篇的各个部分之间是如何延续、展开和转移话题的,因此经验主位是小句的一个基本要素。然而,也可以在该小句中增加一些纯粹的人际和语篇成分的**主位性**(thematicity),在进入该小句的主要内容之前让这些成分得以突显。这是通过将这些成分放在经验主位本身之前,将之作为该小句经验内容的序言。因此,我们可以将一个小句的主位成分①定义为包括经验主位在内的所有成分。我们将在下面的第 5.4 节中讨论人际主位和语篇主位。

回到上面丘吉尔的演讲,我们说丘吉尔一直把主位焦点放在"we"身上,当经验主位从一个小句到下一个小句之间延续时,我们将之称为**固定主位**(constant Theme)。这里需要记住的一点是,**主位**是指称对象,而不管用来指代它的词是什么。重复使用完全相同的单词,例如"we",可以达到修辞效果;或者,如果丘吉尔用"the British public"或"our nation"这样的短语来改变"we"的措辞,那么这就将固定主位与语义演进有趣地结合起来了(见第 2 章)。

在英语中,主位通常是陈述句或是非问句的主语、祈使句中的动词本身,以及特殊疑问句中的 wh 词(见第 4 章)。在这种情况下,我们说该小句具有**无标记的主位**(unmarked Theme)。马丁·路德·金演讲中的以下小句以粗体标出了主位:

3. **Some of you** have come fresh from narrow jail cells.
4. **Some of you** have come from areas where your quest for freedom left you battered

---

① 通常只称为主位,我使用主位成分来避免混淆。出于充分的理由,几位系统功能语言学学者对主位和/或主位成分的范围有不同的定义。为了与韩礼德的术语保持对应关系,我遵循他对经验主题的定义。然而,我对主位成分的使用与韩礼德所说的主位一致,但我也强调了主语在不属于主位成分时所起的衔接作用,这种理念与贝里(1996)、福塞特(2003)和其他人类似。

by the storms of persecution and staggered by the winds of police brutality.

5. **You** have been the veterans of creative suffering.

6. **Continue** to work with the faith that unearned suffering is redemptive.

7. **Go back** to Mississippi,

8. **go back** to Alabama,

9. **go back** to South Carolina,

10. **go back** to Georgia,

11. **go back** to Louisiana,

12. **go back** to the slums and ghettos of our northern cities, knowing that somehow this situation can and will be changed.

13. **Let us not wallow** in the valley of despair.

　　请注意,在第 3 小句和第 4 小句中,主位是一个短语,因为这个短语指的是参与者构成的整体。还要注意的是,第 3—5 小句在某种程度上有一个固定主位,即作为马丁·路德·金的受众"you",不过句子之间还是有所区别,因为前两个小句缩小了指称范围。通过这种方式,既保持了一定程度的连续性,也有了一定程度的变化——这就是语篇性的要旨所在,即衔接和推进。

　　在第 6—13 小句中,主位是祈使动词。由于直接祈使句总是暗示内含第二人称主语(你),因此我们又在这里观察到了连续性和推进,这个隐含的主语保持不变,而作为祈使句焦点的动作本身可能会发生变化(尽管在这里只有轻微变化)。在第 13 小句中,有一个由"let's"引入的第一人称复数祈使句。由于隐含的主语(我们)和过程在这里都发生了变化,因此主位也发生了变化,使马丁·路德·金得以重构他的受众,将他自己包括了进去,从而在他的受众和他自己之间构造了一种团结感,并且将他自己构建成非裔美国人群体的代表。

　　至于例 14,请记住 DO 是一个人际成分(参见第 4 章),它将结构标记为疑问结构,因此它不是经验主位的一部分。

14. Do you want to talk about it outside?

　　涉及 BE 动词的疑问句也是如此。虽然 BE 在关系小句中有经验意义(见第 3 章),但英语的一个特点是,有 BE 的疑问句是通过将 BE 放在句首而不是像我们对其他动词那样引入"假位词"DO 而形成的。在英语的某些方言中，HAVE 也是如此。在这种情况下，小句结构的特征与语篇结构之间存在张力，这是在语言及其他不断发展的系统中必然存在的。因此，在以下情况下，主位是主语，而不是过程：

15. Are you an idiot?
16. Have you any eggs?

在特殊疑问句中，小句语法和语篇发展之间也存在张力(见第 4 章)。英语进化出了一种系统——使疑问词出现在小句的开头，以便从一开始就表明说话人在问问题，而不是提供信息。因此，疑问词是该小句的主位，它还以未知参与者或环境成分的形式编码经验信息。在例 17 中，无标记的主位就是"when"。这是有意义的，因为它标志着语篇焦点向环境要素转变，但它也可以掩盖一个事实，即主语可能维持了主位指称的连续性。也就是说，小句层面(关注问题)和语篇层面(关注连续性)的主位性具有张力。因此，在这些情况下进行主位分析时，最好对疑问词(粗体)和主语(下画线)做出标记：

17. **When** did you get here?

注意，在一些由 WHO 和 WHAT 引导的疑问句中，主语和疑问词是相同的，所以我们只需要标记一个成分就行了：

18. **Who** saw you?
19. **What** happened next?

然而，WHO 和 WHAT 通常指的是该小句的补语(见第 4 章)，那么在这些情况下，如上所述那样把主语标记出来也很有好处。事实上，当我们有一个主位不是主语时，标出主语也是有好处的：[1]

---

[1] 事实上，福西特(1999、2003)将主题分析为主位的一种类型，称为主语主位；贝里(1996 年)将主位分析为包括主语在内的所有成分。

20. **What** did you do next?
21. **Who** did you see?

5.3　有标记主位

在上面的章节中，我们已经考虑了无标记的主位，所以现在我们来考虑一下所谓的有标记主位指的是什么。在马丁·路德·金演讲中的以下小句中，我们看到陈述性小句的第一个经验成分不是主语（如无标记的情况），而是"five score years ago"所表达的时间环境：

22. **Five score years ago**, a great American, in whose symbolic shadow we stand today, signed the Emancipation Proclamation.

马丁·路德·金本可以说：

23. **A great American**, in whose symbolic shadow we stand today, signed the Emancipation Proclamation five score years ago.

在修改后的例子中，环境因素在句尾，主语在句首，大约百分之九十的英语小句都是这样的，这就是为什么我们称之为无标记的情况。然而，马丁·路德·金"选择"以这个短语作为他的小句的开头，这是一种有标记的行为，因此我们需要为这个"选择"寻求更多的解释。第一个原因可以在局部层面找到，因为我们可以看到马丁·路德·金将自己出现在林肯纪念堂（"today"）的时间与林肯本人名垂青史的演讲的时间框架进行对比：

24. **I** am happy to join with you today in what will go down in history as the great-est demonstration for freedom in the history of our nation.
25. **Five score years ago**, a great American, in whose symbolic shadow we stand today, signed the Emancipation Proclamation.

在这里，我们可以看到，使用有标记主位如何明确标志焦点的转移（通常是空间转移,或如本例中的时间转移),而这种语篇推进的明确信号是一种语篇意义。与此类似,为了将法令的高调措辞和美国许多黑人在马丁·路德·金的时代的悲惨境遇进行对比,第 28 小句中又回到了现在:

26. This momentous decree came as a great beacon light of hope to millions of Negro slaves who had been seared in the flames of withering injustice.
27. It came as a joyous daybreak to end the long night of their captivity.
28. But one hundred years later, the Negro still is not free.

因此,有标记主位的使用是明确转移语篇焦点的工具。然而,正如我在上文所说,语篇性既包括连续性,也包括发展性,我们在上面几行中看到,尽管焦点发生了变化,但通过在第 26 小句和第 28 小句中提及"the Negro",便维持了这种连续性。因此,与上文类似,当存在有标记主位时,最好将主语和主位都标示出来:

29. **This momentous decree** came as a great beacon light of hope to millions of Negro slaves who had been seared in the flames of withering injustice.
30. **It** came as a joyous daybreak to end the long night of their captivity.
31. But **one hundred years later**, the Negro still is not free.

因此,我们可以看到,在第 29 小句和第 30 小句之间有一个主位,但在下面的小句中,我们有一个明确的重点转移,这来自有标记主位(我将在下面讨论"but"的主位功能)和一个新的主位"the Negro",它与第 29 小句和第 30 小句相照应。因此,你可能会问,我们为什么不在第 29 小句中把"Negro slaves"列为主位,我稍后会再谈这个问题。

首先,让我们再多看一下这篇文章,其主位推进已被做了标记:

32. **This momentous decree** came as a great beacon light of hope to millions of Negro slaves who had been seared in the flames of withering injustice.
33. **It** came as a joyous daybreak to end the long night of their captivity.
34. But **one hundred years later**, the Negro still is not free.
35. **One hundred years later**, the life of the Negro is still sadly crippled by the

manacles of segregation and the chains of discrimination.

36. **One hundred years later**, the Negro lives on a lonely island of poverty in the midst of a vast ocean of material prosperity.

37. **One hundred years later**, the Negro is still languishing in the corners of American society

38. and finds himself an exile in his own land.

39. So we have come here today to dramatize a shameful condition.

　　这里有两个语法特征需要快评一番。首先，第 39 小句中的"so"一词（与第 34 小句中的"but"一词一样）并没有为该小句增加经验意义，因此不是经验主位的一部分（见下文）。其次，第 38 小句有一个限定动词，但没有明显的主语。这是因为第 37 小句和第 38 小句由一句话组成，两个小句都有相同的主语。发生这种情况时，可以省掉第二个主语。这样做能取得很强的衔接效果，表明这两个过程在某种程度上联系紧密，因此省略被认为是一种衔接手段，也是语篇意义的一部分。因此，我们可以说省略是两个小句中固定主位的一个非常有力的标记，为了表明这一点，我们必须将一个主语置入括号中，将其标记为主位。因为主位指的是指称对象，而不是概念，因此我们用来表示省略主位的具体词汇并不重要，只要指称明确就行。因此，为了便于分析，我们可以将第 37 小句和第 38 小句改写为：

40. **One hundred years later**, the Negro is still languishing in the corners of American society

41. and [**he**] finds himself an exile in his own land.

　　在第 34—37 行这段文字中，有一点非常不寻常（因此值得评论），一是重复"one hundred years later"这一环境成分作为有标记主位，二是重复主语"the Negro"。既然已经明确地转移了时间焦点，马丁·路德·金就没有必要重复有标记主位，同样地，除了第一种情况，他本可以用他、他们或我们来代替"the Negro"。这里的原因似乎是，马丁·路德·金意欲通过重复"one hundred years leater"来反复强调林肯的豪言壮语与现实之间那深阔的鸿沟，而重复"the

Negro"同样强调了当时非裔美国人和白人之间的鸿沟。此外,这段文字呈现了一系列概括的结论(我们将在第6章中探讨),因此重复使用相同的结构有助于强调这样一个观点,即这种不愉快的事态是一个普遍的事实,而不是一个孤立的事件。这种重复是马丁·路德·金的演讲的整体修辞效果的一部分,而且通常只有在这种充满跌宕和情感色彩的话语中才能发现。

现在让我们再次看看以下小句,已重新标示为第42和第43小句:

42. When the architects of our republic wrote the magnificent words of the Constitution and the Declaration of Independence,

43. they were signing a promissory note to which every American was to fall heir.

在这里,我们看到一个**小句复合体**(*clause complex*)(一个句子中包含多个小句),其中小句放在主句(承载句子主旨的小句)之前。由于小句的功能是提供环境信息,而小句通常位于主句之后,因此我们可以说,主句之前的小句在整体上是一个有标记主位。然而,由于主句和小句都有自己的小句结构,我们也可以分别分析它们的主位。为了突显这一点,我们可以将主句前面的小句设为斜体,并用粗体标记每个小句的主位:

44. *When **the architects of our republic** wrote the magnificent words of the Constitution and the Declaration of Independence,*

45. **they** were signing a promissory note to which every American was to fall heir.

小句的语义功能与环境小句非常相似。表5.1列出了小句的主要类别以及引导小句的连词。

表5.1　小句

类别		连词	示例
Temporal	same time	while, when	I called him while he was painting.
	preceding	before	The man was unconscious before he was shot.
	following	after	The man was shot after he was unconscious.

续表

类别		连词	示例
Spatial	same	where	I like to linger where the lovely lilies bloom.
Manner	comparison	as, like	She sings just like he does!
Cause	cause: reason	because	I love you because you understand me.
	cause: purpose	so (that)	We need to save up so we can all go on holiday.
	cause: result	so that	She was so tall that she could pick the apples from the tree.
Condition	positive	if	If it rains we'll stay indoors.
	negative	unless	We'll play football outside unless it rains.
	concessive	even if, although	We'll play football outside even if it rains.

在上面的章节中,笔者试图展示有标记主位如何表明焦点从一个小句到下一个小句的变化,但我在上面说过,它们也有一个不仅限于局部的功能,即贯穿整个语篇或语篇的一部分。为理解这一点,我们来看看马丁·路德·金演讲的前六个有标记主位:

> Five score years ago …
> one hundred years later …
> one hundred years later …
> one hundred years later …
> one hundred years later …
> When the architects of our republic wrote the magnificent words of the Constitution and the Declaration of Independence …

正如我们所看到的,所有这些主位都是时间环境成分,表明语篇的这一部分是从时间的角度设计的。因此,一系列有标记主位表示语篇或部分语篇的发展角度。马丁·路德·金本可以选择从空间角度突显非裔美国人的命运在全国是如何毫无二致的。如果他这样做了,我们可能会看到一系列的处所环境成

分,例如:

> In Alabama ... ,
> In Mississippi ... ,
> In Kansas ... ,
> And even in Washington DC ...

　　然而,马丁·路德·金选择了一个历史的角度,这反映在有标记时间环境成分的使用上。这两种策略在传记、简历和百科全书条目中都很常见——请观察一下它们是如何使用有标记时间或位置主位来标志语篇中的过渡的。让我们再看一段马丁·路德·金的演讲,看看46 至 49 小句:

46. **Now** is the time to make real the promises of democracy.
47. **Now** is the time to rise from the dark and desolate valley of segregation to the sunlit path of racial justice.
48. **Now** is the time to lift our nation from the quick sands of racial injustice to the solid rock of brotherhood.
49. **Now** is the time to make justice a reality for all of God's children.

　　在这里,我们看到时间的概念再次被强调,不是通过有标记时间主位,而是通过将无标记主位"now"用作四个小句的主语。因此,我们可以看到,马丁·路德·金是如何利用时间框架来引导对当前时间的讨论的,以"now"为主位,在四个连续的小句中持续不断地使用无标记主位,他以此为基础,将现在必须做的事情与自林肯演讲以来的一百年来缺乏进展进行对比。

　　总之,有标记主位有两个目的,一是在局部层面上转移小句的重点,二是确定语篇或部分语篇的发展角度。在局部层面上,我们可能会在以下小句中有一个有标记主位,然后是一个主位或一系列主位,这些主位在焦点转移之前立即引用小句的主位或主位,表明发展的连续性和变化:

50. We cannot walk alone
51. *As* **we** *walk*,
52. we must make the pledge ...

　　或者,有标记主位后面可能出现以前没有出现过的主位,标志着语篇发生了较大转变:

53. It came as a joyous daybreak to end the long night of their captivity.
54. But **one hundred years later**, the Negro is still not free.

　　因此,我们可以看到有标记主位和无标记主位是如何共同作用以表明小句的展开方法,也凭此显示了说话人作为编织者的技巧。在下一节中,我们将从整体上观察主位成分中人际成分和语篇成分的功能。在第 5.5 节中,我们将探讨焦点的转移在连贯语篇中是如何穿插的。

练习 5.1

　　阅读以下语篇并回答以下问题。

语篇 5.1　**维基百科上关于拿破仑的词条**

1　Napoleon Bonaparte was a French military and political leader who rose to prominence during the latter stages of the French Revolution and its associ ated wars in Europe.

2　As Napoleon I, he was Emperor of the French from 1804 to 1815.

3　His legal reform, the Napoleonic Code, has been a major influence on many civil law jurisdictions worldwide,

4　but he is best remembered for his role in the wars led against France by a series of coalitions, the so-called Napoleonic Wars.

5　He established hegemony over most of continental Europe

6　and sought to spread the ideals of the French Revolution, while consolidating an imperial monarchy which restored aspects of the deposed *Ancien Régime*.

7　Due to his success in these wars, often against numerically superior enemies, he is generally regarded as one of the greatest military commanders of all time,

8　and his campaigns are studied at military academies worldwide.

9　Napoleon was born at Ajaccio in Corsica in a family of noble Italian ancestry which had settled Corsica in the 16th century.

10　He trained as an artillery officer in mainland France.

11   He rose to prominence under the French First Republic

12   and led successful campaigns against the First and Second Coalitions arrayed
      against France.

13   He led a successful invasion of the Italian peninsula.

14   In 1799, he staged a *coup d'état*

15   and installed himself as First Consul;

16   five years later the French Senate proclaimed him emperor, following a plebi-
      scite in his favour.

17   In the first decade of the 19th century, the French Empire under Napoleon
      engaged in a series of conflicts—the Napoleonic Wars—that involved every
      major European power.

18   After a streak of victories, France secured a dominant position in continental
      Europe,

19   and Napoleon maintained the French sphere of influence through the formation
      of extensive alliances and the appointment of friends and family members to rule
      other European countries as French client states.

20   The Peninsular War and 1812 French invasion of Russia marked turning points
      in Napoleon's fortunes.

21   His *Grande Armée* was badly damaged in the campaign

22   and never fully recovered.

23   In 1813, the Sixth Coalition defeated his forces at Leipzig;

24   the following year the Coalition invaded France,

25   forced Napoleon to abdicate

26   and exiled him to the island of Elba.

27   Less than a year later, he escaped Elba

28   and returned to power,

29   but was defeated at the Battle of Waterloo in June 1815.

30   Napoleon spent the last six years of his life in confinement by the British on the
      island of Saint Helena.

31   An autopsy concluded he died of stomach cancer,

32   but there has been some debate about the cause of his death,

33   as some scholars have speculated

34   that he was a victim of arsenic poisoning.

问题

(1) 找出语篇 5.1 中的主位。存在有标记主位的地方也要标记主语。确定有标记主位的类别。见附录的答案。

(2) 无标记主位和主语所标志的主题焦点和转变是什么?

(3) 语篇暗含着怎样的总体展开或阅读角度?

(4) 现在,阅读下面的语篇,比较有标记和无标记主位在转移、连续性和展开角度方面的使用。记住要考虑小句的位置。

语篇 5.2 **大学规章**

1 6.1.5 Your Address and Contact Details

2 You must keep us informed of your current contact details including Cardiff and home postal addresses, mobile telephone number and email addresses.

3 Should any of this information change during the year

4 you should make the changes via SIMS Online

5 and notify the administrative staff as soon as possible.

6 This is most important.

7 6.1.6 Attendance

8 The University requires all students to be present in Cardiff during the whole of both semesters (including throughout reading weeks, guided study weeks and examination periods).

9 This means that you should plan to be in Cardiff

10 even when you do not have to attend classes or sit examinations.

11 However, if you must miss a lecture or seminar,

12 try to make sure that you collect any handouts which may have been distributed,

13 and find out from others as much as you can about what the session covered.

14 Year 1 students should note that attendance at seminars is compulsory.

15 If you fail to attend any seminar,

16 your seminar tutor will expect an explanation

17 and you must catch up with any work you have missed.

18 If you fail any of your assessments,

19 you must also be available in the summer resit examinations period,

20 which usually falls in the second half of August.

21 Bear this in mind when making plans for the summer vacation.

22 See also Section 10 below and the following website: http://www. cardiff. ac. uk/regis/sfs/regs/index. html.

23 6.1.7 Absence

24 It is important that you inform the School of any period of absence from University.

25 (See 'Failure to Engage with Programme of Study' below)

26 You should do this by contacting the administrative office

27 (see 'School Administration' (1.3) for details).

28 6.1.8 Failure to Engage with Programme of Study/Points of Engagement

29 It is a University requirement that student attendance is monitored at a number of points of engagement throughout the year.

30 Where a student fails to provide evidence of engagement on 2 consecutive points of engagement,

31 the Head of School or nominee will remind the student in writing of their requirement to engage,

32 and will state

33 that continued failure to engage will result in their exclusion from their programme of study.

34 Registry will also be informed of the student's failure to engage.

35 Where a student continues to fail to provide evidence of engagement with their programme of study,

36 or where a student fails to respond to written communication regarding their failure to engage,

37 the Head of School will inform Registry of his/her decision that the student should be excluded from their programme of study.

5.4　人际主位和语篇主位

正如我上面所说的，人际意义和语篇意义的成分可以放在小句的开头，在经验主位之前。这些主位被称为语篇主位和人际主位。我说过，这增加了这些成分的主位性，因为如果我们把经验主位作为小句表达的出发点，那么我们可以看到语篇主位和人际主位突出了在我们开始表达之前需要"处理掉"的想法。

主位成分中的语篇成分通常是连词或并列成分，这些词表示小句之间的逻辑关系，但不增加任何经验意义。我们上文看到了两个例子，其中在经验主位之前出现了"but"和"so"：

55. **One hundred years later**, **the Negro** is still languishing in the corners of American society

56. and [**he**] finds himself an exile in his own land.

57. So **we** have come here today to dramatize a shameful condition.

58. **It** came as a joyous daybreak to end the long night of their captivity.

59. But **one hundred years later**, the Negro still is not free.

如前所述，"so"和"but"显示了一个小句和下一个小句之间的逻辑关系，在第一种情况下，表明两个想法之间存在因果关系，在第二种情况下，存在与预期相反的情况。在这些例子中，我们有两个主要小句连接在一起，形成一个小句复合体，但在其他例子中，我们看到一个小句通过一个连词连接到一个主句，连词表示作为语篇主位的关系：

60. **This sweltering summer of the Negro's legitimate discontent** will not pass

61. until **there is an invigorating autumn of freedom and equality**.

记住，在有标记的情况下，小句可以放在主句之前：

62. When ***the architects of our republic*** *wrote the magnificent words of the Constitution and the Declaration of Independence*,

63. **they** were signing a promissory note to which every American was to fall heir.

丘吉尔的 *On the Beaches* 演讲中有一个更复杂的语篇主位的例子(斜体):

64. **Parliament** has given us the powers to put down Fifth Column activities with a strong hand,

65. and **we** shall use those powers subject to the supervision and correction of the house, without the slightest hesitation

66. until **we** are satisfied, and more than satisfied,

67. that **this malignancy in our midst** has been effectively stamped out.

68. *Turning once again, and this time more generally, to the question of invasion*, I would observe

69. that **there has never been a period** in all these long centuries of which we boast when an absolute guarantee against invasion, still less against serious raids, could have been given to our people.

丘吉尔用"Turning once again, and this time more generally, to the question of invasion"这句话的目的是明确地告诉受众他正在改变焦点。虽然这可能看起来像是该小句经验意义的一部分,并且与之相关,但它实际上更多充当的是后面主旨的序言,即 "there has never been a period… when an absolute guarantee against invasion… could have been given to our people"。它并没有像一个经验环境成分那样,在这个概念中增添如何、什么、何时或为什么,而是明确地说明丘吉尔要如何展开他的语篇,因此可以作为语篇主位进行分析。如果第 69 小句的主要意思是,正如我所说,从来没有一项能保证防止入侵的措施,那么我们如何理解第 68 小句中的"I would observe that"这句话,这句话也因此成为序言的一部分吗? 虽然这个短语可以从经验的角度进行分析,但我认为,在这个例子中,它作为一种归因手段,具有附加的情态效应,就像表达"说"和"想"的动词经常做的那样(见第 4 章)。这个案例很有趣,因为它是自我归因,这可能表明丘吉尔希望他作为首相的文化资本为他的观点提供适当的符号资本。根据这种解释,该短语在整个小句中具有人际功能,而且因为它出现在所有经验成分之前,所以它是一个人际主位。

人际主位更常见的例子是称呼语(例 70)、情态附加语(例 71)和评论附加语(例 72),下面双下画线:

70. <u>Mary</u>, will you marry me please?

71. <u>Perhaps</u> you don't love me?

72. But <u>bizarrely</u>, I think you do!

让我们看看《我有一个梦想》的另一段摘录(经验主位用**粗体字**表示;主语用<u>下画线</u>表示;人际主位用<u>双下画线</u>表示):

73. **Instead of honoring this sacred obligation**, <u>America</u> has given the Negro people a bad check, a check which has come back marked "insufficient funds."

74. But <u>**we**</u> refuse to believe

75. that <u>**the bank of justice**</u> is bankrupt.

76. <u>**We**</u> refuse to believe

77. that **there are insufficient funds** in the great vaults of opportunity of this nation.

78. So **we** have come to cash this check — a check that will give us upon demand the riches of freedom and the security of justice.

79. **We** have also come to this hallowed spot to remind America of the fierce urgency of now.

如上所述,投射小句通常可以被视为以隐喻的方式提供了人际意义,因此我在上面的投射小句上画了双下画线。但这类小句也有经验内容,可能或多或少比较突出,因此我也标记了投射小句的经验主位(这是一个分析者可以根据具体情况做出的决定,取决于分析的角度和投射小句中经验意义的显著性)。在上面的简短摘录中,我们可以看到马丁·路德·金如何在一个层面上介绍他的(共同的)信仰,将之作为第 75 小句和第 77 小句的人际序言,以美国"bank of justice"的金融隐喻提供了一个固定主位,而在另一个层面上,他利用这些被投射小句的主位"we"作为过渡到第 78 小句和第 79 小句的经验主位的手段,第 78 小句和第 79 小句以"we"为固定主位。很聪明,是吧?

当一个小句的主位成分中包含的信息不只经验信息时,我们称之为**复杂主位**(*complex Themes*)。在复杂主位中,顺序总是(语篇主位)^(人际主位)^经验主位,如在下面的例子中,"but"是语篇主位,呼语"Mary"是人际主位,"you"是经验主位:

80. But, Mary, **you** must love me!

在这一点上,你可能会感到困惑——如果主位是一个语篇功能,你怎么能有语篇主位、人际主位和经验主位? 答案是,一个小句的成分可以是多功能的。在上面的小句中,"Mary"作为呼语是一个人际成分,但它被置于经验主位之前,从而被赋予了主位地位;"you"不仅有经验意义,而且因其具有作为经验主位的衔接功能,又具有了语篇意义;而"but"则具有语篇意义,因为它标示了该小句与之前所说或所理解的内容之间的关系,且被置于经验主位之前的主位位置。因此,所有主位都具有语篇性,只有语篇主位具有双重语篇性!

练习 5.2

阅读以下语篇并回答以下问题。

语篇 5.3　University Welcome

1　FOREWORD

2　Welcome, or welcome back, to "ENCAP".

3　As one of the largest Schools in the University, with more than a thousand students (one hundred of them postgraduates), and over fifty academic staff, we pride ourselves in providing an excellent experience for our students, based in a friendly, personalised and supportive environment.

4　There are several ways in which you as a student can contribute to the community, generally by participating fully in lectures and seminars and by engaging with your fellow students and staff in the spirit of mutual respect that we seek to promote in all dealings within the School.

5　As you will be aware,

6 students entering their first year and those in the second year each have their own Facebook page

7 —this is a great way of getting to know each other, sharing experiences and information.

8 You can make a particularly useful contribution by joining the Student-Staff panels associated with the Board of Studies that runs your degree and by standing as a student representative to the Board.

9 In our turn, our job is to help you achieve your best.

10 Your Personal Tutor is there for that purpose

11 —take time to catch up with him or her,

12 and do take advantage of the opportunities for Academic Progress Meetings (APMs) we have introduced.

13 You will find more information about APMs, and much else, in this School Undergraduate Student Handbook.

14 It also contains advice on presentation of work and exam preparation, how staff and students contact each other, personal development and careers, stu-dent support, extenuating circumstances, regulations regarding examinations and assessed work and progression.

15 For more detailed information relating to your programme of study,

16 please refer to your Course Guide,

17 which details academic staff email addresses and research interests, word limits for essays and dissertations, grading/assessment criteria, referencing systems etc.

18 This Handbook and your Course Guide should be read in conjunction with each other.

19 Of course, no handbook can cover every possible detail;

20 if you have any queries or need clarification on any issue

21 your first point of contact are the staff in the Undergraduate Office

22 —they are always happy to help (Humanities Building, Room 2.67).

23 Each programme also has a Deputy Director whose job it is to deal with queries that cannot be resolved by the Office.

24 And, of course, personal matters should be discussed with your Personal Tutor.

25 I hope

26 you both enjoy

27 and profit from your time in the School.

语篇 5.4　Bush's *Bring Them On* Moment

1	Q:	A posse of small nations, like Ukraine and Poland, are materializing to help keep the peace in Iraq,
2		but with the attacks on U.S. forces and casualty rates rising, what does the administration do to get larger powers like France and Germany and Russia to join in the American (xxxx)?
3	B:	Well, first of all, you know, we'll put together a force structure that meets the threats on the ground.
4		And we got a lot of forces there ourselves.
5		And as I said yesterday,
6		anybody who wants to harm American troops will be found and brought to justice.
7		There are some who feel like
8		That if they attack us
9		that we may decide to leave prematurely.
10		They don't understand what they're talking about,
11		if that's the case.
12		Let me finish.
13		There are some who feel like
14		that, you know, the conditions are such that they can attack us there.
15		My answer is bring them on.
16		We got the force necessary to deal with the security situation.
17		Of course we want other countries to help us.
18		Great Britain is there.
19		Poland is there.
20		Ukraine is there,
21		you mentioned.
22		Anybody who wants to help, we'll welcome to help.
23		But we got plenty tough force there right now to make sure the situation is secure.
24		We always welcome help.
25		We're always glad to include others in.
26		But make no mistake about it,

27	and the enemy shouldn't make any mistake about it,
28	we will deal with them harshly
29	if they continue to try to bring harm to the Iraqi people.
30	I also said yesterday an important point,
31	that those who blow up the electricity lines really aren't hurting America,
32	they're hurting the Iraq citizens.
33	Their own fellow citizens are being hurt.
34	But we will deal with them harshly as well.

问题

(1)找出并讨论两个语篇中无标记主位和主语的变动。

(2)讨论有标记主位对两个语篇的语篇意义有何贡献。

(3)找出并讨论两个语篇中复杂主位的使用。

（主位分析见附录。）

5.5 主位推进

在本节中，我们将介绍固定主位之外的**展开方法**（*methods of development*）——**线性主位**（*linear theme*）和**派生主位**（*derived theme*）。

5.5.1 线性主位

在第 5.2 节和第 5.3 节中，我们看到了一些固定主位的例子，并讨论了这些主位在保持或转移语篇焦点时如何与有标记主位相互作用。在这一节中，我们将从另一个角度来研究一个小句的主位可如何同前面的语篇照应。让我们再来看看马丁·路德·金演讲的以下部分。这一次我用粗体标出了主位和主语，并用下画线标出每个小句的前一小句中被照应的成分。同样重要的是要注意连续性体现在指称对象上，而不是确切的措辞上：

81. **I** am happy to join with you today in what will go down in history as the greatest demonstration for freedom <u>in the history of our nation</u>.

82. **Five score years ago**, **a great American**, in whose symbolic shadow we stand today, signed <u>the Emancipation Proclamation</u>.

83. **This momentous decree** came as a great beacon light of hope to millions of Negro slaves who had been seared in the flames of withering injustice.

84. **It** came as a joyous daybreak to end the long night of <u>their</u> captivity.

85. **But one hundred years later**, **the Negro** still is not free.

86. **One hundred years later**, **the life of the Negro** is still sadly crippled by the manacles of segregation and the chains of discrimination.

87. **One hundred years later**, **the Negro** lives on a lonely island of poverty in the midst of a vast ocean of material prosperity.

88. **One hundred years later**, **the Negro** is still languishing in the corners of American society

89. and (**he**) finds himself an exile in his own land.

90. So **we** have come here today to dramatize a shameful condition.

　　我们在这里看到,马丁·路德·金以自己为主位开始演讲,评论他在当天事件中的角色。这种手段也存在于我们之前讨论的塞巴斯蒂安·科和托尼·布莱尔的演讲、亨利叔叔和莎拉的话语贡献中,以及下面我们将讨论的布什和奥巴马的就职演说中。这是重要演讲非常常见的一种开篇方式,可以被视为一种普遍的惯例,一种在特定情景下预期的语言特征。马丁·路德·金接下来做的是,在下一个小句的主位+主语之内纳入了第一个小句的结尾部分(述位):

81.—82. ... the history of our nation>Five score years ago, a great American ...

　　他使用了同样的策略来连接下面的小句:

82.—83. ... the Emancipation Proclamation>This momentous decree ...

　　第 84 小句继续使用相同的主位,由代词"it"表示,但在第 85 小句中,马丁·路德·金再次将前面述位的成分(时间和非裔美国人群体)作为他的主位+主语:

83. It came as a joyous daybreak to end the long night of their captivity.

84. But one hundred years later the Negro still is not free.

马丁·路德·金在第 85—89 小句以及第 90 小句中保持了一个固定主位，但这一次将他自己和他的听众纳入了"the Negro"的指称范围：

85. **But one hundred years later, the Negro** still is not free.

86. **One hundred years later, the life of the Negro** is still sadly crippled by the manacles of segregation and the chains of discrimination.

87. **One hundred years later, the Negro** lives on a lonely island of poverty in the midst of a vast ocean of material prosperity.

88. **One hundred years later, the Negro** is still languishing in the corners of American society

89. and (**he**) finds himself an exile in his own land.

90. So **we** have come here today to dramatize a shameful condition.

当前句述位的成分被纳入了后句主位+主语时（如第 81—82 小句和第 82—83 小句中），我们将之称为**线性主位**或**线性推进**（ linear Theme or linear progression），这不同于前文所说的固定主位。固定主位让说话人可以就同一个指称对象（如第 85—88 小句）提出一系列观点，线性主位让说话人可以推着主位向前，进入新的领域，同时保持着连续性线索。因此，在语篇的这一部分中，我们看到马丁·路德·金在开始他的演讲时遵循了一般的期望，提到自己作为说话人的身份，但随后利用线性推进方式从这里无缝地过渡到美国国家的历史和非裔美国人群体被奴役的地位。然后，他又回到了自己身上，但现在不再是作为站在听众面前并处于权威地位的一个说话人（I），而是作为同一个群体（we）的一员，同属于在过去一百年间被奴役的非裔美国人群体。因此，在第 90小句中使用"we"不仅使马丁·路德·金和他的听众团结一致，而且标志着语篇从前一小句的（以"the Negro"这个一般性范畴框定的）概括性观点转变为个人的评论（见第 6 章），令人对非裔美国人受到的奴役更加感同身受。它还将他的听众带入了演讲这个事件，不是作为与"我"这样的说话人区隔开来的"你们"，而是作为演讲的指示中心的"我们"，是直接语境的核心。①

5.5.2 派生主位

除了固定主位和线性主位之外，还有一种主位推进类型，实际上是两者的结合。这就是**派生主位**（*derived theme*），其中一个小句的述位被其后的一系列小句提取，且每个小句聚焦于其一个方面。派生主位通常出现在学术写作中，用来描述一般性范畴的不同部分或类型。我在下面的例子中使用了粗体和下画线表明短语"the Outer Hebrides"为以下三个小句提供了主位：

91. **The Outer Hebrides** comprise seven principal islands.
92. **Lewis** is the northernmost and the largest of these islands.
93. **Harris** is next, heading south,
94. and **North Uist** is a further hop away, skip and jump across the Minch.

通常，从一个上位范畴衍生出来的主位都会在多个小句上以较长篇幅展开，其中每一部分都具有自己的主位结构，例如，一篇文章的开头段落列出了讨论的主题，而下面的各部分都介绍了其中的一个方面。在本例中，我们讨论的是宏观主位和超主位（参见 Martin and Rose 2003，第 6 章）。由于上位概念及其派生主位之间的关系可以在语篇中以不同的距离分布，因此它们通常是混乱的，难以分析。马丁·路德·金的演讲中有一个相对明确的例子，从描述历史上非裔美国人被奴役开始转到今天需要采取（第 95 小句所确立的）的行动，提供了一个上位概念，然后在其后数个小句的主位中均有照应，并在述位中得到展开：

95. **This** is no time to engage in the luxury of cooling off or to take the tranquilizing drug of gradualism.
96. **Now** is the time to make real the promises of democracy.

---

① 非常感谢我的朋友简·穆德里格（Jane Mulderrig）为我提供了这个想法。

97. **Now** is the time to rise from the dark and desolate valley of segregation to the sunlit path of racial justice.

98. **Now** is the time to lift our nation from the quick sands of racial injustice to the solid rock of brotherhood.

99. **Now** is the time to make justice a reality for all of God's children.

　　当然，一个小句的述位也有可能汲取前面小句中的概念，如：

100. and we will not be satisfied

101. until <u>justice</u> rolls down like waters and <u>righteousness</u> like a mighty stream.

102. I am not unmindful that some of you have come here out of *great trials and tribulations*.

　　在这里，最后一个小句的述位（斜体）通过反义关系（尽管在全文中你可以看到前一节讨论的是不公正现象，所以在更广泛的上下文中，justice 和 righteousness 是反义词）从上一个小句复合体（带下画线）中吸取了一些观点。这是一种称为**扩展**（*expansion*）的主位推进机制，将在下一章中讨论。

练习 5.3

　　选择我们在本章中看过的任何语篇，识别并讨论它们展示的不同类型的主位推进手段。

5.6　语篇完整分析

　　于此章末，我将分析一篇完整的语篇，对迄今为止介绍的观点进行例证和评论，同时也会引入一些新的转折。语篇还是托尼·布莱尔在 2005 年 7 月 7 日伦敦爆炸案后向媒体发表的讲话（另见 O'Grady 2010）：

1　**I** am just going to make a short statement to you on the terrible events that have happened in London earlier today,

2　and **I** <u>hope</u>

3　**you** <u>understand</u>

4　that **at the present time** <u>we</u> are still trying to establish exactly what has happened,

5　and **there is a limit to what information I can give you**,

6　and **I** will simply try and tell you the information as best I can at the moment.

7　<u>It is reasonably clear</u> **that there have been a series of terrorist attacks in London**.

8　**There are obviously casualties**, both people that have died and people seriously injured,

9　and **our thoughts and prayers** of course are with the victims and their families.

10　**It is my intention** to leave the G8 within the next couple of hours and go down to London and get a report, face-to-face, with the police, and the emergency services and the Ministers that have been dealing with this, and then to return later this evening.

11　**It is the will** of all the leaders at the G8 however that the meeting should continue in my absence, that we should continue to discuss the issues that we were going to discuss, and reach the conclusions which we were going to reach.

12　**Each of the countries round that table** have some experience of the effects of terrorism

13　and **all the leaders**> < share our complete resolution to defeat this terrorism.

14　>as **they** will indicate a little bit later<

15　<u>It is particularly barbaric</u> that **this** has happened on a day when people are meeting to try to help the problems of poverty in Africa, and the long term problems of climate change and the environment

16　Just as <u>it is reasonably clear</u> that **this** is a terrorist attack, or a series of terrorist attacks,

17　<u>it is also reasonably clear</u> that **it** is designed and aimed to coincide with the opening of the G8.

18　**There will be time to talk later about this**.

19　<u>It is important</u> however that **those engaged in terrorism** realise

20　that **our determination to defend our values and our way of life** is greater than their determination to cause death and destruction to innocent people in a desire to impose extremism on the world.

21 **Whatever** they do,

22 **it is our determination** that they will never succeed in destroying what we hold dear in this country and in other civilised nations throughout the world.

首先看看第 1—6 小句,我们可以看到,正如《我有一个梦想》一样,布莱尔以自己的说话人身份为经验主位开始了这次公开声明,解释了他为什么会做演讲。在第 2—4 小句中,我们看到"I"被重复为经验主位(第 2 小句),后来这一主位转变为作为普通公众(第 3 小句)的"you",然后是一个外排"we"(即不包括受话人),其中包括作为说话人的布莱尔,但延伸至其他未指明的不在场者,可能也包括政府。以这种方式使用第一人称和第二人称主位,布莱尔能够在作为信息提供者的他自己和政府,以及作为信息接受者的公众之间建立起关系,而后者是整个直接语境中的超主位。正如我们在上文马丁·路德·金的演讲中所看到的,我们可以将第 2 小句作为第 3 小句和第 4 小句的人际序言,也可对其作为小句本身进行分析。这里还有一个迂曲之处,因为第 3 小句本身可以作为第 4 小句的序言来加以分析,也可就该小句本身加以分析。使用这种双重人际主位使布莱尔既能将自己与公众之间的关系主位化,又能将语篇转移到对当天事件的描述上。在第 5—8 小句中,布莱尔向事件描述过渡,不过也强调信息尚不全面。他在第 5 小句中使用了一个**存在主位**(*existential theme*):

there is a limit ...

在这里,我们可以看到,在第 3 章中作为过程类型分析的存在结构也可以作为一种特定的主位类型加以分析,其中存在物作为**增强**主位(*enhanced Theme*)。它之所以被称为增强主位是因为它前面的"假位结构"允许存在物置于一个小句的末尾,因此作为"新"信息而获得声调突出(Halliday and Matthiessen 2004:87-92),即在语气中被强调,标志着这是受话人应该关注的部分。这样一来,"存在物"既是主位又是新信息,这是一种不同寻常的组合,是将新概念或参与者引入语篇的理想选择。在第 6 小句中,布莱尔回转到自己在直接语境中的信息提供者身份,并以己为主位,而在第 7 和第 8 小句中,布莱尔使用平行的存在结构来引入他演讲的主要主位——当天早些时候发生的袭击以及所造成的伤亡。

第 7 小句是另一个增强主位,这次是**增强型评价主位**(*enhanced evaluative Theme*),其中"假位"短语让评价词"clear"获得了声调突出。在第 4 章中,我们认为这种结构是显式客观情态,其中以"reasonable clear"为中值概率的例子。这种结构的另一个效果是布莱尔对情态的使用(一种模棱语形式)也被主位化了。在许多情况下,这可能并不特别重要,毕竟布莱尔使用的"增强"形式比起"更具一致性"的形式"that there have been a series of terrorist attacks in London is reasonably clear",标记性不强。因此,我们可以简单地说,这种结构是实现显式客观情态的一种手段。然而,当我们考察整个语篇时,我们将看到有充分的理由来考虑这一结构的语篇效应,因为布莱尔反复使用这个结构,将他的主张的模糊语和他对各种事件的评价主体化。第 8 小句也暗示了这一点,其中"obviously"是一个隐式客观情态(高概率)的例子,出现在存在主位中,而主位一直延续至存在物"casualties"。

在演讲开场部分,布莱尔以不同方式将三个不同且互相区别的概念主位化:1)他自己与公众和其他政治人物之间的关系;2)当天早些时候发生的事件;3)程度不同的、旨在限定他陈述的模糊限制语。正如我们稍后将看到的,这三个概念在正文的其余部分都有提及。

第 9 小句与第 8 小句并列,其中布莱尔将他对事件的反应主位化,并在此使用了包含公众的内包式"Our"作为主位的一部分。类似地,在第 10 小句中,布莱尔用"It is my intention"将对事件的反应主位化。这是第三类增强主位的一个例子,即**增强型经验主位**(*enhanced experiential Theme*),其中,经验意义的成分位于假位结构"it is"之后,被赋予声调突出。由于短语"my intention"回指"it",所以我将这整个结构标记为主位。请注意,布莱尔本可以说"My intention is to leave the city…"。但也要注意,意图也是一个情态特征。我在这里没有这样分析它(将其标记为人际主位),因为它显然是经验结构的一个组成部分,并且与其他例子不同,它不引导完整的小句。然而,其情态语义是明确的,这里的情态概念被具体化了(变成一个事物),这样就可以将它作为经验意义的一部分来加以讨论,而且就像在这个例子中这样将其主位化。另一种分析可以将"it is my intention"作为人际主位,并将其后的所有 to do 小句作为小句进行分析。通过这一分析可以看出,布莱尔作为这些小句中的隐性动作者被主位化了,我们的主位从情感反应转向了物质行动。两种分析都提供了对本语篇的洞见,分析的模糊性也是如此,允许情态和行为的双重主位化。结合这些分析可以看出,我们既有一个固定的情态主位,从概率(第 7 小句)转移到意图(第 10 小句),也有一个经验主位,从布莱尔的情绪和意图(第 2、6、9 和 10 小句)转移到布莱尔作为动作者——一个不仅在情绪上做出反应,而且还根据这些情绪采取行动的人(第 10 小句)。第 11 小句将这一主位与另一个强调执掌权力者行动意愿的增强经验主位并列起来并加以展开,但动作者换成了携手合作的里约集团领导人。

第 12—14 小句更直接地将主位重点放在里约集团领导人及其所代表的国家上,有三个无标记主位,(这在本文中似乎很特别!)每个都是以领导人或他们的国家为主位。

第 15 小句是另一个增强评价主位的例子,这次以非情态成分"barbaric"为主位。正如我们在第 4 章中看到的,评价和情态作为人际意义的要素紧密相连,它们之间的界限往往是模糊的。因此,第 14 小句中的增强评价主位照应了前面的情态增强评价主位。由于这个强化的主位后接一个完整的小句,所以我们可以把它作为一个人际主位来分析,这使得"this"(指当天的事件)成为经验主位。因此,我们再次看到主位在事件、反应和情态之间的分布,这些变动促进了整个语篇的展开。

第 16 小句也是如此,我们有一个情态增强评价主位(概率:中值)充当人际主位,后接经验主位"this",而这个经验主位与前一小句保持一致。第 17 小句重复了这一策略，之后第 18 小句使用了增强存在主位，引入了一个新概念"time to talk about this"，这与到目前为止本语篇的大量模糊限制语在语义上有某些相似之处。

第 19 小句使用另一个人际增强评价主位，后跟对比语篇主位"however"（一种罕见的情况，即语篇主位紧跟着人际主位，这是由该小句的有标记结构而得以实现的），以强调尽管行动不会立即发生，但是一旦发生，该行动将会是强而有力的。因此，这里与先前的主位转变有一定的相似性（作为感知者的布莱尔转变为作为动作者的布莱尔）。第 20 小句照应了这个想法，用了另一个主位"determination"，这是具体化情态的另一个例子，这次是意图：高值，而第 11 小句中是意图：中值。请注意，在第 20 小句中，"determination"只能被分析为经验主位，而不是增强人际主位。

演讲的最后，将第 21 小句主位中参与恐怖主义的人的行为与国家对此的回应进行对比，这是通过增强经验主位（意图：高值）"our determination"来实现的。在这最后一个小句中，增强主位后接一个完整的小句，因此它作为人际主位或经验主位的地位是有争议的——但考虑到语篇的展开方式，这似乎是完全恰当的——它是关于具体化的情态还是当天的事件？因此，作为整个语篇的**超新信息**（*hyperNew*），这些结束语既捕捉到了贯穿全文的主位模糊性，同时，如果从第 4 章评价内容的角度来回顾并对该语篇进行分析，这篇演讲强烈表达了"our"价值观的胜利，尽管敌人表现出了决心。它似乎在说"我们必须为一场漫长的战斗做好准备，前方有许多不确定因素，但我们的决心最终会胜出"——这是一条复杂的信息，通过布莱尔在这篇错综复杂的语篇中使用的许多主位手段，赋予该信息以连贯性。

练习 5.4

比较布莱尔和布什的演讲，讨论他们在说话人的定位、当代事件的故事情节（包括事件之间的关系）和不同受众这三方面的差异。不要忘了布什的讲话

（很大程度上?）是脱稿的,而布莱尔的讲话显然措辞非常谨慎。

5.7　总结

在这一章中,我们研究了如何使用各种主位手段来表示语篇之间的连续性和推进。分析语篇主位时,需要考虑八个核心要点:

(1)找出经验主位。

(2)主位是有标记的还是无标记的?

(3)如果有标记,还要找出主语。

(4)主位之间的推进方法是什么(固定、线性或衍生)?

(5)哪些主题主位化了,语篇如何在主题之间变换?

(6)有标记主位提供了什么阅读角度?

(7)主位是简单还是复杂?

(8)哪些人际成分被主位化了? 为什么?

处理了这些基本问题(参见 Thompson 2007,该书旨在进行总结,非常不错,可读性很强)之后,我们可以讨论语篇变量在构造语篇和突出某些角度和特征的过程中所发挥的功能,然后考虑语篇元功能如何在构建说话人的定位和作为话语的语篇的功能/效果方面所起的作用。

第6章　空间、时间和语篇块

6.1　引言

在第 2 章中,我们看到了语篇的各个部分是如何维持和转移话语语场的,其中往往混合了直接语境和移位语境。在上一章中,我们看到了主位的语法资源是如何将这些动作编织成语篇的。因此,我们可以说,主位的作用是使语篇本身具有连贯性,并显示语篇是如何实现整体性的。在这一章中,我们将探讨**连贯**(*coherence*)的另一个不同但相关的方面,即语篇是如何围绕说话人和他们的听众——语篇作为话语的指示中心——加以编织的。指示中心是指言语行为即时的此时此地、最直接的目的**位点**(*locus*)或场所。然而,正如我们所看到的,语篇往往集中在非直接的、移位的语境上,因此在这一章中,我们将探讨(一段)语篇可以被移位的不同程度,对此进行标志的语法手段,以及不同程度的移位的**修辞功能**(*rhetorical function*)。具有相同移位程度的语篇节段被称为**修辞单位**(*rhetorical units*),英语简写为 RU(Cloran 2010①)。然后,我们将再次重温主位问题,看看它们是如何用来标记连续修辞单位在功能上的关系的。

在第 2 章中,我们思考了构建同一子语场的语篇节段。修辞单位提供了一种

---

① 克洛兰称之为语境化/去语境化的程度,但由于语篇构建了语境,我更喜欢称之为移位语境距直接环境的位移程度。

将语篇分割成一致的节段的替代方法;如果再加上构建一致语旨的语篇节段,我们就有了三种不同的语篇划分方式,每个元功能一种。① 这些不同的划分可能重叠,也可能不重叠,正是重叠和离散的结合,使说话人能够通过混合连续性和变化来展开语篇——正是这些特征使其成为语篇。按照格雷戈里的理念,我们可以将在所有三个元功能上显示出连续性的语篇节段称为一个**阶段**(*phase*),这样当三个元功能中的任何一个发生重大变化时,我们就有了一个新阶段。

在某种程度上,阶段是本书的核心分析单位,我们之前一直在为其做铺垫。早前我们讨论过语场的变化可能对应着语旨的变化,因为说话人可能会随之采取不同的定位。现在,我们将扩展这一思想来讨论语场、语旨和语式(从修辞单位来看)的不同组合如何对应说话人在那个节点上的话语中的定位。哈桑(Halliday and Hasan 1985:55)将语场、语旨和语式的结合称为**语境结构**(*contextual configuration*),并强调了将所有三种元功能一起处理的重要性。阶段的变化也与互动社会语言学中的**框架**(*frame*,大致相当于语场,但在一定程度上也对应着语式)和**基脚**(*footing*,大致相当于语旨)的变化非常接近。通过观察不同的语境结构和转移,我们可以看到说话人如何通过在他们的话语行为中结合不同的经验意义、人际意义和语篇意义来为自己构建复杂而连贯的定位组合,还可以看到这些不同的定位如何依赖于环境的特征,以便被一个或多个受众接受或合法化。

6.2 修辞单位的类型

在下一节中,将通过乔治·布什第二次总统就职演说的开头 28 小句(语篇 6.1)来介绍如何进行修辞单元分析。完成分析后,我们将比较布什的演讲和奥

---

① 克洛兰将修辞单元视为源于所有三个元功能的语篇部分,但在我看来,它们本质上是语篇,因此我将把它们视为语篇连续性的代表。

巴马的第一次总统就职演说之间的异同。

语篇 6.1

1 Vice President Cheney, Mr. Chief Justice, President Carter, President Bush, President Clinton, reverend clergy, distinguished guests, fellow citizens: On this day, prescribed by law and marked by ceremony, we celebrate the durable wisdom of our Constitution,

2 and recall the deep commitments that unite our country.

3 I am grateful for the honor of this hour,

4 mindful of the consequential times in which we live,

5 and determined to fulfill the oath that I have sworn and you have witnessed.

6 At this second gathering, our duties are defined not by the words I use, but by the history we have seen together.

7 For a half century, America defended our own freedom by standing watch on distant borders.

8 After the shipwreck of some countries came years of relative quiet, years of repose, years of sabbatical

9 —and then there came a day of fire.

10 We have seen our vulnerability

11 —and we have seen its deepest source.

12 For as long as whole regions of the world simmer in resentment and tyranny—prone to ideologies that feed hatred and excuse murder—violence will gather,

13 and multiply in destructive power,

14 and cross the most defended borders,

15 and raise a mortal threat.

16 There is only one force of history that can break the reign of hatred and resentment, and expose the pretensions of tyrants, and reward the hopes of the decent and tolerant,

17 and that is the force of human freedom.

18 We are led, by events and common sense, to one conclusion:

19 The survival of liberty in our land increasingly depends on the success of liberty in other lands.

20 The best hope for peace in our world is the expansion of freedom in all the world.

21 America's vital interests and our deepest beliefs are now one.

22 From the day of our Founding, we have proclaimed that every man and woman on this earth has rights, and dignity, and matchless value, because they bear the image of the Maker of Heaven and earth.

23 Across the generations we have proclaimed the imperative of self-government,

24 because no one is fit to be a master,

25 and no one deserves to be a slave.

26 Advancing these ideals is the mission that created our Nation.

27 It is the honorable achievement of our fathers.

28 Now it is the urgent requirement of our nation's security, and the calling of our time.

（来源：白宫）

在分析修辞单位时，我们需要考虑两个语义特征的组合：被讨论的**中心实体**（*central entities*）和语篇节段的**事件朝向**（*event orientation*）。布什演讲的前五个小句很像塞巴斯蒂安·科和亨利叔叔的语篇的开头，都集中在直接活动上——布什站在观众面前做演讲。这一节段的中心实体——在语法上被体现为主语——是观众（第 1、2 小句）和布什本人（第 3—5 小句，在第 4、5 小句中省略）。布什和听众可以被称为话语中的**互动者**（*interactants*）、说话人和受话者。**事件朝向**（*event orientation*），语法上以所使用的时态表示，与说话时刻共时（即时）。当我们以互动者为中心实体，并且有**同时的**（*concurrent*）时间朝向时，我们便将语篇的节段称作**评论**（*Commentary*），这是最直接的修辞单位之一。

在第 6 小句中有一点不同。核心实体仍然是布什和他的（更广泛的）受众，但布什所指的"duties"并不像他站在那里那样直接——最好将之描述为**习惯性的**（*habitual*）。当我们有互动者作为中心实体，并且有习惯性事件朝向时，我们将修辞单位标记为**反思**（*Reflection*）。那么，请注意布什是如何通过中心实体来保持连续性，但却从事件朝向的角度来推进语篇的。

在第 7—11 小句中，事件朝向不再是共时的，而是**事先的**（*prior*）（尽管第 10 小句和第 11 小句中的现在完成式可以被视为过去和现在的结合）。每当我们有事先的事件朝向时,无论中心实体是谁或什么,我们都将修辞单位标记为**追述**(*Recount*)。

第 12—15 小句再次改变了事件朝向,以情态"will"表示**预测**(*Prediction*)。预测可以指任何中心实体,尽管也有一个**计划修辞单位**(*Plan* RU),它以互动者为中心,但更为明确(例如,以非情态的 WILL 或是 GOING TO 为标志)。

第 16—20 小句提供了另一种类型的修辞单位,即一种**描述**(*Account*),其中心实体(这里分别体现为"human freedom""liberty"和"peace"——这是一个有趣的语义展开的例子)不存在于直接环境中(克洛兰称为物质情境环境,或 MSS),事件朝向是习惯性的。请注意,第 18 小句在意义上主要是人际的,因此不作为单独的评论进行分析。

第 21 小句是另一个反思;第 22—27 小句是另一次追述;第 28 小句是进一步的反思。语篇中有几种修辞单位类型没有出现:**行动**(*Actions*),涉及控制直接语境的修辞单位,通常是祈使句(正如我们在《我有一个梦想》中看到的)或使用情态语的间接命令;**观察**(*Observations*),即 MSS 中存在的非互动者的习惯性朝向;**报告**(*Reports*),即 MSS 中不存在的人或事物的共时或持续的(而不是习惯性的)朝向;**概括**(*Generalisations*),即整个群体的人或事物的习惯性朝向;还有**猜测**(*Conjectures*),它们比预测有着更多的假设性。其中一些类型在含义上非常接近,例如,如果布什在第 12 小句中说,在这种情况下"violence gathers",而不是预测它"will gather",那么修辞单位将是一种概括,而不是预测;如果他说它"might gather",那将是一种猜测。因此,在分配修辞单位标签时,并不是总能够完全确定,这是说话人可以利用的语言"模糊"边界的一个例子!

表 6.1 提供了修辞单位类型的完整图式。下面是一个连续体,大致表明了不同的修辞单位类型的(从在构建语境中对其他行为最具辅助性的,到最具构成性的)顺序。或者,换句话说,从那些构建最直接的语境的修辞单位,到那些构建移位最远的修辞单位。我说,这只是一个大致的分类,因为涉及 MSS 之外的人或事的追述可能会被认为比涉及互动者本身的计划或猜测移位更远(要更

全面地了解修辞单位,请参见 Cloran 2010)。

表 6.1　修辞单位的类型

事件朝向	习惯性的	已然	事先	非已然	
中心实体		共时		物品/服务交换	信息交换
在 MSS 内			追述	行动	预测　猜测性的
互动者	反思	评论			计划/预测　猜测
其他:人/物	观察				预测
不在 MSS 内					
人/物	叙述	报告			预测
类	概括				

［附注］

语言在社交过程中角色的连续体:

辅助性的［例如直接的］　　　　　　　　　　　　　构成性的［例如移位的］

动作—评论观察—反思报告—追述、叙述、计划—预测、猜测、概括

　　在表 6.2 中,我添加了几列,列出了语场和语旨的变化,以补充上述语式(修辞单位)的展开。语场包括**题材**(*subject matter*),可能包括**关键主题**(*motifs*)项下不断变化的词汇,以及主要的及物性类型。语旨包括语气特征、情态特征和评价特征。

表 6.2　布什演讲中的修辞单位

小句	阶段	语场	语旨	语式/修辞单位
1—5	**Positioning of self as leader and servant**, one among many Americans recalling the past	President/oath Verbal, mental, and relational processes of remembrance	I as President as sworn representative of the people	评论

续表

小句	阶段	语场	语旨	语式/修辞单位
6	**Linking common past to present duties**.	Memories defining duties	Presidential role (I) as secondary to shared history (we)	反思
7—11	**US as witness to change from peace to troubles**	We become "America" Behavioural and mental processes of watching as peace turned to trouble	Our shared history as defenders of American dream of freedom	追述
12—15		"Vulnerability" identified as other nations' tyranny Material processes of evil spreading	International others appraised negatively (−Judgement; −Affect)	预测
16—20	**Identification of America's historic mission as the overcoming of evil**.	Freedom as antidote to tyranny.	Contrast of positive and negative appraisal in international context (+/− Judgement); common sense conclusions of 'right' (+Judgement)	叙述
21		Freedom identified as simultaneously US ideal and protector of interests i	Dual positive Appraisal (+ security) and (+social sanction)	反思
22—27		Verbal processes of America proclaiming liberty becoming clauses identifying America's destiny as the overcoming of evil.	We and founding fathers as one, appraised positively as evaluators (+Judgement)	追述
28	**Historic and present mission identified**	America destiny again identified as the overcoming of evil.	Strong positive Judgement of positive action.	反思

有标记主位也可以包含在语式列中,因为这些通常是角度转移的语篇标记。该表还显示了语篇整体节段的阶段性推进,即语境结构的变化。注意,对第 7—15 小句和第 16—27 小句,我只给了这两个阶段一个标签,尽管这两个阶段内语境结构都有变化。这是因为我认为两者虽然有所不同,但每一节中的各节段共同作用而达到了相同的效果。当然,如果觉得有用的话,还是可以对二者进行区分。

练习6.1

表 6.3 是我对奥巴马第一次总统就职演说开头 17 小句(语篇 6.2)的阶段性分析。看看这个篇章,并将其与布什的讲话进行比较,然后回答下面的问题。

表6.3 奥巴马演讲中的修辞单元

小句	阶段	语场	语旨	语式/修辞单位
1—2	Positioning of self as leader and servant	President/oath Verbal/behavioural processes and lexis of speaking. Oath taken in good times and bad.	I as President, entrusted by people = personal authority within context of history. Positive appraisal of fortitude (+Judgement)	评论
3—4			I as President and one of line; oath as sign of duty, before God	追述
5			Duty in hardship; contrastive appraisal of prosperity (+/−Affect)	叙述
6—8	Establish theme	Americans'	We the People	追述

续表

小句	阶段	语场	语旨	语式/修辞单位
	of vagaries of history and	endurance in general facing problems.	throughout history; positive appraisal	反思
9	shared endurance of leaders and populace	Relational Processes and lexis of endurance.	of loyalty to founding documents (+Judgement)	行动
10—16	Establish theme	Present hardships.	We the People	反思
17	of shared present problems	Relational Processes with America as Carrier and Attributes of crisis. Material Processes of deterioration becoming a token of general problems.	now; common sense understanding; 'our' shared problems; negative evaluation of current domestic situation (-Affect)	概括

语篇 6.2

1 My fellow citizens: I stand here today humbled by the task before us, grateful for the trust you have bestowed, mindful of the sacrifices borne by our ancestors.

2 I thank President Bush for his service to our nation, as well as the generosity and cooperation he has shown throughout this transition.

3 Forty-four Americans have now taken the presidential oath.

4 The words have been spoken during rising tides of prosperity and the still waters of peace.

5 Yet, every so often the oath is taken amidst gathering clouds and raging storms.

6 At these moments, America has carried on not simply because of the skill or vision of those in high office,

7　but because We the People have remained faithful to the ideals of our forbearers, and true to our founding documents.

8　So it has been.

9　So it must be with this generation of Americans.

10　That we are in the midst of crisis is now well understood.

11　Our nation is at war, against a far-reaching network of violence and hatred.

12　Our economy is badly weakened, a consequence of greed and irresponsibility on the part of some, but also our collective failure to make hard choices and prepare the nation for a new age.

13　Homes have been lost; jobs shed; businesses shuttered.

14　Our health care is too costly;

15　our schools fail too many;

16　and each day brings further evidence that the ways we use energy strengthen our adversaries and threaten our planet.

17　These are the indicators of crisis, subject to data and statistics.

问题

(1) 你认为这两个演讲的开头与更具体的话题(topics)和主题(motifs)的展开之间有什么相似之处? 你如何解释这些相似之处?

(2) 你认为这两个语篇的展开方式有什么不同? 为了一方面保持连续性、另一方面推进语篇,二者用了什么样的语言手段?

(3) 这两个语篇以何种方式在直接语境和移位语境之间变动? 这会产生什么影响? 它与就职演说语篇的相关性是什么?

(4) 考虑到不同的说话人和语篇产生的历史环境,你如何将这些语篇差异与演讲话语联系起来?

(5) 看看下面奥巴马演讲的后一部分,描述一下奥巴马的定位。

(6) 什么样的环境条件"允许"奥巴马采取他在本节中的定位? 想想摘录的语境结构,以及这与奥巴马个人身份(尤其是作为美国第一位非裔总统)的联系,他演讲的各种受众,以及美国近代(以及相对近期)历史的故事情节。

语篇 6.3

奥巴马第二次总统就职演说的后面部分

1　And for those who seek to advance their aims by inducing terror and slaughtering innocents, we say to you now

2　That "Our spirit is stronger and cannot be broken.

3　You cannot outlast us,

4　and we will defeat you."

5　For we know

6　that our patchwork heritage is a strength, not a weakness.

7　We are a nation of Christians and Muslims, Jews and Hindus, and nonbelievers.

8　We are shaped by every language and culture,

9　drawn from every end of this Earth.

10　And because we have tasted the bitter swill of civil war and segregation

11　and emerged from that dark chapter stronger and more united,

12　we cannot help but believe

13　that the old hatreds shall someday pass;

14　that the lines of tribe shall soon dissolve;

15　that as the world grows smaller,

16　our common humanity shall reveal itself;

17　and that America must play its role in ushering in a new era of peace.

18　To the Muslim world, we seek a new way forward, based on mutual interest and mutual respect.

19　To those leaders around the globe who seek to sow conflict or blame their society's ills on the West, know

20　that your people will judge you on what you can build, not what you destroy.

21　To those who cling to power through corruption and deceit and the silencing of dissent, know

22　that you are on the wrong side of history,

23　but that we will extend a hand if you are willing to unclench your fist.

24　To the people of poor nations, we pledge//to work alongside you to make your farms flourish and let clean waters flow; to nourish starved bodies and feed hungry minds.

6.3 修辞单位之间的关系

上面的分析给人的印象是修辞单元是按线性顺序推进的,但这并不是其全貌。正如我前面所说,主位和述位是构建语篇的另一种主要语法手段,它们参与了修辞单位的推进。让我们先来看看前一章所描述的"固定主位"与"线性主位"的关系,以及布什演说中修辞单元的变化。下面的描述非常简短,如果您在阅读时同时参考前面的语篇 6.1 和后面的表 6.4,将会有所帮助。修辞单位的第一个变化是在第 5 小句和第 6 小句之间。第 6 小句的主位是"At the second gathering"。因为这是一个有标记主位(时间/地点环境),所以看主位推进时,我们也应该考虑主语"our duties"。有标记的主位和主语照应了第 1 小句的"ceremony"和第 5 小句的"the oath that I have sworn"的语义。当在一个新修辞单位的主位中照应前面的概念时,我们说该修辞单位**嵌入**(*embedded*)到了另一个修辞单位(即**矩阵修辞单位** *matrix* RU)中。这是因为新的修辞单位通过深化旧的修辞单位的一个特定方面来展开旧的修辞单位。因此,第二个修辞单位在矩阵修辞单位中起一定作用,并被视为矩阵修辞单位的一部分。正如所暗示的那样,其信号就是嵌入修辞单位的主位并不完全是新的。严格地说,新的修辞单位并不是完全新的或独立的,因为它形成了矩阵修辞单位的一部分,并且其本身就是一个修辞单位。为了显示这种嵌入,从第 6 小句开始的修辞单位被标记为 1 并被置于方框中以表示它完全在其矩阵修辞单位内。

如发生在第 6 小句和第 7 小句之间修辞单位的下一个变化所示,嵌入行为可能很复杂。这里我们有另一个环境成分,"For a half century"和主语"America"。"America"一词的使用显然继承了(并推进了)前一小句(及之前)中"we"的概念,因此我们有了另一层嵌入。这意味着从第 7 小句开始的修辞单位是双重嵌入的,既嵌入了从第 6 小句开始的矩阵修辞单位,又嵌入了该矩阵修辞单位的矩阵修辞单位(从第 1 小句开始的)。换言之,这里仍在深入探讨同样的话题。为了表示这种双重嵌入,从第 7 小句开始的修辞单位被标记为 1.1,并被完全置于编号为 1 的修辞单位的方框中。所以,我们便有了一个方框里的方框。

从第 12 小句开始的下一个修辞单位是进一步的嵌入,因为有标记主位和主语都照应和推进了"our vulnerability",将之归结为来自他者的"resentment and tyranny"以及"ideologies"的"violence"。因此,这个修辞单位被标记为 1.1.1,这是一个三重嵌入,用两重方框里的方框表示!

然后,我们在第 16 小句中有了一些不同的内容,它用"the reign of hatred and resentment… and the pretensions of tyrants"这些言语照应了前面所说的"tyranny"。然而,由于这些概念是在述位中表达的,而不是在主位中表达的,因此这里没有再继续深入探究最初的概念,而是用一个新的主位元素"one force in history"对这个概念进行**扩展**(*expansion*),然后可以加以推进。然而,由于这一主位照应了第 6 小句中的"history"概念,因此该修辞单位被嵌入到修辞单位 1 中,并被标记为 1.2(因为 1.1 已经出现)。因此,从第 16 小句开始的修辞单位既是前面修辞单位的扩展,又嵌入了从第 6 小句开始的修辞单位中。这通过编号和方框的设置来表示,与之前的修辞单位分开,但嵌入从第 6 小句开始的修辞单位中(而该单位本身又已嵌入在从第 1 小句开始的修辞单位中)。

修辞单位的下一个变化发生在第 21 小句和第 22 小句之间。在这里,通过"every man and woman… Maker of Heaven and Earth"照应了第 21 小句中"America's deepest beliefs"的概念。这是第 22 小句的述位,因此我们又看到了另一个扩展的例子。然而,主位"From the day of our founding"和主语"we"再次照应了前面的概念,因此这个修辞单位就嵌入到了从第 6 小句开始的修辞单位中。这通过编号和方框的设置来显示。也许可以说,"we"这个主语照应了前一个小句中的"America",但我认为我的分析更好地抓住了整体趋势。当我们处理像这样紧密衔接的语篇时,通常会有可以讨论的空间,而所做的分析往往需要做出改变,直到整个语篇的框架实现整体性。

　　同样地,我把修辞单元中在第 27 小句和第 28 小句之间最后一个变化标记为一个扩展,因为我认为述位中对前面思想的阐述是这一小句的核心推进方式。我将这个修辞单位标记为嵌入从第 6 小句开始的修辞单位中,因为在有标记主位"now"中的时间指称回到了第 6 小句中早些时候提到的"at this second gathering"。

　　请注意,嵌入和**细化**(*elaboration*)仅在修辞单位发生变化时才被标记。如果语场或语旨发生变化,而修辞单位没有变化,则不会标记任何关系(尽管这将代表一个不同的阶段)。

　　当一个新的修辞单位没有从以前的修辞单位中吸取概念时,我们可以分两种情况来分析。如果新的修辞单位吸取了前文修辞单位的概念,我们可以说它是**不连续的**(*discontinuous*)。如果没有连续性,那么无论出于何种意图和目的,我们都说这是一个新的语篇,因为韩礼德和哈桑(Halliday and Hasan 1976)将语篇定义为连贯的语言节段。然而,许多语篇中包含的序言可能与下文没有衔接,但显然是语篇的一部分。

　　尽管,正如我们在两篇演讲以及在其他语篇中看到的那样,演讲者通常会设法在序言和后面的内容之间建立一种衔接。这是修辞艺术的一部分。所有这些可能看起来非常复杂,是一种分析的精巧招数,但没有真实地反映说话人对语篇所做的处理。然而,我相信如果你观察表 6.4 中的分析时思考一下嵌入和扩展意味着什么,你会感觉到,真真切切地感受到,这就是实情,这就是语篇的实现连贯和展开的方式。

练习 6.2

(1)讨论表 6.4 中标记的修辞单位之间的关系,并解释一下这些关系是如何表明整个演讲在这个节段的推进的。

表 6.4 布什演讲中修辞单位间的关系

	评论
Vice President Cheney, Mr. Chief Justice, President Carter, President Bush, President Clinton, reverend clergy, distinguished guests, fellow citizens:	
On this day, prescribed by law and marked by ceremony, we celebrate the durable wisdom of our Constitution, and recall the deep commitments that unite our country. I am grateful for the honor of this hour, mindful of the consequential times in which we live, and determined to fulfill the oath that I have sworn and you have witnessed.	
At this second gathering, our duties are defined not by the words I use, but by the history we have seen together.	1 反思
For a half century, America defended our own freedom by standing. watch on distant borders. After the shipwreck of some nations came years of relative quiet, years of repose, years of sabbatical-and then there came a day of fire. We have seen our vulnerability-and we have seen its deepest source	1.1 追述
For as long as whole regions of the world simmer in resentment and tyranny—prone to ideologies that feed hatred and excuse murder—violence will gather, and multiply in destructive power, and cross the most defended borders, and raise a mortal threat.	1.1.1 预测

There is only one force of history that can break the reign of hatred and resentment and expose the pretensions of tyrants, and reward the hopes of the decent and tolerant, and that is the force of human freedom. We are led, by events and common sense, to one conclusion: The survival of liberty in our land increasingly depends on the success of liberty in other lands. The best hope for peace in our world is the expansion of freedom in all the world. America's vital interests and our deepest beliefs are now one.	1.2 描述
From the day of our Founding, we have proclaimed that every man and woman . on this earth has rights, and dignity, and matchless value, because they bear the image of the Maker of Heaven and earth. Across the generations we have proclaimed the imperative of self-government, because no one is fit to be a master, and no one deserves to be a slave. Advancing these ideals is the mission that created our Nation. It is the honorable achievement of our fathers.	1.3 追述
Now it is the urgent requirement of our nation's security, and the calling of our time.	

（2）看看布什演讲中的这些有标记主位，讨论这些主位如何标志语篇的推进角度，以及它们如何与修辞单位的变化相互作用。

（3）现在来看下表中奥巴马的演讲开场白中对修辞单位关系的分析，并讨论两个语篇之间的相似性和差异，以及它们如何对应作为历史语境中的话语的这两个语篇。

表 6.5　奥巴马就职演讲中修辞单位之间的关系

1	My fellow citizens: I stand here today humbled by the task before us, grateful for the trust you have bestowed, mindful of the sacrifices borne by our ancestors.	评论

2	I thank President Bush for his service to our nation, as well as the generosity and cooperation he has shown throughout this transition.	
3	Forty-four Americans have now taken the presidential oath	追述
4	The words have been spoken during rising tides of prosperity and the still waters of peace.	
5	Yet, every so often the oath is taken amidst gathering clouds and raging storms.	1 叙述
6	At these moments, America has carried on not simply because of the skill or vision of those in high office,	1.1 追述
7	but because We the People have remained faithful to the ideals of our forbearers, and true to our founding documents.	
8	So it has been.	
9	So it must be with this generation of Americans.	1.1.1 行动
10	That we are in the midst of crisis is now well understood.	1.2 评论
11	Our nation is at war, against a far-reaching network of violence and hatred.	
12	Our economy is badly weakened, a consequence of greed and irresponsibility on the part of some, but also our collective failure to make hard choices and prepare the nation for a new age.	
13	Homes have been lost; jobs shed; businesses shuttered.	
14	Our health care is too costly;	
15	our schools fail too many;	
16	and each day brings further evidence that the ways we use energy strengthen our adversaries and threaten our planet.	
17	These are the indicators of crisis, subject to data and statistics.	1.2.1 概括

6.4　总结

在这一章中,我们研究了修辞单位以及语篇各部分与说话人和受话人在说话时构成的指示中心之间的关系。与第 2 章中介绍的直接语境和移位语境的概念相比,它提供了一个更精细的区别。我们还看到了修辞单位之间的联系,这些联系建立在第 5 章介绍的主位推进的分析之上,并有所拓展。

因此,通过对修辞单位的研究,我们对这三种元功能意义的探讨便结束了。我在这里提出了一种分析这三种意义如何在说话人定位方面相互作用的方法,并在这三个方面比较了布什和奥巴马就职演讲的开场部分。在本书的最后一章,我们将对我们目前为止分析的一些语篇再做全面分析,然后要考虑一些可以用我们的分析方法来说明和讨论的社会语言学和话语分析问题。

第 7 章　声音与混合

7.1　引言

在第 2 章到第 6 章中，我们依次研究了相关词汇和语法特征，它们被用来构建三种不同类型的意义——体验意义、人际意义和语篇意义。以这种方式分析语篇的目的是为更宏观的探究做好铺垫，以研究它们在现实生活中如何运作、它们可能服务于什么目的以及它们需要什么条件才能有效等方面的问题。为了便于呈现内容，我们逐一讨论了这些意义的各个方面。然而，虽然从语篇的角度看，每一个分析领域都是可能的，但在探究语篇如何作为话语发挥功能时，最重要的是任一节点上不同类型意义的相互作用，以及不同阶段的组合顺序。在前一章中，我们就此稍作思考，然后在最后一章中，我们将更详细地探讨语篇中不同类型的意义如何在话语中协同发挥作用。这里的讨论将集中在我在圭亚那的实地调查中的例子上，但也会探讨社会语言学和批评语言学中的一些关键概念以及它们与定位和权力的关系，包括声音、语篇互文性和话语互文性、角色和混合。

7.2　关键概念 2

为了介绍本章中讨论的一些关键概念，让我们再看看在第 1 章中讨论过的坎特伯雷大主教的圣诞布道,在此复制为语篇 7.1。这将为我们做好铺垫,以便更细致地分析通过莎拉和亨利叔叔解释可持续利用区的过程(我们已经在第 2 章中讨论过)而引入的概念。

语篇 7.1

1　The most pressing question we now face, we might well say, is who and where we

2　are as a society.

3　Bonds have been broken,

4　trust abused and lost.

5　Whether it's an urban rioter mindlessly burning down a small shop that serves his

6　community or a speculator turning his back on the question of who bears the ultimate

7　cost for his acquisitive adventures in the virtual reality of today's financial world,

8　the picture is of atoms spinning apart in the dark. But into that dark, the word of God

9　has entered, in love and judgement,

10　and has not been overcome

11　… in the darkness … the question sounds as clear as ever:

12　to each of us, and to our church and our society: Britain, where are you?

我从语篇 7.1 中所观察到的第一点是,它似乎混合了来自两种不同**话语** (*Discourses*)的语言。首字母 D 大写的"Discourses(话语)"指的是关于某一特定主题的全部谈话以及关于讨论方式的所有传统。例如,我们可以提到马克思主义、女权主义或关于开发的话语。因此,大 D 话语与小 d 话语是不同的,小 d 话语是任一语境中的谈话。(又是出于必要,本章汉语译文中将以"话语(d)"来表示小 d 话语,而"话语"则是指大 D 话语。——译者注)这两者当然有着错综复杂的联系,因为话语的传统带给我们(我试图在定位大卫之星中表达正确)话

语的约束和功能可供性。已经确立的语篇特征通常有较高的可识别性,语言学界已经开展了大量工作,以确定话语之间的语言差异,并从社会政治的角度讨论这些差异的作用(Fairclough 1992;Young and Fitzgerald 2006)。最近的一个趋势是,尤其在批评性话语分析(CDA)中,研究一种话语的语言特征是如何**殖民**(*colonise*)其他话语的。例如,当教育话语呈现出营销术的语言特征(即被营销话语(d)所殖民)时,这被称为话语互文性,费尔克劳夫(Fairclough 2003:218)将其定义为:"[语篇]所依据的语类、话语(d)和风格的特定组合,以及不同语类、话语(d)或风格在语篇中的表现方式(或'共同作用')。"

"殖民"一词暗含有利于殖民者的权力失衡状态。但**话语互文性**(*interdiscursivity*)也允许权力关系逆转,因为主导性话语的特征可以为少数群体**所挪用**(*appropriate*),并为他们自己的目的服务(见下文和 Bartlett 2012a)。在这种情况下,定位之星上所有的点可以被视为扰动现状的战略操纵区。

话语互文性是指一系列语言特征从一种话语进入另一种话语,它不同于通过引用或释义简单地将语言片段从一个语篇转入另一个语篇。二者都被称为互文性,但是,按照费尔克劳夫的理念,我们在本书中采用的方法是将互文性一词的意义限定为费尔克劳夫所说的互文性(Fairclough 2003:218):"语篇的互文性是指语篇中存在其他语篇的构成元素⋯⋯这些语篇也许有着各种各样的联系。"

在语篇7.1中,有一个明显的互文性例子,"But into that dark, the word of God has entered, in love and judgement, and has not been overcome",这与《以赛亚书(9:2)》产生了特别的共鸣,"The people that walked in darkness have seen a great light: they that dwell in the land of the shadow of death, upon them hath the light shined",这是圣诞节时人们经常在教堂里读的经文。这句话还与大量其他基督教圣经语录产生了共鸣,这些语录显示了彼此之间高度的互文性。这样的引用和释义是基督教布道的主要内容,因此在这里我们不应该感到惊讶;更令人感兴趣的是布道的开头部分,其中提到了城市暴徒和鲁莽的投机者,以及最近事件的经济代价和社会代价。在政治演讲中听到这样的语言(就内容和表达而言），我们就不会那么惊讶了。因此，在布道中使用这样的语言便使之成为一个话语互文性的例子。如果这是事情的全部，那么话语互文性的概念将意味着存在稳定且易于识别的话语，让我们能识别一种话语的特征何时进入了另一种话语的领域。但一个事实被忽略了，即今天的稳定话语是昨天的话语互文性的产物（Foucault 1972），而今天看起来是有标记的用法明天将变得司空见惯。例如，尽管语篇 7.1 可能仍然被标记为混合了两种话语（d），但在我们这个时代神职人员进入政治辩论语境变得越来越寻常，因此语篇 7.1 的混合特征正逐渐变成**自然化的**（*naturalised*）单一话语的特征。

话语互文性这个词经常与**语类理论**（*genre theory*）联系在一起使用。"语类"一词指的是在给定的社区中通过语言进行社会行为的公认方式，许多语言学工作都涉及语类描述，从服务会面（见第 2 章）到大学章程、学术论文和政治访谈。因此，语类的重点在于已经存在的稳定的做事方式，而话语互文性是一种解释不同话语语类中新特征的侵入方式。虽然到目前为止，我们在这本书中介绍过的许多工具都可以用于语类描述，但我在本章余下部分将采取一个相当不同的角度，因为我的重点不是描述通过语言行事时既定方式的语言特征（尽管这很有用），而是关注人们的社会差异会产生什么样的模式，以及他们在语言上构建这些差异的方式。因此，虽然语类分析侧重于语言用于不同目的时的可见结构模式，但我们更关注的是语言中不那么结构化但同样系统化的社会关系模式，即被体现的各种**声音**（*voices*）。

声音这个社会语言学概念指的是某个社区特定的说话方式，以及语言在该社区中发挥的社会功能。以下引用自戴尔·海姆斯（Blommaert 2005：70 中的1996：45），他是关于声音模式的主要理论家之一。在这本书中，他将说话方式或语言功能组织的概念与沃尔夫的语言相对性概念进行了比较，后者认为语言结构的差异揭示了不同群体用物理手段构建世界的方式：

> 第二种语言相对性涉及语言的各种功能，它的意义不仅仅是批判性、警示性的。作为一种社会语言学方法，它呼吁人们关注社会互动中语

言特征的组织。相关研究已经逐渐表明,对说话方式的描述可以揭示基本的文化价值观和取向。所揭示的世界不是沃尔夫所关注的物理关系的本体论和认识论世界,而是社会关系的世界。所揭示的不是对空间、时间、振动现象等的取向,而是对人、角色、地位、权利和义务、尊重和行为的取向。

显然,语言编码"对人、角色、地位、权利和义务、尊重和行为的取向"的方式一直是本书的中心思想。海姆斯的声音概念的不同之处在于,在前几章中,我们一直看的是话语的个别实例,以了解这些取向是如何被策略性地操纵的,而声音则暗示有一些通过语言来进行的社会行为方式是深嵌于社区之中的。正如海姆斯在上面的引文中所指出的,这提出了有关社会互动、资源获取和流动性的重要问题。我们将在本章末再回头谈谈这些概念。现在,我们将重新看看莎拉和亨利叔叔就可持续利用区向当地社区所做的解释,以详细探究声音的概念,并思考当不同的声音聚集于一个话语中时,会发生什么,这是一种看待话语互文性的不同方式。

7.3 声音、角色和混合

我们在第 2 章中看到,尽管莎拉和亨利叔叔在解释同一个概念——可持续利用区——但他们所构建的语场却是十分不同的。在那一章中,笔者还指出两个语篇中直接语境和移位语境的混合是不同的——这一观点在第 6 章引入修辞单元概念后得到了展开。我们现在可以更详细地了解这些想法,在我们的分析中加入人际特征,看看两位说话人在说话方式上的差异是否能揭示出不同社区的声音的某些规律。

第 2 章中解释过在莎拉(和其他人)尝试向受众解释可持续利用区的概念后,亨利叔叔作出了他的话语贡献,并且大家一致认为亨利叔叔在其他人失败的地方取得了成功。这让我好奇亨利叔叔话语贡献的语篇特征是如何使这成为可能的。因为当时我刚刚接触到修辞单位,让我颇为欣喜,于是我决定对这两个语篇进行修辞单位分析。这里限于篇幅,不能复制全篇的分析(如果想了解更多,请参阅 Bartlett 2012a),只是在下面节选了亨利叔叔的话语贡献中具有代表性的一节:

语篇 7.2　NRDDB **会议** 4/11/2000

叙述

2　So you have(TAPE TURNS)…

3　…(slender)lines,

4　so that you can observe … changes.

5　How things changes?

6　How do they form?

7　What happen within a year after, within a year, five year, a ten year, a fifteen year period?

1.1 预测

8　So, you would get to understand the forest better

9　and those things would be left in their normal state.

1.2 反思

10　Because there are other important issues which we,

11　because we live among them,

12　we live inside,

13　it's a way of life, we take it for granted.

14　We are not(x),

15　many of us do not have sense of value,

16　don't know how valuable those things are to us,

17　and we just discard it, like many of us who pushing fire in the savannah

18　you know how many innocent birds' lives you destroying

19　(probably, even though xx xxx)?

20　If a snake(xxxxxxx xxxxx)inside your house?

1.2.1 行动

21 So, don't blame the snakes

22 where you can't put fire in the savannah,

1.2.1.1 反思

23 it's not good,

24 it's a very bad habit, like poisoning,

25 all these things are detrimental.

26 But because we never study it in depth,

27 we don't know how disastrous it is.

1.3 评论

28 So these are things which we are now asked to participate in our knowledge (about it), to find certain things.

29 And when we come to sustainability of the forest,

30 it does not confine that to Iwokrama alone,

31 we have to look on the other communities way outside.

1.3.1 猜测

32 Because you might not find

33 (when it—

34 when the plant come,) to assess it:

35 "What do we have?

36 Okay, this piece of thing, yeah yeah,

37 we'll try this for sustainable utilisation."

38 What is there that we can use sustainably?

39 One of the things you have to do is research.

1.4 追述

40 A lot has been done with animals, reptiles, birds, and all those things.

41 Bit of a botanical collection was done,

42 there's a lot more to be done.

43 The greenhearts of Iwokrama, that was one of the key elements they (classified).

1.4.1 描述

44　They want to do（away with them）now.

45　Because no sense putting up all the Wilderness Preserve

46　and then there's no greenheart in there.

1.4.1.1 预测

47　And we leave that for commercial harvesting, sustainable ....

48　in a short while it will disappear.

49　So they have to pinpoint those areas.

1.5 评论

50　Now they have a good idea,

51　but I'm still a bit sceptical about certain areas I notice that are for sustainable

1.5.1 描述

53　"Oh oh of course it just ends there",

54　and to have a wilderness preserve,

55　and you have a sustainable portion（xxxxxxx）

1.5.1.1 预测

56　to my mind it will backfire after you get（x）population,

57　because this wildlife（is our stuff）

58　as soon as applications start here,

59　（we're started … xx）.

60　And once they adapt,

61　there are migration uhm migratory routes which they will take

62　and they will find themselves right up in Pakaraimas for the next.

63　So these are things still to be discussed

64　because there is not—

> 65　I don't think that that is already confirmed where (x),
>
> 66 those are just tentative demarcation (x).

莎拉和亨利叔叔的话语贡献都是从描述他们参加的会议开始的(叙述和重述)(莎拉贡献的语篇见第 2 章),但后来发生了一些有趣的事情——莎拉接着使用了大量非语境化的语言(即构建移位语境的语言),比如概括,而亨利叔叔反复将自己的观点语境化,手段是通过在他的追述中嵌入(见第 6 章)评论和反思(如语篇 7.2 所示),以及通过命令和警示之类的行动,使这些概念更接近他的受众和社区的生活方式。图 7.1 展示了通过多重嵌入实现情境化的最典型的例子(来自亨利叔叔话语贡献中的其他部分)。

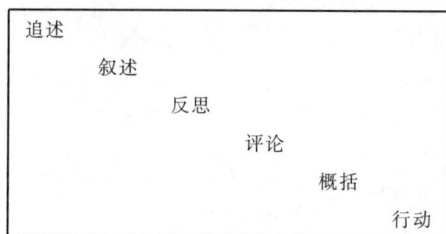

图 7.1　亨利叔叔话语贡献中其他部分的修辞单位结构

作为我的实地调查工作的一部分,我撰写了一份关于北鲁普努尼大草原生活的民族志报告,揭示了社区传递环境、农业和狩猎相关信息的正常方式实际上是通过提供他们正在做的事情的评论,以便他们的孩子通过观察来学习。这样,亨利叔叔使用高度语境化的语言,在语篇性方面更接近于社区的声音或说话方式。

在经验意义和人际意义方面也可以观察到类似的规律。如第 2 章所述,莎拉和亨利叔叔以非常不同的方式构建了可持续利用区——莎拉的角度是会议、团体和组织,以及营销方面;与此相对,亨利叔叔解释可持续利用区的角度是森林资源和社区关于这些资源的知识以及他们与环境互动的日常实践。注意,上述海姆斯的声音概念似乎忽视了经验意义,而倾向于声音的人际方面,将理解世界被语言描述的方式归结为沃尔夫式的、结构性的语言相对性概念。然而,沃尔夫的概念与这里的情况有着重要的区别。沃尔夫讨论了关键概念在不同语言的语法中的不同编码方式，以及其如何反映世界观的差异，而我认为我们在这里讨论的是对（通过持续的社区对话以及作为社会行动的语言所创造出的）世界的理解。从这些角度看，声音既包含人际特征的方面，又包含对世界的各种经验表达方面，以及语境化情况下的语篇特征和修辞单位。理解了这一点后，我们可以说亨利叔叔基于社区关于森林的知识及其与森林的互动而对可持续利用区做出的表述也是社区声音的一个特征。

再说说人际关系。莎拉话语贡献的一个特点是它在很大程度上是通过无情态的陈述句体现的，依靠她作为知识渊博的局外人的身份赋予她以权威。相比之下，亨利叔叔的话语贡献则充满了"必须"和祈使句，这反映了他作为社区长者的地位和他能够吩咐社区做事的权威。这两种贡献之间的另一个明显的人际差异是，对于萨拉来说，Iwokrama 是"我们"，而社区是"你们"，而对亨利叔叔来说，社区是"我们"，但通常正如我们将在下文中看到的，情况并非总是如此。通过这种方式，亨利叔叔能够将权威与团结结合起来，这同样符合他在社区中的地位。因此，在人际方面，跟经验和语篇方面一样，亨利叔叔的话语贡献比莎拉更接近社区的声音。

因此，我们可以看出，系统功能语言学中语言三种意义的概念在分析话语和声音时是十分有用的。如果我们认为声音是一个语码，并牢记说话人的地位和受众的性质的重要性，那么我们还可以看到这与第 2 章中介绍的定位大卫之星相吻合。表 7.1 列出了语篇 7.2 的（按照元功能）三维分析。然而，从大卫之星的角度来进一步思考莎拉和亨利叔叔的贡献，我们对这里的相关情况的理解将会更为复杂。

首先，很明显，莎拉无法使用与亨利叔叔相同的语言，因为她没有适当的文化资本。她描述可持续利用区的方式或多或少是她唯一的选择。

表 7.1 亨利叔叔演讲中的阶段和语境结构

行数	修辞功能	语场	语旨	语式
2—9	Importance of observation of changes as transition to call for collaborative	Community Sen and Beh of material processes of change.	Pedagogic [+knowledge/+control]: Dialogic engagement through rhetorical questions.	Account of observation and change leading to Prediction of enhanced understanding.
10—27	Problematises local familiarity with respect to sustainability	Community abuse of forest resources (lexis) resulting from familiarity and lack of knowledge (mental and behavioural processes). knowing. Negative Judgement of processes of Appreciation-. Instructional context projecting regulatory.	WE as community, but becoming YOU for worst errors. Bare imperative [+moral authority] through distance within solidarity. Negative and interrogative mood for processes of	Multiple embeddings contextualising concept of change in community experience.
28—49	Research carried out on various natural resources of the forest as necessary complement to traditional knowledge and potential problems.	Community asked to be Sensers and Actors in processes of participation and research; Iwokrama as Actors in Assigners in processes of research with local ecology as Scope and Identified.	Operates symbolic capital as elder[+solidarity/+control] through WE and direct imitated speech mixed with statement of obligations. Contrast with symbolic capital as external experts[−solidarity/+knowledge] of Iwokrama as THEY carrying out research. Regulatory context with instructional embeddings. Positive appraisal of sustainability [+Appreciation]	Commentary on proposed role in knowledge relations embedding Conjecture of possible problems paralleled with Recount of important but incomplete outside research and Conjecture of potential problems.
50—66	UF's knowledge used to question imported knowledge.	UH as Sen and Ca of cognitive Ats concerning Iwokrama's practice of classifying (including relational processes of meronymy). Potential material results of poor classsification and mapping. Menta processes of future discussions	I as sceptic = [+power/knowledge] of communities over Iwokrama and of UH within community. Regulatory projecting interpersonal and instructional. Negative appraisal of actions [−Judgement]	Commentary: Uncle Henry's evaluation of Iwokrama's knowledge embedding Account of Iwokrama's classification and Prediction of further work needed.

其次，亨利叔叔对情态和代词的使用并不像我所暗示的那样直截了当。在他的话语贡献的不同阶段，亨利叔叔非常清楚地将自己从他的受众中分离了出来，称受众为"你们"，有时还声称外部知识比当地关于森林的经验和知识更有益。此外，这两件事往往同时发生。换句话说，亨利叔叔在同一个话语中为自己创造了两个不同的定位——作为当地的长者和外部科学专家。鉴于他作为当地长者的身份，以及他在与政府和国际专家一起建立 Iwokrama 的过程中所发挥的重要作用，也只有他有能力做到这一点。语篇 7.2 的第 50 至 66 行突显了这一独特的定位，亨利叔叔现在是"我"，他怀疑外界的知识，并权衡着讨论双方的证据。

亨利叔叔这样做的方式表明，在三种元功能的语境结构中，同时考虑三者的重要性，因为正是通过这三种功能的组合，才能确立定位，实现不同的声音。

这里需要注意的另一个重要点是亨利叔叔采取的不同定位没有体现出由于一个单一身份而浑然一体的一组角色，就像医生从诊断师的角色转变为顾问的角色那样（Sarangi 2010,2011）；相反，它们涉及根植于不同社区的不同身份，因此可以被视为**混合声音**（*hybrid voice*）的一个例子。与此相对，说话人从单一身份（角色集合）衍生为多个角色的语篇被描述为**复合语类**（*complex genres*）（Sarangi 2010,2011）。

更复杂的是，我想说亨利叔叔在解释可持续利用区方面的成功很大程度上源于萨拉解释的失败。实际上，亨利叔叔借助了莎拉所做的技术性解释和她作为外部科学家的身份，在他贡献的不同阶段将其**纳入**（*subsuming*）自己的论述中，这得益于他独特的混合身份。这两个人的话语都对讨论作出了贡献，这个事实表明 NRDDB 会议利用了话语互文性，因此，他们在其内的话语贡献可以视为混合语类。当然，当这样一种混合的说话方式在这种语境中自然化了的时候，我们就没有话语互文性和混合声音了，而是新的话语和新的声音。

这提出了与声音概念相关的另一个问题——我们怎么能说莎拉和亨利叔叔二人来自不同背景的、非常不同的说话方式都是这种新声音的代表呢？对此,我的回答是,虽然有人将声音视为代表整个社会群体的单一概念,但我们的观点是当说话人的话语语境结构实现了在特定社区内被认可的角色时(理想的情况是他们由于在该社区中的地位而有权扮演该角色),才能认为某种声音在发挥作用。这取代了一种相当本质化的概念,认为社区是只有一种说话方式的同质群体。与此相反,一个社区内不同的人有不同的说话方式,所有这些方式的结合就是社区的声音。正如一个社区有多种相互关联的说话方式一样,一个说话人也可以属于多个社区,他可以用不同的声音说话,正如亨利叔叔所展现的那样。最后,一旦可识别的角色(每个角色都有自己的说话方式,无论其来源如何)已经融入一个给定的社区中,那么我们可以说,这些不同的说话方式都代表了该社区的声音。在这个例子中,这是北鲁普努尼地区发展委员会(NRDDB)的声音,而不是当地社区本身的声音。回到前面的一个例子,在马丁·路德·金的《我有一个梦想》演讲中宗教和政治声音融在一起不应该被视为一种混合,因为它已经成为当时民权运动(某些派别)演讲的自然化方式,因此代表了该群体的独特声音。

练习 7.1

(1)对托尼·布莱尔的7/7演讲进行阶段分析。将第一个修辞单位标记为1,将嵌入其中的任何修辞单位标记为1.1,依此类推。用另一个数字,比如2、3等,来标记扩展,同时将嵌入标记为2.1、3.1等,将多重嵌入标记为2.1.1、3.1.1等。我在附录附上了我的分析,你的分析与我的可能有点不同,但希望差异不要过大。

(2)讨论你的阶段分析,特别是对语场和语旨之间的任何重叠进行评论。

(3)识别托尼·布莱尔采用重新调整直接语境和移位语境以及对团结和权威的构建这两种手段,为自己、其他领导人和公众所构建的不同定位。这与文化资本的概念有什么关系?

(4)思考一下这是一个复合语类的例子(其中不同的定位体现源于单一的角色

集和单一身份的不同角色)还是一个混合的例子(其中聚合了不同的话语和声音)。当然,答案可能并不简单。

7.4　结论

前几章中的所有内容做好了铺垫,到本章就水到渠成了。所以虽然本章很短,但总结了笔者一直以来所做过的思考。希望我已经阐明,在分析语言中的权力时,定位和声音是多么重要的概念,而在讨论作为话语的语篇时,仅仅看语言是不够的。虽然从本质上讲,这本书关注的是语篇特征,但它始终着眼于如何在定位之星的启发式模型中解释这些特征。这里概述的方法源于我在圭亚那的实地研究,以及我完成博士学位后十年的思考。毫无疑问,还有很多事情需要考虑而且模型还需要修改,所以希望我能继续研究一段时间。

我在读博期间主要关心的社会问题是少数群体如何能让那些有权作出决定、控制自己生活的人听到他们的声音。本章的分析在某种程度上触及了这种**跨文化交流**(*intercultural communication*),但仅限于一个例子,一个相对较小且同质的群体与一个有同情心的把关者打着交道。社会语言学的一个主要的新趋势是考虑更多的多样性语境。现代移民模式加上技术的进步,意味着越来越多的话语涉及不同语言背景的人,不仅涉及他们所说的“语言”,还涉及他们的说话方式和声音。这被称为**超多样性**(*superdiversity*)。这本书中概述的方法和我提出的声音概念是否有助于讨论超多样化世界中的话语,还有待观察。在这样的背景下布鲁马特(Blommaert 2005:255)提出声音相当于“让自己被理解的能力”,但我不确定这理论是否充分,至少在对“被理解”意味着什么的表面理解上是这样。我个人的观点是,被理解只是成为重要话语的合法参与者的第一步。我希望本书中的方法将有助于在不断变化的社会世界中进行一些有社会意义的研究。

附　录

隐藏语篇

语篇文本 1.2

9　　But into that dark, the word of God has entered, in love and judgment,

10　　and has not been overcome

11　　... in the darkness ... the question sounds as clear as ever:

12　　to each of us, and to our church and our society: Britain, where are you

（讲话人是时任坎特伯雷大主教的罗文·威廉姆斯,引文源自其 2011 年圣诞布道的内容。）

题目(6)—(15)的参考答案

(6) The sermon was given at a time of unrest in Britain, just after there had been rioting in the streets of major cities and in the wake of popular discontent with the banks who had been bailed out by the government after their investments had failed but who had continued to pay large bonuses to their top executives and healthy dividends to their shareholders.

(7)(i) The Archbishop portrays contemporary society in negative terms as, among other things, greedy, mindlessly violent and lacking in social cohesion.

(ii) The Archbishop generally orients himself to his listeners as part of the same social group— through the use of the pronoun "we", the common nouns "community" and "society" and the proper noun "Britain". While the rioters and bankers are not referred to as "we", they are included within the ideas of community, society and Britain, and so there is possibly an idea that, even if we are not directly responsible for the behaviour of these groups, we are in some way responsible as a society.

(8) In criticising the behaviour of both bankers and rioters the Archbishop includes both those perceived of as rich and as disadvantaged, the targets of both the left-wing and right-wing press, in his criticism.

(9) The pomp and ceremony of the occasion serve to emphasise the Archbishop's socially sanctioned

status as the head of the Church of England.

(10) The Archbishop's status imbue his words with a degree of authority (at least to some people …) that they would not have if uttered by someone else.

(11) In this particular text the Archbishop would seem to betaking on the role of social commentator rather than that of spiritual advisor, though there are, of course, elements of both.

(12) Social issues have not always been considered within the authority of religious leaders in Britain and for some within the Church of England this is still a matter of some debate. Rowan Williams, in particular, is well known for becoming involved in social issues. We can thus distinguish between the position of "Archbishop of Canterbury" in general and "Rowan Williams as Archbishop" more specifically.

(13) I would say that the Archbishop is addressing at least three different audiences. Most directly, but not necessarily primarily in this case, he is addressing the assembled congregation. Beyond that he will be aware that his sermon will be broadcast on national television and also that it is likely to cause debate in the daily papers and other media (including YouTube and, though I'm sure he did not consider this, students of discourse analysis). I suppose he may also have God in mind as an audience. It therefore is an interesting question how his sermon was worded to appeal to these different audiences simultaneously.

(14) I would think that his sermon and the Archbishop's status will attract different responses from regular churchgoers, religious people in general, non-religious people and staunch atheists (to put it a little simply), as well as politicians. However, these are questions for discussion and research and not facts that we can glean from the text alone.

(15) My own personal feeling (and therefore an idea needing further research) is that the Archbishop is not only suggesting a religious solution to a particular problem, but also trying to show that the Church of England is socially involved and a relevant institution in the modern world.

(16) The two extracts are held together by the theme of light and darkness (at least) with the social problems of the day characterised by the metaphor of "darkness" which is then contrasted with the traditional Christmas theme of the Nativity as the coming of light into darkness. The way in which speakers and writers create a continuity in their texts while developing different themes is an important point we will consider later, in particular inasmuch as it serves to make their message appear, on the surface at least, to be logical and consistent.

术语表

An **Adjunct** is a non-essential element of the clause. *Cf.* **nucleus**.

Agnate clauses differ in specific features of meaning, usually only one. They are useful in testing for **cryptogrammar** and so distinguishing between process types, for example, I always eat steak/Right now I'm eating steak (material) *cf.* I always think I'm going to fail/Right now I think I'm going to fail (mental).

Anaphoric reference is when a pronoun, etc. refers to something that has previously been mentioned.

Ancillary language works alongside material action (or pictures, etc.) to **construe** a **context**. *Cf.* **constitutive**.

The **angle of development** of a **text** is the basic organising principle, such as moving from one time or place to another or setting out conditions for regulations. The angle of development can often be identified by looking at the **marked Themes** across a text.

Appraisal analysis is a means of identifying and categorising different forms of evaluation in a text.

Appropriation of a dominant discourse is its use by more marginalised groups. *Cf.* **colonisation**.

Attribution of an idea is when you cite someone else as the source.

Attributive. A subtype of **relational** processes, see Chapter 3.

The **audience** or **audiences** of a text are the people who are intended to hear it. See **marketplace**.

Behavioural processes. See Chapter 3.

Capital. See **cultural capital** and **symbolic capital**.

Cataphoric reference is when a pronoun, etc. refers to something that appears later in the clause.

The **central entity** is a concept used in analysing **rhetorical units**. It refers to the person or thing that the clause is primarily talking about and is usually realised in the **lexicogrammar** by the **Subject**.

Circumstances are elements of the **clause** that tell you how, where, when and why (etc.) an event happened.

A **clause complex** is the main clause plus any **subordinate clauses**. Clause complexes realise a single **discourse function**.

A **code** is the way a specific social group uses language.

A text is **coherent** if it is all makes sense together. *Cf.* **cohesion**.

Cohesion refers to the way the **lexicogrammar** signal show parts of a **text** are joined together. It generally helps **coherence** but does not guarantee it.

Colonisation of a **discourse** is when key features of another, usually more powerful, **discourse** begin to become the norm within it. *Cf.* **appropriation**.

A **Comment Adjunct** is an adverb-like word or phrase, such as "hopefully" or "bizarrely", that realises non-modal speaker evaluation of a **proposal** or **proposition**. *Cf.* **Modal Adjunct**.

The **Complement** of a clause is any participant, apart from the **Subject**, that must be included for the clause to be fully "grammatical".

A **complex genre** is one in which participants play a variety of **roles** which are all part of the same **role set** appropriate to single **statuses**. *Cf.* **hybrid**.

Congruence is when the **lexicogrammar** and the **semantics** are in alignment and follow the usual relationship, for example, when an **interrogative** is used to ask a question.

Constitutive language construes a context entirely on its own. *Cf.* **ancillary**.

Speakers **construe** a **context** through language. This captures the ideas that a context does not exist prior to language and that different speakers may construe similar situations differently.

Context refers to the situation that is **construed** through language. Other authors use this term to refer to either what is called **environment** or what is called the **cotext** in this book. See also the definition in Chapter 1 under Key Concepts.

The **contextual configuration** of a **phase** of text is the combination of **experiential**, **interpersonal** and **textual** meanings it realises.

A **contextualisation cue** is a verbal or non-verbal signal that a situation should be understood in a particular way.

Cotext refers to other parts of the same **text**.

Cultural capital is the prestige a speaker has because of their education, experise or social position. See Chapter 1. *Cf.* **symbolic capital**.

A clause is in the **declarative mood** when the **Subject** precedes the **Finite**. *Cf.* **interrogative** and **imperative**.

The **deictic centre** is the immediate here and now: the speaker and the audience at the time of speaking.

Delicacy refers to the level of detail in a linguistic description; for example, relational:attributive is a more delicate description of a process than relational. Note the use of colons in the labels.

Deontic modality is used when a speaker signals how much they want an event to come about or how necessary it is, for example, "You must be home by eleven". *Cf.* **epistemic**.

With a small letter, **discourse** refers to text as a real-time, socially situated event. A **Discourse**, with a capital letter, refers to the accepted ways of talking about an idea, for example, "the Discourse of development". *Cf.* **text**.

The **discourse function** of an utterance refers to its **semantics** in terms of whether it is making a statement, asking a question, asking someone to do something or making an offer. *Cf.* **mood**.

A **displaced** field or context refers to a **field** or **context** that is not part of the immediate event. See Chapter 2. *Cf.* **immediate**.

Ellipsis is when a word or words are missed out but are understood and which would be necessary to make a clause fully "grammatical".

An **embedded** rhetorical unit (RU) is one that takes up and develops the matrix RU through the Theme of its first clause. *Cf.* **expansion**.

Endophoric reference is when a pronoun, etc. refers to something anywhere within the same text. *Cf.* **exophoric**, **homophoric**.

Enhanced themes are when a clause begins with "it is" followed by an adjective of evaluation (**enhanced evaluative theme**, for example, "It's strange that you should say that") or an element of experiential meaning (**enhanced experiential Theme**, for example, "It's you that I want"). See Chapter 5.

The **environment** of a text refers to all the non-linguistic features of the situation as well as to previous discourse that may be relevant to what the text means. Other authors use **context** in this way.

Epistemic modality is used when a speaker signals how likely they think it is that an event will come about, for example, "He must be home by now". *Cf.* **deontic**.

Event orientation is used in analysing **rhetorical units**. It refers to the temporal relation of the utterance to the deictic centre and is realised grammatically by the **Finite**.

Evidentiality is a semantic area concerning why or how we think something is true, as in "She looks like an interesting woman".

Evoked evaluation is extra evaluative meaning we can get from a word or phrase according to the situation or cotext. It would not bean essential part of a dictionary definition. *Cf.* **inscribed**.

Existential process. See Chapter 3.

An **existential Theme** is one introduced by the Subject "there" as in "There's a man with a bill at the door".

Exophoric reference is when a pronoun etc. refers to something in the immediate environment rather than the text itself. *Cf.* **endophoric**, **homophoric**.

Expansion is when a rhetorical unit (RU) takes up and develops the previous RU through the Rheme of its first clause. *Cf.* **embedded**.

The **experiential metafunction** refers to a speaker's representation of events. *Cf.* **interpersonal** and **textual**.

Explicit modality is marked by the lexicogrammar as being either **subjective** (usually through the word "I", as in "I think it will rain") or **objective**, (usually through the word "it", as in "It's likely that it will rain"). *Cf.* **implicit**.

The **field** of discourse is that part of the **context** that relates to the activity taking place and the subject matter. It is **congruently realised** by the **experiential metafunction**. *Cf.* **tenor** and **mode**.

The **Finite** verb in a clause realises tense or **modality**.

A **genre** is the way a particular social group carries out an activity through language and possibly other means. See also Chapter 7.

Hedging is downplaying the force of an utterance. *Cf.* **intensifier**.

Homophoric reference is when we need shared background information to identify the referent, for example, "the Prime Minister". *Cf.* **endophoric**, **exophoric**.

A **hybrid genre** or **voice** is one that draws on the norms of different social groups or which involves different **role sets**. *Cf.* **complex**.

Identifying processes are a subset of **relational** processes. See Chapter 3. *Cf.* **attributive**.

The **immediate context** is what is happening here and now, the present activity. *Cf.* **displaced**. See Chapter 2.

A clause is in the **imperative mood** when the **Subject** and **Finite** are not realised or can be omitted without change in discourse function. *Cf.* **declarative** and **interrogative**.

Implicit modality is when the **subjective** or **objective orientation** is not overtly marked, for example, "You must be home by now" (implicit:subjective) and "He's surely home by now" (implicit:objective). *Cf.* **explicit**.

Inscribed evaluation is when a word or phrase carries a positive or negative meaning according to its dictionary definition. *Cf.* **evoked**.

An **intensifier** heightens the evaluation of a word or clause. *Cf.* **hedge**.

Interdiscursivity is the mixing of different discourses or ways of speaking in the same text. See Chapter 7. *Cf.* **intertextuality**.

The **interpersonal metafunction** is concerned with how speakers' opinions and judgements and the relations between speakers are construed through language. *Cf.* **experiential** and **textual**.

A clause is in the **interrogative mood** when the **Finite** precedes the **Subject**. *Cf.* **declarative** and **imperative**.

Intertextuality is when a text, or a paraphrase of it, appears in a different text. Some authors include interdiscursivity within intertextuality. See Chapter 7. *Cf.* **interdiscursivity**.

Investment refers to whether **modality** is either **explicit** or **implicit**.

The **lexicogrammar** of a language is how the words and grammar of that language make meanings.

Locally contingent meanings and relations depend upon the particular text or environment.

A **macrophenomenon** is a whole event seen as a Phenomenon, as in "I saw them crossing the road". See chapter 3. *Cf.* **metaphenomenon**.

A **marked Theme** is when a **Circumstance**, or occasionally a **Complement** is the **Theme** of a clause. See Chapter 5. *Cf.* **unmarked Theme** and **enhanced Theme**.

Marketplace refers in this book to the set of speakers and the different audiences within a discourse, each with their own linguistic **codes**, social values and expectations.

Material process. See Chapter 3.

Meaning potential is a functional way of referring to the lexicogrammar as a resource for meaning making rather than as a set of rules. See Chapter 1.

Mental process. See Chapter 3.

The **metafunctions** are the groupings of the **semantic** and **lexicogrammatical** resources of a language in terms of their **experiential**, **interpersonal** and **textual** functions.

A **metaphenomenon** is a fact, act, idea or quote (locution) **realised** as a **Phenomenon** or a **projection**. *Cf.* **macrophenomenon**.

The **method of development** of a text is how it progresses in terms of the **Themes** used.

A **Modal Adjunct** is an adverb-like word or phrase, such as "possibly" or "usually", that realises an option in **implicit objective modality**. *Cf.* **Comment Adjunct**.

The **modal auxiliaries** or **modal verbs** are verbs like "must", "may" and "should" that are the **Finite** element in a clause and realise an option in **implicit subjective modality**.

Modality refers to the means a speaker has of evaluating a **proposition** or **proposal** in terms of how usual or probable an event is, how necessary it is, or how willing they or others are to carry it out.

Mode is that aspect of a **context** that relates to its **cohesion**, its **textuality** and, in this book, its relation to the **deictic centre**. *Cf.* **field** and **tenor**.

Mood is a **grammatical** system with the options **declarative**, **interrogative**, and **imperative**. *Cf.* **discourse function**.

The **mood element** of a clause comprises the **Finite** and **Subject** and any intervening **modal Adjuncts**.

A **motif** is a topic or theme developed by a speaker or writer. These terms are not used as they have specific meanings in linguistics.

Naturalisation of a **genre**, **voice** or way of speaking is when it becomes accepted as the norm within a particular social group. *Cf.* **hybridity**.

A **nominal group** is a group of words referring to a single thing, usually a noun plus any article and adjectives.

The **nucleus** of a clause comprises the **Subject**, the **process** and any **Complements**. *Cf.* **Adjunct**.

Objective modality is when a speaker does not take personal responsibility for their evaluation. *Cf.* **subjective**.

Orientation refers to whether **modality** is **objective** or **subjective**.

A **participant** is a person, thing, quality or role that is realised as the **Subject** or **Complement** of a clause, or as part of a **Circumstance**.

A **participant role** is the relation of one **participant** to another in terms of **transitivity** and **process types**, for example, Actor or Attribute.

A **phase** is a stretch of text with a constant **contextual configuration**.

A speaker's **position** is the set of rights and responsibilities they take up in discourse. See Chapter 1.

A **probe** is a grammatical means of testing a clause (usually) to see what process type is involved, usually through re-expressing it. *Cf.* **agnate**.

The **process** in a clause refers to the type of event being **construed** in terms of the **transitivity** relations between **participants**. It is usually realised by the man verb.

A **process type** refers to how **transitivity relations** between the **participants** are **construed** in a clause. There are six main types: material, mental, verbal, behavioural, relational and existential. See Chapter 3.

A **proposal** is a request for or offer of goods and services, as in "You must be home by 11" or "I'll do that for you". *Cf.* **proposition**.

A **proposition** is the giving or requesting of information, as in "He'll be home by now!" or "Are you a ninny?" *Cf.* **proposal**.

A **pseudomodal** is when a process of thinking or hoping, etc. acts as a way of expressing modality, as in "I think it'll rain tomorrow".

A **rankshifted** clause is a clause or part-clause that plays a function *within* a group or another clause (as in "the man who came to dinner").

Realisation refers to the way abstract levels of language are made more concrete, for example, **context** is realised through **semantics** and **semantics** is realised though **lexicogrammar**.

If you **recalibrate** a **storyline** or a **position** you change it in real time through your **discourse**.

Relational process. See Chapter 3.

A **rhetorical unit** (RU) is a stretch of text, such as a Recount, that has a constant relation in time and space to the **deictic centre**. See Chapter 6.

A **role** is a way of acting within an activity, for example, as counsellor. See Chapter 7. *Cf.* **status**.

A **role set** is a group of **roles** that are all part of the same job or are connected with the same **status** relations, for example, when a doctor is both counsellor and diagnostician.

A **semantic domain** is a range of ideas with interconnected meaning.

Semantic prosody is when a text or stretch of texts contains many similar forms of evaluation.

Semantics are the meanings that can be or are made. The semantics realise the context and the **lexicogrammar** realises the semantics.

A **semimodal** is a verb like "have to" which has some properties of modality but not all. See Chapter 4.

Semiotic means related to meaning-making.

A speaker's **speech role** refers to whether they are making a statement, asking a question, asking someone to do something or making an offer.

A speaker's **status** in a discourse is their social position in relation to other speakers, for example, doctor or patient. *Cf.* **role**.

The **storyline** (**s**) of a discourse are the continuing social activities and histories to which the discourse contributes.

The **Subject** of a clause is the **participant** that the truth or otherwise of the clause is based on and negotiated around. See Chapter 4. *Cf.* **Complement.**

Subjective modality is when a speaker takes personal responsibility for their evaluation. *Cf.* **objective**.

A **subordinate clause** is introduced by a conjunction and cannot stand alone; it acts as a kind of **Circumstance** to the main clause.

Symbolic capital refers to the value that a speaker's language takes on because of the **cultural capital** of that speaker within a specific **marketplace**.

A **system** is a set of options, a choice in meaning with minimal difference.

Tenor is that aspect of a **context** that relates to the interpersonal relations between speakers. *Cf.* **field** and **mode**.

A **text** is any stretch of language that forms a unified whole, without consideration of any non-linguistic features of its use. *Cf.* **discourse**

The **textual metafunction** refers to the semantic and lexicogrammatical resources for creating textuality and cohesion. *Cf.* **experiential** and **interpersonal**.

Textuality is the property of a stretch of language as being a unified whole.

The **thematic element** of a clause is made up of the experiential Theme and any textual or interpersonal Themes that precede it. See Chapter 5.

The **Theme** of a clause usually refers to the first element with **experiential** meaning, though this is properly called the experiential Theme as **interpersonal** and **textual** Themes are also possible. See Chapter 5.

Transitivity refers to the relations between **participants** in terms of their involvement within the **process** construed. See Chapter 3.

An **unmarked Theme** is the **Subject** of a **declarative** clause, the **Subject** or wh-word in an **interrogative** clause and usually the main verb in an **imperative** clause. Cf. **marked Theme** and **enhanced Theme**.

Value in **modality** is high, median or low.

Verbal process. See Chapter 3.

Voice refers to the way the social organisation of a particular group is realised through their ways of speaking. See Chapter 7.

答　案

练习 2.2

凡指涉对象可从语篇内外得以明确的,都突出显示。

1　I stand here today because of the inspiration of the Olympic Movement.

2　When I was 12, about the same age as Amber,

3　I was marched into a large school hall with my classmates.

4　We sat in front of an ancient, black and white TV

5　and watched grainy pictures from the Mexico Olympic Games.

6　Two athletes from our home town were competing.

7　John Sherwood won a bronze medal in the 400m hurdles.

8　His wife Sheila just narrowly missed gold in the long jump.

9　That day a window to a new world opened for me.

10　By the time I was back in my classroom,

11　I knew

12　what I wanted to do

13　and what I wanted to be.

14　The following week I stood in line for hours at my local track just to catch a glimpse of the medals the Sherwoods had brought home.

15　It didn't stop there.

16　Two days later I joined their club.

17　Two years later Sheila gave me my first pair of racing spikes.

18　35 years on, I stand before you with those memories still fresh. Still inspired by this great Movement.

19　My journey here to Singapore started in that school hall

20　and continues today in wonder and ingratitude. Gratitude that those flickering images of the Sherwoods, and Wolde, Gammoudi, Doubell and Hines drew me to a life in that most potent celebration of humanity Olympic sport.

21 And that gratitude drives me and my team to do whatever we can to inspire young people to choose sport.

22 Whoever they are,

23 wherever they live

24 and whatever they believe.

25 Today that task is so much harder.

26 Today's children live in a world of conflicting messages and competing distractions.

27 Their landscape is cluttered.

28 Their path to Olympic sport is often obscured.

29 But it's a world we must understand and must respond to.

30 My heroes were Olympians.

31 My children's heroes change by the month.

32 And they are the lucky ones.

33 Millions more face the obstacle of limited resources and the resulting lack of guiding role models.

34 In my travels over the last two years, speaking with many of you, I've had many conversations about how we meet this challenge.

35 And I've been reassured

36 and I've been uplifted

37 we share a common goal for the future of sport.

38 No group of leaders does more than you to engage the hearts and minds of young people.

39 But every year the challenge of bringing them to Olympic sport becomes tougher.

40 The choice of Host City is the most powerful means you have to meet this challenge.

41 But it takes more than 17 days of superb Olympic competition.

42 It takes a broader vision. And the global voice to communicate that vision over the full four years of the Olympiad.

43 Today in Britain's fourth bid in recent years we offer London's vision of inspiration and legacy.

44 Choose London today

45 and you send a clear message to the youth of the world:

46 more than ever, the Olympic Games are for you.

47 Mr President, Members of the IOC: Some might say

48 that your decision today is between five similar bids.

49 That would be to undervalue the opportunity before you.

50 In the past, you have made bold decisions: decisions which have taken the Movement forward in new and exciting directions.

51 Your decision today is critical.

52 It is a decision about which bid offers the vision and sporting legacy to best promote the

Olympic cause.

53 It is a decision about which city will help us show a new generation why sport matters. In a world of many distractions, why Olympic sport matters. And in the 21st century why the Olympic Ideals still matter so much.

54 On behalf of the youth of today, the athletes of tomorrow and the Olympians of the future, we humbly submit the bid of London 2012.

55 Mr President, that concludes our presentation.

56 Thank you.

练习 3.1

参与者以粗体显示。

1 **I** [α] am happyto [α Ac] <u>join</u> with you today in **what** (Ac) will <u>go down</u> in history as the greatest demonstration for freedom in the history of our nation.

2 Five score years ago, **a great American** (Ac), >< <u>signed</u> **the Emancipation Proclamation** (Go).

3 >in whose symbolic shadow west and today,<

4 **This momentous decree** (Ac) <u>came</u> as a great beacon light of hope to millions of Negro slaves **who** (Go) had been <u>seared</u> in the flames of withering injustice.

5 **It** (Ac α) <u>came</u> as a joyous daybreak to [α Ac] <u>end</u> **the long night of their captivity** (Go).

6 But one hundred years later, the Negro still is not free.

7 One hundred years later, **the life of the Negro** (Go) is still sadly <u>crippled</u> by **the manacles of segregation and the chains of discrimination** (Ac).

8 One hundred years later, **the Negro** (Ac) <u>lives</u> on a lonely island of poverty in the midst of a vast ocean of material prosperity.

9 One hundred years later, **the Negro** (Ac) is still <u>languishing</u> in the corners of American society

10 and finds himself an exile in his own land.

11 So **we** (Ac α) have <u>come</u> here today to [α Ac] <u>dramatize</u> **a shameful condition** (Go).

12 In a sense **we** (Ac α) have <u>come</u> to our nation's capital to (α Ac) <u>cash</u> **a check** (Go).

13 When **the architects of our republic** (Ac) <u>wrote</u> **the magnificent words of the Constitution and the Declaration of Independence** (Go: cre),

14 **they** (Ac) were <u>signing</u> **a promissory note to which every American was to fall heir** (Go).

15 This note was a promise that all men, yes, black men as well as white men, would be guaranteed the unalienable rights of life, liberty, and the pursuit of happiness.

16 It is obvious today that **America** (Ac) has <u>defaulted</u> on this promissory note

17　insofar as her citizens of color are concerned.

18　Instead of［α Ac］honoring **this sacred obligation** (Go)，**America** (Ac α) has given **the Negro people** (Rct) **abad check** (Go)，a check **which** (Ac α) has come back ［α Go］ marked "**insufficient funds.** " (At)

19　But were fuse to believe

20　that the bank of justice is bankrupt.

21　We refuse to believe

22　that there are insufficient funds in the great vaults of opportunity of this nation.

23　So **we** (Ac α) have come to ［α Ac］cash **this check** (Go) — a check **that** (Ac) will give **us** (Rect) upon demand **the riches of freedom and the security of justice** (Go).

24　**We** (Ac) have also come to this hallowed spot to remind America of the fierce urgency of now.

练习3.2

前引号表示投射。

1　**I** (Sayer) am just going to make **a short statement** (Vb) to **you** (Recr) on **the terrible events** (Ac) that have happened in London earlier today

2　and **I** (Sen:cog[①]) hope

3　"**you** (Sen:cog) understand

4　"that at the present time **we** (Sen:cog) are still trying to establish exactly **what** (Ac) **has happened** (Phen)，

5　and there is a limit to **what information** (Go) **I** (Ac) can **give you** (Rect)，[②]

6　and **I** (Sayer) will simply try and tell **you** (Rect) **the information** (Vb) as best I can at the moment.

7　It is reasonably clear that there have been a series of terrorist attacks in London.

8　There are obviously casualties，both **people** (Ac) that have died and **people** (Go) seriously injured，

9　and our thoughts and prayers of course are with the victims and their families.

10　It is my intention to ［Blair Ac］leave the G8 within the next couple of hours and ［Blair］go down to London and ［Blair Ac］get **a report** (Go)，face-to-face，with the police，and the emergency services and the Ministers **that** (Ac) have been dealing with **this** (Go)，and then to ［Blair Ac］return later this evening.

11　It is the will of all the leaders at the G8 however that **the meeting** (Ac) should continue in my absence，that **we** (Sayer α) should continue to discuss **the issues that we were going to discuss** (Tg[③])，and ［α Sen:cog］reach **the conclusions** (Sc) **which** (Sc) **we** (Sen:cog) were going to reach.

12　Each of the countries round that table have some experience of the effects of terrorism

13 and **all the leaders** ［a］> < share our complete resolution to （α Ac） <u>defeat</u> **this terrorism** （Go）.

14 >as **they** （Sayer④） will <u>indicate</u> a little bit later<

15 It is particularly barbaric that **this** （Ac） has <u>happened</u> on a day when **people** （Ac α） are <u>meeting</u> to （α Ac） try to <u>help</u> **the problems of poverty in Africa, and the long term problems of climate change and the environment** （Go）

16 Just as it is reasonably clear that this is a terrorist attack, or a series of terrorist attacks,

17 it is also reasonably clear that it is designed and aimed to coincide with the opening of the G8.

18 There will be time to ［leaders? Beh］ **talk** later about this.

19 It is important however that **those engaged in terrorism** （Sen：cog） <u>realise</u>

20 "that our determination to ［us Ac］ <u>defend</u> **our values and our way of life** （Go） is greater than their determination to ［they Ac］ <u>cause</u> **death and destruction** （Sc） to innocent people in a desire to ［they Ac］ <u>impose</u> **extremism** （Go）on the world.

21 **Whatever** （Go） **they** （Ac） <u>do</u>,

22 it is our determination that **they** （Ac） will never succeed in <u>destroying</u> **what we hold dear in this country and in other civilised nations throughout the world** （Go）.

练习3.2 注释

①从意念角度看,这肯定像意愿过程,而从语法角度看,很明显这是认知过程。
②字体不够用,难以完全标示这个复杂的句子。希望读者能厘清其中各种关系。
③这可能值得商榷,但从语法来看,似乎是最为恰当的。
④可以认为"as"是投射言语。

练习3.3

1 I am just going to make a short statement to you on the terrible events that have happened in London earlier today,

2 and I hope

3 you understand

4 that at the present time we are still trying to establish exactly what has happened,

5 and there <u>is</u> **a limit to what information I can give you** （Ex）,

6 and I will simply try and tell you the information as best I can at the moment.

7 It is reasonably clear that there have <u>been</u> **a series of terrorist attacks in London** （Ex）.

8 There <u>are</u> obviously **casualties** （Ex）, both people that have died and people seriously injured,

9 and **our thoughts and prayers** （Ca） of course <u>are</u> **with the victims and their families** （At：circ）.

10 It <u>is</u> **my intention** （Val①） **to leave the G8 within the next couple of hours and go down**

to London and get a report, face-to-face, with the police, and the emergency services and the Ministers that have been dealing with this, and then to return later this evening (Tk).

11   It is **the will of all the leaders at the G**8 (Val) however **that the meeting should continue in my absence, that we should continue to discuss the issues that we were going to discuss, and reach the conclusions which we were going to reach** (Tk).

12   **Each of the countries round that table** (Ca) have **some experience of the effects of terrorism** (At: pos)

13   and **all the leaders** (Tk^②) > < share **our complete resolution to defeat this terrorism** (Val).

14   >as they will indicate a little bit later<

15   It is **particularly barbaric** (At) **that this has happened on a day when people are meeting to try to help the problems of poverty in Africa, and the long term problems of climate change and the environment** (Ca)

16   Just as it is **reasonably clear** (At) **that this** (Ca) is **a terrorist attack, or a series of terrorist attacks** (At) (Ca), ^{③}

17   it is also **reasonably clear** (At) **that it** (Ca) is **designed and aimed to coincide with the opening of the G**8 (At) (Ca). ^{④}

18   There will be **time to talk later about this** (Ex).

19   It is **important** (At) however **that those engaged in terrorism realise**

20   **that our determination to defend our values and our way of life** (Ca) is **greater than their determination to cause death and destruction to innocent people in a desire to impose extremism on the world** (At) (Ca). ^{⑤}

21   Whatever they do,

22   it is **our determination** (Val) **that they will never succeed in destroying what we hold dear in this country and in other civilised nations throughout the world** (Tk).

练习3.3 注释

①这是有标记的主位结构(见第5章)。

②这比较奇怪,但是是一个可逆关系过程。

③这里的确令人迷惑,可以认为所分析的关系如下: "**this** (Ca) is **a terrorist attack, or a series of terrorist attacks** (At)" and "**that this is a terrorist attack, or a series of terrorist attacks** (Ca) is **reasonably clear** (Ca)"。

④这里也很难。作者分析如下: "**that it is designed and aimed to coincide with the opening of the G**8 (Ca) is also **reasonably clear** (At)" and "**it** (Ca) is **designed and aimed to coincide with the opening of the G**8 (At)"。第二例也可以分析为被动物质过程。

⑤这里也有难度,一些读者应该可以自己厘清其中的两种关系。

练习 4.1

1	S：	Okay, so ... so the activity ... is ... to do what? WH INT Q[①]
2		>To get a reservoir ... set up ... in the village? < Right? ANSWER + CHECK
3		That's the activity? DEC Q
4	N?：	Yeah. ANSWER
5	S：	Right. CONFIRM
6		And then ... how does that fit with ... with all these other things in terms of
7		of agricultu：re, health, and all of those ... is the next thing you're talking
8		about? WH-INT Q
9		Makes it more accessible, makes it easier ... maybe healthier, those kind of
10		stuff, right? DEC Q
11		So ... so, let's just back up. 1PLIMP SUGGESTION
12		So, you wanna ↑ do ... ↓ three.
13		(15s)
14		And remember this from yesterday ... the various points we've built, right?
15		IMP REQ +CHECK
16		(5s)
17		Right? CHECK
18		And re ... re ... and so ... that's one, it is "How does it ↑ fit with other things
19		in the
20		village?",
21		and you're saying it makes it more accessible an' easier.
22		So ...
23		(6s)
24		Any other ... things [to go with] INT Q
25	N：	[Safer], it was safer.
26	S：	Sa：fer. ((writing it down?)) ECHO
27	W：	(xxx) safer (xxx). ECHO
28	S：	(xxx).
29		(9s)
30	S：	Because drinking water is such a straightforward thing, these two collapse into
31		one basically.
32		I mean 'cause it's not like you're talking about lo：gging or ... or cutting
33		down trees to do agriculture, right? DEC STATEMENT + CHECK
34		So 1 and 2 would ...

35 N: Less time taken to ... t= =for your water. SUGGESTED ITEM

36 S: Yeah. 1 and 2. Less time taken to acquire (our) water. CONFIRM AND

37 ECHO

38 So, less labour, right? SUGGESTED ITEM + CHECK

39 ?: ((grunt of assent))

40 (14s)

41 S: Mm-hmm. Anything else? INT^{②} Q

42 (6s)

43 W: Encourage agr ... kitchen gardens. SUGGESTED ITEM

44 S: Encourage agriculture, right? CHECK ITEM

45 (20s)

46 Anything else? INT Q

47 W: Is it okay that hoping they erm ... a flush toilet system (xxxxx)? INT Q

48 S: In the future? CHECK ELEMENT

49 W: Mm-hmm.

50 S: But that's not meant to be activity right now? DECL Q

51 (Eh,) the activity right now is to find somebody to fund ... the reservoir. . and

52 the pipes ... to

53 certain points, right? DEC STATEMENT + CHECK

54 So, potential future ... so that's potential. ITEM

55 N: I think maybe we should put that part. DEC SUGGESTION

56 ((Wand N mutter a while)) (12s)

57 S: We have ... you talked about this yesterday, activity (xx), how it's going to each

58 home and ... and ...

59 N: We could have taken it from under ... easier access, (xxx).

60 (12s)

61 S: (What about other) sanitation, Walter? WH INT Q

62 Flush toilet system, (? sanitary towel) system. (This is to put under) positive=

63 N: =We don't see water in the home as something that should be automatic.

64 ((mumbling from floor)) (16s)

65 S: They would get what? WH INT Q

66 ((further mumbling, with N's voice suddenly becoming prominent.)) (6s)

67 N: ... not a necessity,

68 you could collect (more than) water from outside).

69 I mean, which can happen,

70 S: [Could everyone] INT REQUEST

71 W: [When we] talked about the flush toilet, it was the ... around the nearby

72		well ... (xxxxx). Nearby homes to the wells, because of er ... (away then
73		from) the shit-
74		juice bringing into the wells and the water stream.
75	S：	Right. CONFIRM
76		So it links (xxxx).
77		Sanitation, right? ITEM + CHECK
78	W：	Right. CONFIRM
79	S：	We also talked yesterday about ecotourist things ... having better water supply.
80		So that if we collapse ... in here we could do one and two together, kind of
81		collapse it
82		in ... okay? DEC SUGGESTION
83		So ...
84		((mumbling leading to laughing, especially from N)) (23s)

练习4.1　注释

①这是个标记性很高的 wh-问句,暗示发问者可能知晓答案或是相当有把握。
②这取决于读者认为这里是信息有所省略,还是在对事项进行核对。

练习 4.3

Modality

1　I am just going to make a short statement to you on the terrible events that have happened in London earlier today,

2　and I hope (*explicit*; *subjective*; *inclination*; *median*)

3　you understand

4　that at the present time we are still trying to establish exactly what has happened,

5　and there is a limit to what information I can give you,

6　and I will (*? implicit*; *subjective*; *inclination*; *median*) simply try and tell you the information as best I can at the moment.

7　It is reasonably clear (*explicit*; *objective*; *probability*; *median*) that there have been a series of terrorist attacks in London.

8　There are obviously (*implicit*; *objective*; *probability*; *high*) casualties, both people that have died and people seriously injured,

9　and our thoughts and prayers of course (*implicit*; *objective*; *probability*; *high*) are with the victims and their families.

10 It is my intention (*explicit*; *objective*; *inclination*; *median*) to leave the G8 within the next couple of hours and go down to London and get a report, face-to- face, with the police, and the emergency services and the Ministers that have been dealing with this, and then to return later this evening.

11 It is the will (*explicit*; *objective*; *inclination*; *median*) of all the leaders at the G8 however that the meeting should continue in my absence, that we should continue to discuss the issues that we were going to discuss, and reach the conclusions which we were going to reach.

12 Each of the countries round that table have some experience of the effects of terrorism

13 and all the leaders>< share our complete resolution to defeat this terrorism.

14 >as they will (? *implicit*; *subjective*; *probability*; *high*) indicate a little bit later<

15 It is particularly barbaric that this has happened on a day when people are meeting to try to help the problems of poverty in Africa, and the long term problems of climate change and the environment.

16 Just as it is reasonably clear (*explicit*; *objective*; *probability*; *median*) that this is a terrorist attack, or a series of terrorist attacks,

17 it is also reasonably clear (*explicit*; *objective*; *probability*; *median*) that it is designed and aimed to coincide with the opening of the G8.

18 There will (? *implicit*; *subjective*; *probability*; *high*) be time to talk later about this.

19 It is important however that those engaged in terrorism realise

20 that our determination to defend our values and our way of life is greater than their determination to cause death and destruction to innocent people in a desire to impose extremism on the world.

21 Whatever they do,

22 it is our determination (*explicit*; *objective*; *inclination*; *high*) that they will never succeed in destroying what we hold dear in this country and in other civilised nations throughout the world.

Appraisal

1 I am just going to make a short statement to you on the terrible (*inscribed*; *judgement*: *social sanction*: *–propriety*) events that have happened in London earlier today,

2 and I hope

3 you understand

4 that at the present time we are still trying to establish exactly what has happened,

5 and there is a limit to what information I can give you (*inscribed*; *judgement*: *social esteem*: *–capacity*),

6 and I will simply try and tell you the information as best I can (*inscribed*; *judgement*: *social esteem*: *+capacity*) at the moment.

7　It is reasonably clear that there have been a series of terrorist (*inscribed*; *judgement*: *social sanction*: −*propriety*) attacks (*incribed*; *affect*: −*security*) in London.

8　There are obviously casualties (*evoked*; *affect*: − *happiness*), both people that have died (*evoked*; *affect*: −*happiness*) and people seriously injured (*evoked*; *affect*: *happiness*),

9　and our thoughts and prayers (*inscribed*; *affect*: *inclination*) of course are with the victims (*evoked*; *affect*: −*happiness*) and their families.

10　It is my intention (*inscribed*; *affect*: *inclination*) to leave the G8 within the next couple of hours and go down to London and get a report, face-to-face, with the police (*incribed*; *affect*: +*security*), and the emergency (*incribed*; *affect*: − *security*) services and the Ministers that have been dealing with (*inscribed*; *judgement*: *social esteem*: +*capacity*) this, and then to return later this evening.

11　It is the will (*inscribed*; *affect*: *inclination*) of all the leaders (*inscribed*; *judgement*: *social esteem*: +*capacity*) at the G8 however that the meeting should continue (*inscribed*; *judgement*: *social esteem*: +*tenacity*) in my absence, that we should continue (*inscribed*; *judgement*: *social esteem*: +*tenacity*) to discuss the issues that we were going to discuss, and reach (*inscribed*; *judgement*: *social esteem*: +*tenacity*) the conclusions which we were going to reach.

12　Each of the countries round that table have some experience of the effects of terrorism (*inscribed*; *judgement*: *social sanction*: −*propriety*)

13　and all the leaders (*inscribed*; *judgement*: *social esteem*: + *capacity*) >< share our complete resolution (*inscribed*; *judgement*: *social esteem*: +*tenacity*) to defeat (*inscribed*; *judgement*: *social esteem*: +*tenacity*) this terrorism (*inscribed*; *judgement*: *social sanction*: −*propriety*).

14　>as they will indicate a little bit later<

15　It is particularly barbaric (*inscribed*; *judgement*: *social sanction*: − *propriety*) that this has happened on a day when people are meeting to try to help (*inscribed*; *judgement*: *social sanction*: +*propriety*) the problems of poverty (*inscribed*; *judgement*: *social esteem*; −*capacity*) in Africa, and the long term problems of climate change and the environment (*incribed*; *affect*: −*security*)

16　Just as it is reasonably clear that this is a terrorist (*inscribed*; *judgement*: *social sanction*: −*propriety*) attack (*incribed*; *affect*: −*security*), or a series of terrorist (*inscribed*; *judgement*: *social sanction*: −*propriety*) attacks (*incribed*; *affect*: −*security*),

17　it is also reasonably clear that it is designed and aimed (*inscribed*; *affect*: +*inclination*) to coincide with the opening of the G8.

18　There will be time to talk later about this.

19　It is important (*inscribed*; *appreciation*: +*valuation*): however that those engaged (*inscribed*; *affect*: +*inclination*) in terrorism (*inscribed*; *judgement*: *social sanction*: −*propriety*) realise

20　that our determination (*inscribed*; *judgement*: *social esteem*: +*tenacity*) to defend (*inscribed*; *judgement*: *social esteem*: + *tenacity*) our values and our way of life (*inscribed*; *judgement*:

social sanction:+*propriety*) is greater than their determination (*inscribed*; *judgement*:*social esteem*:+*tenacity*) to cause death and destruction (*inscribed*; *judgement*: *social sanction*: −*propriety*) to innocent (*inscribed*; *judgement*: *social sanction*: +*propriety*) people in a desire (*inscribed*; *affect*: *inclination*) to impose (*inscribed*; *judgement*: *social esteem*: +*tenacity*) extremism (*inscribed*; *judgement*:*social sanction*: +*propriety*) on the world.

21　Whatever they do,

22　it is our determination (*inscribed*; *judgement*:*social esteem*:+*tenacity*) that they will never succeed in destroying (*inscribed*; *judgement*:*social sanction*:−*propriety*) what we hold dear (*inscribed*; *judgement*: *social sanction*: +*propriety*) in this country and in other civilised (*inscribed*; *judgement*:*social sanction*:+*propriety*) nations through out the world.

练习 5.1

主位用粗体表示;非主位主语用下画线表示;标记主位类别用括号表示;省略内容用方括号表示。

1　**Napoleon Bonaparte** was a French military and political leader who rose to prominence during the latter stages of the French Revolution and its associated wars in Europe.

2　**As Napoleon I** (Circ: guise), he was Emperor of the French from 1804 to 1815.

3　**His legal reform**, the Napoleonic Code, has been a major influence on many civil law jurisdictions worldwide,

4　but **he** is best remembered for his role in the wars led against France by a series of coalitions, the so-called Napoleonic Wars.

5　**He** established hegemony over most of continental Europe

6　and [**he**] sought to spread the ideals of the French Revolution, while consolidating an imperial monarchy which restored aspects of the deposed *Ancien Régime*.

7　**Due to his success in these wars** (Circ: reason), **often against numerically superior enemies** (Circ: manner), he is generally regarded as one of the greatest military commanders of all time,

8　and **his campaigns** are studied at military academies worldwide.

9　**Napoleon** was born at Ajaccio in Corsica in a family of noble Italian ancestry which had settled Corsica in the 16th century.

10　**He** trained as an artillery officer in mainland France.

11　**He** rose to prominence under the French First Republic

12　and [**he**] led successful campaigns against the First and Second Coalitions arrayed against France.

13　**He** led a successful invasion of the Italian peninsula.

14　**In** 1799 (Circ:temp), he staged a *coup d'état*

15　and [**he**] installed himself as First Consul;

16　**five years later** (Circ: temp) **the French Senate** proclaimed him emperor, following a plebiscite in his favour.

17　**In the first decade of the** 19**th century** (Circ: temp), the French Empire under Napoleon engaged in a series of conflicts—the Napoleonic Wars—that involved every major European power.

18　**After a streak of victories** (Circ: temp), France secured a dominant position in continental Europe,

19　and **Napoleon** maintained the French sphere of influence through the formation of extensive alliances and the appointment of friends and family members to rule other European countries as French client states.

20　**The Peninsular War and** 1812 **French invasion of Russia** marked turning points in Napoleon's fortunes.

21　**His** Grande Armée was badly damaged in the campaign

22　and [**it**] never fully recovered.

23　**In** 1813 (Circ: temp), the Sixth Coalition defeated his forces at Leipzig;

24　**the following year** (Circ: temp) the Coalition invaded France,

25　[**it**] forced Napoleon to abdicate

26　and [**it**] exiled him to the island of Elba.

27　**Less than a year later** (Circ: loc), he escaped Elba

28　and [**he**] returned to power,

29　but [**he**] was defeated at the Battle of Waterloo in June 1815.

30　**Napoleon** spent the last six years of his life in confinement by the British on the island of Saint Helena.

31　**An autopsy** concluded he died of stomach cancer,

32　but **there has been some debate about the cause of his death**,[①]

33　**as some scholars** have speculated

34　that **he** was a victim of arsenic poisoning.

练习5.1 注释

①这是后面要讲到的存在主位。

练习5.2

主位用粗体表示;非主位主语用下画线表示;标记主位类别用括号表示;人际主位用双下画线表示;从句主位用斜体表示;省略内容用方括号表示。语篇主位不做标记,因此经验主位前任何未标记的元素都是语篇主位。

语篇5.3　University Welcome

1　　FOREWORD

2　　Welcome, or welcome back, to "ENCAP".

3　　**As one of the largest Schools in the University, with more than a thousand students (one hundred of them postgraduates), and over fifty academic staff** (Circ:guise), we pride ourselves in providing an excellent experience for our students, based in a friendly, personalised and supportive environment.

4　　**There are several ways in which you as a student can contribute to the community,**[①] generally by participating fully in lectures and seminars and by engaging with your fellow students and staff in the spirit of mutual respect that we seek to promote in all dealings within the School.

5　　*As you will be aware*,

6　　 **students entering their first year and those in the second year** each have their own Facebook page

7　　—**this** is a great way of getting to know each other, sharing experiences and information.

8　　**You** can make a particularly useful contribution by joining the Student-Staff panels associated with the Board of Studies that runs your degree and by standing as a student representative to the Board.

9　　**In our turn** (Circ: manner), our job is to help you achieve your best.

10　　**Your Personal Tutor** is there for that purpose

11　　—**take time** to catch up with him or her,

12　　and **do take advantage** of the opportunities for Academic Progress Meetings (APMs) we have introduced.

13　　**You** will find more information about APMs, and much else, in this School Undergraduate Student Handbook.

14　　**It** also contains advice on presentation of work and exam preparation, how staff and students contact each other, personal development and careers, student support, extenuating circumstances, regulations regarding examinations and assessed work and progression.

15　　**For more detailed information relating to your programme of study** (Circ:reason),

16　　please **refer** to your Course Guide,

17　　**which** details academic staff email addresses and research interests, word limits for essays and dissertations, grading/assessment criteria, referencing systems etc.

18　　**This Handbook and your Course Guide** should be read in conjunction with each other.

19　<u>Of course</u>, **no handbook** can cover every possible detail；

20　if you have any queries or need clarification on any issue（Clause：condition）

21　**your first point of contact** are the staff in the Undergraduate Office

22　— **they** are always happy to help（Humanities Building, Room 2.67）.

23　**Each programme** also has a Deputy Director whose job it is to deal with queries that cannot be resolved by the Office.

24　And,<u>of course</u>, **personal matters** should be discussed with your Personal Tutor.

25　<u>I hope</u>

26　**you** both enjoy

27　and［**you**］profit from your time in the School.

语篇 5.4　Bush's *"Bring Them On"* *Moment*

1　Q：**A posse of small nations, like Ukraine and Poland,** are materializing to help keep the peace in Iraq,

2　but **with the attacks on U. S. forces and casualty rates rising**（Circ：reason）, <u>what</u> does the administration do to get larger powers like France and Germany and Russia to join in the American（xxxx）?

3　B：Well, first of all, <u>you know</u>, **we'll** put together a force structure that meets the threats on the ground.

4　And **we** got a lot of forces there ourselves.

5　<u>And as I said yesterday</u>,②

6　**anybody who wants to harm American troops** will be found and brought to justice.

7　**There are some**③ who feel like

8　That if they attack us（clause：condition）

9　that **we** may decide to leave prematurely.

10　**They** don't understand what they're talking about,

11　if that's the case.

12　**Let** me finish.

13　**There are some** ④ who feel like

14　that,<u>you know</u>, **the conditions** are such that they can attack us there.

15　**My answer** is bring them on.

16　**We** got the force necessary to deal with the security situation.

17　<u>Of course</u> **we** want other countries to help us.

18　**Great Britain** is there.

19　**Poland** is there.

20　**Ukraine** is there,

21   you mentioned. [⑤]

22   **Anybody who wants to help**（Complement），we'll welcome to help.

23   But **we** got plenty tough force there right now to make sure the situation is secure.

24   **We** always welcome help.

25   **We**'re always glad to include others in.

26   But **make** no mistake about it,

27   and **the enemy** shouldn't make any mistake about it,

28   **we** will deal with them harshly

29   if they continue to try to bring harm to the Iraqi people.

30   I also said yesterday an important point,[⑥]

31   that **those who blow up the electricity lines** really aren't hurting America,

32   **they**'re hurting the Iraq citizens.

33   **Their own fellow citizens** are being hurt.

34   But **we** will deal with them harshly as well.

练习5.2　注释

①这是另一个存在主位。
②这是语篇信息和人际信息的混合。
③这是一个经验主位,一直延伸到"prematurely"这个词。
④另一个存在主位,一直延伸到"attack us there"。
⑤我将此分析为非主位性的人际信息。
⑥这是语篇信息和人际信息的混合。

练习7.1

表 7.2 练习 7.1 答案

Clause Nos.	Phase	Field	Tenor	Mode (RU)
1—6	Blair establishing his role a spokesman	Blair as Sayer, public as Recipients and Sensers	Information as plain declaratives; Blair's hope for understanding from audience construes tenor of authority and solidarity	1 Commentary
7	Introduction to events of the day	attacks	−judgement；social sanction	1.1 Recount
8	Establishing details	Casualties and victims	− Affect: happiness	1.1.1 Report
9	Creating empathy		−Affect: happiness; + Affect: inclination; empathy Blair and public	1 Commentary
10—11	Establishing determined Response of leaders	Plans of the leaders.	+Affect：inclination and +judgement：social esteem： tenacity of leaders in response to-judgement；social sanction of terrorists. Leaders as responding on behalf of people.	2 Plan
12—13	Establishing joint cause	Shared experiences and	Solidarity of leaders of other countries with UK and joint	2.1 Report
14	with other leaders.	determination of other leaders.	+judgement；social esteem；tenacity.	2.1.1 Plan
15—17	Barbarism of attack in contrast with Good intentions of leaders.	Aims of the attack	−judgement；social sanction of terrorists	3 Report①

续表

Clause Nos.	Phase	Field	Tenor	Mode (RU)
18	Establishing response as considered.	Leaders and public as joint talkers.	Establishing solidarity in response.	3.1 Prediction
19	Establishing response a strong.	Superior determination of leaders and public.	Solidarity of + judgement: social esteem: tenacity between leaders and public	4 Action[2]
20—22	Triumphal coda.	Strength of tenacity of leaders and people.	Greater + judgement: social esteem: tenacity of leaders and public; solidarity in shared values of leaders and people; triumph of good over evil.	4.1 Plan[3]

Notes

①The present perfect can be analysed as primarily concerned with the present or the past and I've analysed this as a Report of the present situation, though the evaluation is obviously the central idea here.

②I've analysed this as a call for the terrorists to recognise Blair and the other leaders' position.

③I've analysed these projected clauses as embedded in the projecting clause.

参考文献

Austin, J. J. (1962) *How to Do Things with Words: The William James Lectures Delivered at Harvard University in* 1955. Edited by J. O. Urmson and Marina Sbisà. Oxford: Clarendon Press.

Banks, D. (forthcoming) "On the (non)necessity of the hybrid category behavioural process".

Bartlett, Tom (2008) "Wheels within wheels or triangles within triangles: time and context in positioning theory". In M. Fathali, Rom Harré Moghaddam and Naomi Lee (eds) *Global Conflict Resolution through Positioning Analysis*. New York: Springer.

Bartlett, Tom (2009) "Legitimacy, comprehension and empathy: the importance of recon textualisation in intercultural negotiations". *European Journal of English Studies* 13(2). Special Edition on Intercultural Negotiation.

Bartlett, Tom (2012a) *Hybrid Voices and Collaborative Change: Contextualising Positive Discourse Analysis*. London and New York: Routledge.

Bartlett, Tom (2012b) "Lay metalanguage on grammatical variation and neutrality in Wikipedia's entry for Che Guevara". *Text and Talk* 32(6).

Bauman, Richard and Briggs, Charles L. (1990) "Poetics and performance as critical perspectives on language and social life". *Annual Review of Anthropology* 19: 59-88.

Bednarck, Monika (2006) "Epistemological positioning and evidentiality in English news discourse: a text-driven approach". *Text and Talk* 26(6): 635-60.

Bernstein, Basil (1971) *Class, Codes and Control, Volume* 1: *Theoretical Studies towards a Sociology of Language Learning*. London and Boston: Routledge and Kegan Paul.

Bernstein, Basil (2000) (Revised Edition [1996]) *Pedagogy, Symbolic Control and Identity: Theory, Research, Critique*. Lanham, Boulder, CO, New York and Oxford: Rowman and Littlefield Publishers Inc.

Berry, Margaret (1996) "What is theme? A(nother) personal view". In M. Berry, C. Butler, R. P. Fawcett and Guowen Huang (eds) *Meaning and Form: Systemic Functional Interpreta tions*. New Jersey: Ablex.

Blommaert, J. (2005) *Discourse: A Critical Introduction*. Cambridge: Cambridge University Press.

Bourdieu, Pierre (1977) "The economics of linguistic exchanges". In *Social Science Information*

16（6）: 645-68.

Bourdieu, Pierre（1991）*Language and Symbolic Power*. Cambridge: Polity Press. Brazil, David
（1995）*A Grammar of Speech*. Oxford: Oxford University Press.

Brown, Penelope and Levinson, Stephen C.（1987）*Politeness*. Cambridge: Cambridge University
Press.

Cloran, C.（2010）"Rhetorical unit analysis and Bakhtin's chronotope". *Functions of Language* 17
（1）: 29-70.

Coffin, C. and O'Halloran, K. A.（2006）"The role of APPRAISAL and corpora in detecting
covert evaluation". *Functions of Language* 13（1）: 77-110.

Fairclough, Norman（1992）*Language and Social Change*. Cambridge: Polity Press. Fairclough,
Norman（2001）（2nd edn）*Language and Power*. London: Longman.

Fairclough, Norman（2003）*Analysing Discourse: Textual Analysis for Social Research*. London and
New York: Routledge.

Fawcett, R. P.（1999）"On the subject of the Subject in English: two positions on its meaning
（and on how to test for it）". In *Functions of Language* 6（2）: 243-73.

Fawcett, R. P.（2003）"The many types of 'theme' in English: their semantic systems and their
functional syntax"（115 pp.）. Available from the Systemic Paper Archive at micko@ wagsoft. com.

Fawcett, R. P.（2007）"Auxiliary extensions: six new elements for describing English". In R.
Hasan, C. Matthiessen and J. J. Webster（eds）*Continuing Discourse on Language: A
Functional Perspective*. London and Oakville, CA: Equinox.

Foucault, M.（1972）*The Archaeology of Knowledge*. New York: Pantheon.

Halliday, M. A. K.（1978）*Language as Social Semiotic: The Social Interpretation of Language
and Meaning*. Baltimore, MD: University Park Press.

Halliday, M. A. K.（2002）*On Grammar: Volume 1 of the Collected Works of Michael Halliday*.
London and New York: Continuum.

Halliday, M. A. K. and Greaves, W. S.（2008）*Intonation in the Grammar of English*. London:
Equinox.

Halliday, M. A. K. and Hasan, R.（1976）*Cohesion in English*. London and New York:
Longman.

Halliday, M. A. K. and Hasan, R.（1985）*Language, Context and Text: Language in a Social-
Semiotic Perspective*. Victoria: Deakin University Press.

Halliday, M. A. K. and Matthiessen, C. M. I. M.（2004）（3rd edn）*An Introduction to
Functional Grammar*. London: Hodder Arnold.

Harré, Rom and Van Langenhove, Luk（eds）（1999）*Positioning Theory*. Oxford and Malden,
MA: Blackwell.

Hasan, R.（1995）"The conception of context in text". In P. Fries and M. Gregory（eds）
Discourse in Society: Systemic Functional Perspectives. Meaning and Choice in Language:

Studies for Michael Halliday. Westport, CT and London: Ablex.

Hasan, R. (1996) "Semantic networks: a tool for the analysis of meaning". In C. Cloran, D. Butt and G. Williams (eds) *Ways of Saying, Ways of Meaning: Selected Papers of Ruqaiya Hasan* (pp. 104-131). London: Cassell.

Hasan, R. (2009) "The place of context in a Systemic Functional Model". In M. A. K. Halliday and J. J. Webster (eds) *The Continuum Companion to Systemic Functional Linguistics*. London and New York: Continuum.

Hasan, R. (in press) "Choice taken in the context of realization". In L. Fontaine, T. Bartlett and G. O'Grady (eds) *Systemic Functional Linguistics: Exploring Choice*. Cambridge: Cambridge University Press.

Hasan, R. and Cloran, C. (1990) "A sociolinguistic interpretation of everyday talk between mothers and children". In M. A. K. Halliday, J. Gibbons and H. Nichols (eds) *Learning, Keeping and Using Language: Volume* 1 (pp. 67-100). Amsterdam: John Benjamins.

Hasan, R., Matthiessen, C. and Webster, J. J. (eds) (2007) *Continuing Discourse on Language: A Functional Perspective: Volume* 2 (pp. 921-52). London and Oakville, CA: Equinox.

Hymes, D. (1996) *Ethnography, Linguistics, Narrative Inequality: Towards an Understanding of Voice*. London: Taylor and Francis.

Jones, Owen (2012) *Chavs: The Demonization of the Working Class*. London: Verso.

Kress, G. and Van Leeuwen, T. (2001) *Multimodal Discourse: The Modes and Media of Contemporary Communication*. Arnold: London.

McCarthy, M. (2000) "Mutually captive audiences". In J. Coupland (ed.) *Small Talk* (pp. 84-109). Harlow: Longman.

Martin, J. R. (1992) *English Text: System and Structure*. Philadelphia, PA and Amsterdam: John Benjamins.

Martin, J. R. and Rose, David (2003) *Working with Discourse: Meaning above the Clause*. London and New York: Continuum.

Martin, J. R. and White, P. R. R. (2005) *The Language of Evaluation: Appraisal in English*. Basingstoke: Palgrave Macmillan.

Martin, J. R., Matthiessen, C. M. I. M. and Painter, Clare (1997) *Working with Functional Grammar*. London, New York, Sydney and Auckland: Arnold.

O'Grady, Gerard (2010) *A Grammar of Spoken English Discourse: The Intonation of Increments*. London and New York: Continuum.

O'Halloran, K. A. and Coffin, C. (2004) "Checking overinterpretation and underinterpretation: help from corpora in Critical Linguistics". In C. Coffin, A. Hewings and K. A. O'Halloran (eds) *Applying English Grammar: Functional and Corpus Approaches*. London: Hodder-Arnold.

Sarangi, S. (2010) " Reconfiguring self/identity/status/role: the case of professional role performance in healthcare encounters". *Journal of Applied Linguistics and Professional Practice* 7(1): 75-95.

Sarangi, S. (2011) " Role hybridity in professional practice". In S. Sarangi, V. Polese, G. Caliendo (eds) *Genre (s) on the Move: Hybridization and Discourse Change in Specialized Communication*. Naples: Edizioni Scientifiche Italiane.

Tench, Paul (1996) *The Intonation Systems of English*. London: Cassell.

Thompson, G. (2007) "Unfolding theme: the development of clausal and textual perspectives on theme". In R. Hasan, C. Matthiessen and J. J. Webster (eds) *Continuing Discourse on Language: A Functional Perspective* (pp. 671-96). London and Oakville, CA: Equinox.

Ventola, E. (1983) "Contrasting schematic structures in service encounters". *Applied Linguistics* 4 (3): 242-58.

Watts, R. (2003) *Politeness*. Cambridge: Cambridge University Press.

Widdowson, H. G. (2004) *Text, Context, Pretext*. Blackwell: Oxford, Malden MA and Carlton, Australia.

Young, Lynne and Fitzgerald, Brigid (2006) *The Power of Language: How Discourse Influences Society*. London and Oakville, CA: Equinox.